PAGAN LIGHT

DREAMS OF

FREEDOM

AND BEAUTY

IN CAPRI

PAGAN
LIGHT

JAMIE JAMES

FARRAR,
STRAUS
AND
GIROUX
New York

Farrar, Straus and Giroux
175 Varick Street, New York 10014

Owing to limitations of space, illustration credits
can be found on page 321.

Library of Congress Cataloging-in-Publication Data
Names: James, Jamie, 1951– author.
Title: Pagan light : dreams of freedom and beauty in Capri / Jamie
    James.
Description: First edition. | New York : Farrar, Straus and Giroux,
    [2019] | Includes bibliographical references and index.
Identifiers: LCCN 2018033300 | ISBN 9780374142766 (hardcover)
Subjects: LCSH: Capri Island (Italy)—History. | Capri Island
    (Italy)—Intellectual life. | Expatriate artists—Italy—Capri
    Island—History. | Expatriate authors—Italy—Capri Island—
    History.
Classification: LCC DG975.C2 J36 2019 | DDC 945/.73—dc23
LC record available at https://lccn.loc.gov/2018033300

Designed by Richard Oriolo

Our books may be purchased in bulk for promotional,
educational, or business use. Please contact your local
bookseller or the Macmillan Corporate and Premium Sales
Department at 1-800-221-7945, extension 5442, or by e-mail at
MacmillanSpecialMarkets@macmillan.com.

www.fsgbooks.com
www.twitter.com/fsgbooks • www.facebook.com/fsgbooks

1   3   5   7   9   10   8   6   4   2

For Bonita,
who took me there

CONTENTS

Blue Grotto

Gulf of Naples

N

PALAZZO A MAR[...]

VILLA SAN MICHELE

**ANACAPRI
VILLAGE**

VILLA MACKENZIE

Monte Solaro

CAPRI

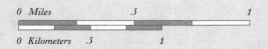

0 Miles		.5		1

0 Kilometers	.5		1

BASILICA OF
SAN COSTANZO

MARINA
GRANDE

VILLA LYSIS

VILLA JOVIS

Monte Tiberio

VILLA
TORRICELLA

VILLA CASTELLO

CAPRI
VILLAGE

VILLA CERCOLA

VILLA FEDERICO

VILLA DISCOPOLI

*Grotto of
Matermania*

VILLA MALAPARTE

*Grotto of
Fra' Felice*

VILLA ALLERS

MARINA
PICCOLA

BELVEDERE
CANNONE
(MALERPLATTE)

Faraglioni

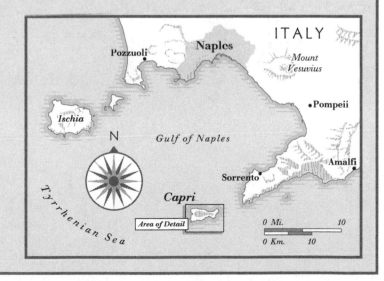

ITALY

Pozzuoli

Naples

*Mount
Vesuvius*

•Pompeii

Ischia

Gulf of Naples

N

Amalfi

Sorrento

Tyrrhenian Sea

Capri

Area of Detail

0 Mi. — 10

0 Km. — 10

PAGAN LIGHT

F ROM THE MAINLAND, Capri looks tantalizingly near, peaking up from the sea like a perfect meringue, just out of reach, but it has always been a world apart. The island is just twenty-two nautical miles from Naples, yet until the twentieth century, getting there was an adventure. The Gulf of Naples is often crossed by storms, and high seas are common even in fine weather. The island is girdled by rocky cliffs, with two small coves: the Marina Grande, a ridiculous misnomer, which was barely large enough to accommodate seagoing ships until the Fascists modernized the port in the 1920s, and the Marina Piccola, little more than an anchorage, with no beach to make landfall. Even when steamships were making transatlantic travel routine, a cruise to Capri was scarcely less perilous than it was when Goethe attempted to visit there, in 1787. The poet breathed a sigh of relief when his ship turned away during a terrifying electrical storm, and "we left that dangerous rocky island behind us."

The main reason that Capri managed to remain aloof throughout most of its history was its poverty, extreme even by the standards of southern Italy. The island made a poor prize for invaders. Its stony, precipitous terrain was unsuitable for agriculture apart from lemons, which grew in prodigious plenty on the mainland, and grapes, but Capriote wine was notoriously bad. The island had little to offer except lovely views, admired by everyone who came to visit but worthless until the twentieth century, when the boom of mass tourism made the island rich.

On historical maps, Capri turns from pink to blue to purple, to represent it as a territory claimed by whatever empire was holding dominion over Naples, always the island's true liege. Greeks, then Romans, the Byzantine and the Ottoman Empires, Napoleon and the Bourbons, swapped the island around like a bad banknote. By comparison with the architectural heritage of the mainland, Capri's imperial overlords left scanty remains, with the spectacular exception of the emperor Tiberius, who ruled the Roman Empire from Capri during the last years of his reign. He built a vast palace atop the island's highest cliff, but little of it has survived except brick arches and ramparts. The tiny municipal museum in Capri village just manages to fill two rooms, and the most interesting objects there are fossils. With the unification of Italy in the nineteenth century, Capri became a part of the newly created Kingdom of Italy, but in name only. Setting aside the omnipresent Neapolitans, mainland Italians were only slightly less exotic in Capri than the foreign visitors.

Capri's most valuable asset is intangible: its robust life as a symbol. Like any good symbol, it can be taken in many ways, but the island most often serves as an emblem of freedom. Since antiquity, Capri has been a hedonistic dreamland, a place where the rules do not apply: a Mediterranean prototype of Las Vegas. Twenty-two miles proved to be just far enough to liberate the island from the canting religious morality of Europe and the stern laws that came with it. For many of the artists who sought refuge there, Capri was still under the imperishable influence of its first foreign occupants, the Greeks: a relic of archaic Hellas, before the rise of the polis, with its demands on the citizen, where the individual lived in harmony with nature, saturated in sunlight between sky and sea. The promise of personal freedom brought with it a fantasy of pleasure without limit. In plain words, like Las Vegas, Capri got a reputation as a place where easy sex of every variety was available in abundance and not unduly fraught with consequences.

Capri did not give rise to a culture of its own: Las Vegas was built by gangsters, and Capri's isolated situation made it a favorite haunt of pirates and smugglers, also not ordinarily known as patrons of the arts; the island never had a prince. The native population was too small, and paradoxically the island was too close to the mainland to nurture its own artistic traditions. There was never a Capriote style of pottery, no indigenous school of lyrical poetry. Foreign visitors brought their culture with them. In the nineteenth century, as the global economy transformed great swaths of northern Europe into industrial parks and poured smoke into urban skies, writers, artists, and other dreamers voyaged to distant island paradises described by early explorers and exploited in trashy fiction. Tahiti, Bali, and other tropical islands off the main trade routes promised a simple life, free from the material demands of the modern world. Capri radiated a similar primeval glamour and felt exotic, although it was near at hand. It was a place lost in time: even by the 1920s, telegrams and telephones were rare, and donkeys were the principal mode of transport.

The pursuit of freedom and pleasure that flourished in Capri was not entirely in service to the senses; it brought with it an alluring promise of unloosing creative powers. For an enchanted interlude that began in the Romantic era and lasted until the chaotic years after the Second World War, Capri was a haven for an international community of artists and writers, where anything was acceptable except the commonplace. The simplicity of life on the island made it dirt cheap, always an attraction for artists. German poets went there to write Greek poetry, American painters to paint French paintings, French writers to write English novels, and Russians to plot world revolution. The island's history as a global nexus of artistic creativity may not be apparent to the millions of contemporary tourists who come for the views and the shopping, but it is an integral part of the island's fabric. Even visitors who know nothing about Capri's cultural history can feel the genius of the place. It is in the air, waiting to be discovered.

Norman Douglas, the British novelist and travel writer resident in Capri throughout the first half of the twentieth century, captured the intoxicating atmosphere of freedom that emanates from Capri's pagan past, and its power to inspire the imagination, in his novel *South Wind*. Douglas's mouthpiece, an antiquarian swindler, attempts to lure a visiting Anglican bishop from the straitened paths of righteousness. As

they bask in the glow of a summer sunset, sitting on a terrace high above the Gulf of Naples, he declares that in Capri
"the sage surrenders his intelligence and grows young again.
He recaptures the spirit of his boyish dreams. He peers into
worlds unknown. See! Adventure and discovery are lurking
on every side. These painted clouds with their floating banners and citadels, yonder mysterious headlands that creep
into the landscape at this hour, those islets emerging, like
flakes of bronze, out of the sunset-glow—all the wonder of
The Odyssey is there!"

Notwithstanding its rhapsodic tone, Douglas's homage
has a firm textual basis. The dream of Capri began in *The
Odyssey*, with a myth about the perils of beauty. In book 12,
Odysseus endures one of his most dangerous trials when
he sails past the island of the Sirens, horrid bird-women whose
surpassingly beautiful song lures mariners to ruin on the
dangerous shores of their frightful lair. Homer describes it as
a small island topped by a flowery meadow, bestrewn with
the bleached bones of the Sirens' victims. Wily Odysseus, as
everyone knows, was the first and only mortal to hear the
Sirens sing and live to tell the tale. He ordered his crew to
bind him fast to the mast and plug their own ears with wax.
When the ship approached, the Sirens broke into their delicious,
deceitful chant: "Come hither, renowned Odysseus, and hear
our song, for never yet has anyone rowed past this isle in his
black ship without stopping to hear our sweet voices and
going away a happier and wiser man. We know everything
the Greeks and Trojans suffered at the hands of the gods in
the wide plains of Troy, and all things that come to pass
upon the all-nourishing earth."

The location of the Sirens' island is a perennial enigma, amusing to ponder because it is insoluble. A prime contender by tradition is Li Galli, a cluster of islets off the Amalfi Coast that formerly called themselves the Sirenuse, as if to endow their claim to ancient notoriety with preemptive clout. However, they are little more than big rocks, with no place that could have sheltered a flowery meadow, the only physical feature specified in Homer's poem. In 1924, the Russian dancer and choreographer Léonide Massine took possession of Gallo Lungo, the largest of the islets, and built a villa there, which Le Corbusier later renovated. After Massine's death, Rudolf Nureyev bought it and spent the last years of his life there in sybaritic seclusion.

Yet few would challenge Capri's claim, supported by centuries of cheap souvenirs, to be the Siren Island. Anyway, it can never be disproved; for the rhapsodes who chanted *The Odyssey*, the islands of the Tyrrhenian Sea were remote, legendary places that only venturesome sailors had ever seen. A noncanonical Homeric myth adds corroboration to Capri's claim. After Odysseus eluded the Sirens' claws, one of them, named Parthenope, was so despondent that she drowned herself. Her body washed ashore on the little island of Megaride, just off the mainland across the bay, and the city of Naples was founded on the spot, now occupied by the Castel dell'Ovo. When French revolutionary forces liberated Naples from the tyranny of the Bourbons, in 1799, they renamed the city after the Siren from Capri. The Parthenopean Republic lasted only six months, but modern Neapolitans still call their city *la città Partenopea*.

Capri's first appearance in history, as opposed to myth, is

also touched by magic. In 29 B.C., when Octavian (soon to take the title Augustus) was cruising home to Rome to celebrate his victory over Antony and Cleopatra and take possession of his empire, he stopped at Capri and fell in love with the place. In *The Twelve Caesars*, Suetonius reports that when the young conqueror passed by a withered oak tree, its drooping branches miraculously recovered their vitality. Delighted by this propitious omen, he promptly bought the island from Naples and thereby set the paradigm for many future visitors who came to Capri on a holiday and found that they could not leave.

Augustus coined a Greek nickname for Capri, Apragopolis, which might be translated as the Land of Doing Nothing—a classical prototype of *dolce far niente*, "how sweet to do nothing," Italy's unofficial motto. He built the island's first holiday villa on a rugged strip of seashore at the foot of a cliff near the Marina Grande. Augustus despised excessive luxury, preferring modest palaces (a quintessentially Augustan paradox), which, according to Suetonius, "were adorned not so much with sculpture and painting as with colonnaded terraces and ornamental groves, and things that were curious either for their antiquity or rarity, such as, in Capri, the gigantic limbs of monsters and wild beasts, which were called the bones of giants, and the weapons of famous heroes." In modern times, Suetonius got a reputation as an unreliable historian, and his report of Augustus's cabinet of curiosities in Capri was cited as an example of his penchant for exaggeration.

Yet in 1906, when the foundations were being dug for an expansion of the Quisisana Hotel, in Capri village, Neolithic tools and the fossil remains of Pleistocene fauna such as the mastodon and pygmy elephants and hippopotamuses were unearthed, which gave Suetonius's claim a measure of credibility. Norman Douglas plausibly called the emperor's collection "the first paleontological museum in the world." The French archaeologist Salomon Reinach speculated that the weapons of famous heroes in Augustus's collection might be identified with the flint axes excavated at the Quisisana dig, but it is doubtful whether the emperor would have been impressed by such crude artifacts. It is just as reasonable to conjecture that unscrupulous dealers duped the emperor into buying bogus relics of the Trojan War.

When Augustus fell sick at Rome with a chill that would be the cause of his death (unless you believe the ancient gossip that his wife, Livia, smeared poison on the figs in his garden), he made a final visit to Capri for a four-day holiday cure, where he gave himself up to rest and relaxation. The emperor loved romping with the island's boys. On this visit, as usual, he spent hours watching them exercise and wrestle at the *ephebeum*, the gym for ephebes, the Greek word for adolescents at the threshold of manhood. He entertained the young athletes at a banquet, where he played games with them, tossing fruit and trinkets to the winners. He had cloaks made as party favors, in the Greek style for the Italians and Roman togas for the Greeks, and insisted that the Greeks speak Latin and the Romans speak Greek. On his fourth day in Capri, he took a turn for the worse and returned to Rome, where he summoned his stepson Tiberius, who would succeed him, for a long meeting behind closed doors. After that, Augustus took no further interest in affairs of state and died a few days later.

THE PALPITATING HEART of Capri village is the Piazzetta, at the junction of the road from the Marina Grande, the upper terminus of the funicular that rises from the shore, and the footpath to the island's northeastern tip, where Tiberius built his palace, Villa Jovis (House of Jove). *Piazzetta* is an appropriate diminutive of *piazza*. In the high season, when the tiny square's four competing cafés set out their outdoor tables, pedestrians must jostle one another to thread a path to the other side. No one complains: in southern Italy, jostling and being jostled is viewed as a stimulating pastime more than a nuisance. Overhead, strings of little white lights crisscross the square, twinkling in the briny air. On special nights when semiprofessional programs of opera arias and Neapolitan songs are performed, the Piazzetta achieves its destined metamorphosis into a stage set for a comic operetta, the metaphor employed by every writer who has undertaken to describe it.

On the south side of the Piazzetta, the island's parish church of Santo Stefano sits haughtily atop a flight of stone stairs, with its entrance at an oblique angle to the square. The church had the status of a cathedral until the Parthenopean Republic abolished the island's bishopric. The steps leading up to Santo Stefano are always crowded with footsore tourists sitting in front of signs asking them not to do so. The almost painfully picturesque bell tower that calls the faithful to the celebration of the Mass is detached from the church, located just opposite, at the main entrance to the square. A kiosk at its base sells soccer newspapers and toys.

The priest of Santo Stefano, Don Vincenzo Simeoli, is one of the most popular personalities in the village. Strolling across the Piazzetta with him, one proceeds slowly as he stops to greet parishioners who call out his name respectfully when he passes by.

Almost nothing remains of Augustus's Palazzo a Mare, but if anyone has a claim to being its caretaker, that would be Don Vincenzo. When I met him in the sacristy of Santo Stefano, he told me that he had collected more than three thousand fragments of the emperor's Villa by the Sea in his garden and the fields surrounding the Marina Grande, the site of the island's earliest settlement. Most of them are tiny scraps of marble and mural painting or single mosaic tesserae. "I have a large family," he explained, "and all my life they have been bringing me pieces for my collection." When I asked him if I could see it, he solemnly shook his head. "No one knows where I keep it," he said. "I keep everything locked up. According to the law, whoever finds ancient relics owns them, but I am responsible for them. If someone stole them, I would go to jail." The prospect of Don Vincenzo being sent to jail seemed remote, but I didn't press the point. He gave me a tour of Santo Stefano, pointing out the brilliantly colored marble pavements that came from Villa Jovis. When I took my leave, Don Vincenzo invited me to take a tour of Augustus's Villa by the Sea. "I will meet you at San Costanzo tomorrow afternoon at four," he said, "unless someone dies and I have to perform a funeral."

Deo gratias the health of the parish remained sound, and Don Vincenzo turned up on time at the Basilica of San Costanzo, the oldest church in Capri. It was built in the fourth century on the site of a Mithraic temple. The cult of Mithras, a mystery religion of Persian origin, was established in Rome during the early empire and quickly found a passionate following, particularly with soldiers. Membership was men only. The cult, unencumbered by any sort of philosophy, put a strong emphasis on animal sacrifice, specifically bulls, in subterranean rites. The appeal was magical and therefore theatrical, with spooky rituals that drenched the celebrants in buckets of blood. Don Vincenzo points out a few columns in the basilica that survive from the original structure and then leads me to the crude brick annex that covers the site of the *mithraeum*, which is nothing more than a hole in the ground. Then we set off to see what there is to see of Augustus's palace.

Slim and fit, with roses blooming in his cheeks and a thick brush of white hair, Don Vincenzo is in his early seventies but looks much younger. He springs up and down the crude stone stairs cut in the hillside with easy grace. We pass an imposing mansion painted Pompeii red behind high walls, which he says occupies the site of a villa that Tiberius built to complement that of Augustus on the shore below. When I ask Don Vincenzo who lives there now, he gives me a canny glance and rubs his thumb against his fingertips: a rich man. As we descend to the sea, he confidently points out which bits of stone wall are Augustan and which are not. Don Vincenzo himself restored the arches that supported the ancient road leading to the Bagni di Tiberio, the Baths of Tiberius. In the niches, he installed the pride of his collection, a Greek amphora dating to the fifth century B.C., and in the adjoining arch a marble bust of Augustus looking young and handsome, which he commissioned from a sculptor in Naples.

The only structural remains of the Palazzo a Mare are a

brick wall abutting the cliff, twenty feet high, with a series of vaulted recesses, the remnants of private chambers. True to Suetonius's description, the living quarters were modest in size. The villa was sited bang on the sea's edge, so its terraces must have been washed by waves when the sea was rough. In the shallows directly in front of it, a modern stone breakwater creates a calm, shallow tidal pool where children can splash in safety on fine days and small boats are moored during a storm. Near the fragmentary ruins of the villa, there is a row of private changing rooms and a trattoria called Bagni Tiberio, which is owned by Don Vincenzo's nephew Peppino.

At the conclusion of our tour, Don Vincenzo brings me to his house, a trim white frame cottage midway along the Roman road to San Costanzo. The house is surrounded by a small vineyard, where he raises grapes from vines that he discovered when he was digging his garden. He believes they are relics of Augustus's own vineyard. Proudly, he says, "I make wine from the vines of the *imperatore*."

～～～

WE FEEL THAT we know Augustus, but Tiberius, his successor, presents a dark, shape-shifting enigma as elusive as the Sirens. If the phrase fits anyone, Augustus was a Great Man of History, possessed by unbounded ambition, which wrought the empire that dominated Europe and the Mediterranean for a millennium. He ruled with ruthless resolve, yet his triumph owed as much to his personal charm as to military genius and statecraft. In his personal habits, he was a man of simple tastes with a passion for gardening who preached and practiced the homely virtues of family life.

Augustus was adored by the soldiers who marched to his orders and revered by the Roman people, who made a god of him long before his posthumous deification by a decree of the Senate. Tiberius was his bipolar opposite, a gloomy, secretive monarch who ascended to the throne with obvious reluctance. He was a brilliant general with a distaste for political intrigue, at least in the beginning of his career, who was propelled to power by his mother, the formidable Livia. As emperor, Tiberius was as irresolute as his predecessor was decisive, incapable of taking any action until he had sought the advice of everyone around him. Pliny the Elder called him *tristissimus hominum*, saddest of men.

It is impossible to make an objective assessment of the personality and reign of Tiberius, because the surviving sources of information are biased and unreliable and conflict with one another about everything except the bare facts. Among those, none was more influential to the course of history than Tiberius's decision in A.D. 26 to move from Rome to Capri. It was unprecedented. Norman Douglas wrote, "For the first time, the center of the world was displaced, the spell of the Eternal City broken." It was a wobble in imperial history that set the precedent for future dislocations of the seat of power, to Milan, Ravenna, Nicomedia, and finally Byzantium. Augustus was enchanted by the Siren Island and visited it often throughout his long life, but Tiberius's move to Capri was permanent: the Gulf of Naples was his Rubicon in reverse. He ruled the world from Villa Jovis, his palace overlooking the gulf, until his death more than ten years later. This final phase of his life dominated his reputation for posterity, and the reports of Tiberius's residency in Capri also had a potent influence on the island's own reputation.

The principal historians of the early empire, Tacitus and Suetonius, paint a lurid portrait of a depraved monster governed by irrational cruelty and perverted sexual appetites. Tacitus, much the more esteemed of the two by his contemporaries and modern historians, wrote his *Annals* eighty years after Tiberius's death. Like most intellectuals of his era, he deplored the monarchy and nurtured a hopeless dream of restoring the republic that had ruled Rome for centuries until the dictatorship of Julius Caesar. The god Augustus was untouchable, commanding respect even after his death, so Tacitus poured his republican convictions into his chronicle of the second emperor's reign. He wrote that Tiberius's professed reason for moving to Capri was a desire to escape the rancorous intrigues of the capital, in particular the relentless scheming of his domineering mother, but "for the most part I am moved to ascribe the motive of his removal more truly to his cruelty and lust, which his actions proclaimed even as he concealed them in a distant place."

Tacitus has nothing but praise for Capri itself. In the *Annals*, the historian is absorbed by the foibles and follies of his imperial subjects and takes but little interest in writing descriptions of places that his readers would have known for themselves. Capri elicited the only description of a landscape that survives in his long book:

> The solitude of the place was, I believe, what pleased [Tiberius] most. It is surrounded by a harborless sea with few places of refuge for even the meanest vessels, and no one can land there and escape the notice of a practiced lookout. The air in winter is soft, for the island is protected from the fury of the winds by a

mountain. In the summertime, the West Wind wafts it, and the open sea all around it makes it a pleasant place. Moreover, it commands the most beautiful view of the bay, at least before flaming Mount Vesuvius altered the appearance of the coast.

Tacitus's description is still a concise, accurate geographic survey of Capri. After Tiberius moved there, Tacitus says, he built a dozen villas, each dedicated to a sign of the zodiac, implying that he moved from one palace to the next following the astrological calendar. This aspect of Tacitus's history is probably apocryphal, or heavily embroidered: the remains of his residence in Damecuta, at the island's western end, suggest that it was a large, lavish palace, and tradition supports the previous existence of a villa above Augustus's Palazzo a Mare, on a site now occupied by a rich man's house, but no trace of the other palaces survives either in stone or in legend, as one would expect of "huge villas." Virtually every event in the historical record of Tiberius's reign takes place at Villa Jovis.

From a diplomatic and military perspective, Tiberius was a successful monarch, who strengthened Rome's control of distant provinces and extended its reach. For most citizens of the empire, it was a prosperous time, and even his sternest critics begrudgingly credit him with being just and generous in his dealings with plebeians. The historians' most interesting material was the ceaseless cycle of murderous intrigues in the capital. One after another Tiberius discovered (or was persuaded to find) traitors in the Senate, the army, and his own family who were subjected to show trials and sentenced to banishment or execution by enforced suicide.

Many of these inquisitions were instigated by his chief adviser, Sejanus, the commander of the Praetorian Guard, whom Tiberius called his *socius laborum*, the partner in his toils. Tiberius eventually turned over most of the day-to-day tasks of running the imperial city to him. Sejanus consolidated his control over the suspicious, vacillating monarch by turning him against anyone who stood in the way of his own ambition, which aimed at nothing less than the throne. After the death of Drusus, Tiberius's son and heir (probably as the result of poisoning by his wife, whom Sejanus had seduced), the emperor wearied of Rome and made his move to Capri, leaving his treacherous helpmate to rule in his place.

It was not the first time Tiberius had run away from Rome. Early in his career, after Augustus made him supreme commander of the Eastern Empire, in 6 B.C., he announced an abrupt retirement from public life, at the age of thirty-six, and moved to Rhodes. The decision was probably motivated at least in part by a desire to escape his miserable marriage to Julia, Augustus's daughter. Tiberius adored his first wife, Vipsania, but Augustus forced him to divorce her and marry his only natural child while she was still in mourning for her husband, Agrippa. Julia was spoiled and headstrong and by every account unrestrained in her quest of sexual adventure. Everyone in Rome except her father knew that she was sleeping with many of the empire's most powerful men. After Augustus found out about her wanton sex life, he ordered a divorce in Tiberius's name and exiled her to the tiny islet of Pandateria, where she was deprived of wine and the company of any men except eunuchs until her death. Tacitus suggests that Tiberius's early, short-lived retirement from public life might have been a sort of trial run of the Orgy in

Capri: "In the years that he went into exile in Rhodes under the guise of retirement, he had no other thoughts than meditating wrath, hypocrisy, and secret sensuality."

Once Tiberius had installed himself in Villa Jovis, after he finally learned the full extent of Sejanus's treachery, he ordered him to be arrested by the very Praetorian Guards that were supposed to be under Sejanus's direct control, a deft stroke that rooted out every vestige of Sejanus's shadow regime. Everyone related to him was executed. A notorious detail of this bloody purge is the execution of the traitor's young children. To satisfy the demands of the convention that children be exempted from execution, the boy was dressed in the toga virilis, the emblem of manhood, before his throat was cut, and the little girl was raped by a guard before she was murdered, to avoid the damnable sin of killing a virgin.

Suetonius records that the emperor received the news of the executions at Villa Jovis, where he kept "a constant watch from the highest cliffs for the signals he had ordered to be raised on the mainland." Sixteen centuries before the first telescopes, such signals could only have been transmitted by beacons or perhaps smoke signals. This passage has excited scholarly speculation about how Tiberius was able to rule the empire from such an isolated place. The most obvious explanation would be fires lit at nighttime, which could be used to send messages, perhaps employing a prototype of Morse code. One modern military historian has mooted the possibility that the Romans developed an early heliograph, creating a bright flash on a large reflective surface that was visible in daytime.

Even after the massacre of Sejanus and his ilk, which

left the capital in turmoil, Tiberius did not budge from his island retreat. He made occasional forays to the mainland of Campania, but never again entered the city of Rome. What kept him in Capri, which for all its natural beauty is a small island, is one of the murkiest of the Tiberian enigmas. Tacitus's sensational explanation is that the monarch, now in his seventies, was so much given over to cruelty and sexual lust that he had lost touch with the realities of empire: "The more intent he had formerly been upon public cares, he became now so much the more buried in dark debauches." Maliciously, he adds that Tiberius might also have been prompted to live in solitude because he was embarrassed by his appearance; although he had a handsome figure, he was bald and his face was disfigured by erupting cankers, which he covered with plasters.

Tacitus was a serious writer, a master rhetorician famed for the symmetry and high polish of his prose. He evoked a sense of terror in his narrative not with graphic shocks but rather with dark insinuations that left the details to his reader's imagination. He leaves his indictment of Tiberius's cruelty deliberately vague. Suetonius, on the other hand, is explicit, and glories in the gory details. His recital of horrors is extensive. One famous passage describes the Salto di Tiberio, Tiberius's Leap: "In Capri, they point out the scene of his executions, from which he used to command those condemned to die, after long and exquisite tortures, to leap into the sea before his eyes. Below, his marines battered the bodies of the victims with pikes to ensure that no breath of life remained, and then shoved the bodies back into the sea." The Salto di Tiberio is the steepest cliff on the island, a principal feature of boat excursions for modern tourists, whose guides recite Suetonius's tale, just as he predicted they would. One of Tiberius's favorite tortures, according to Suetonius, was to profess friendship with the victim and encourage him to drink enormous quantities of wine; then, before the man had a chance to urinate, guards would seize him and tie up his penis with a cord, preventing him from purging his bladder.

Tacitus also enforces a decorous vagueness in his descriptions of the emperor's sexual perversions. This passage is the closest he comes to a pornographic description of Tiberius's orgy:

Like a royal despot, he defiled and committed
outrages on freeborn youths. His lust was excited not
only by a beautiful face and a graceful body but also
in some cases by their youthful innocence and in
others by noble ancestry. At this time words came into
use that were previously unknown, the Sellarii and
Spintriae, one expressing the filthiness of the place
and the other the manifold postures and methods of
buggery.* Slaves were charged with procuring and
bringing youths to service him, with gifts for the
willing and threats against the recalcitrant; and if
their parents or guardians put up resistance, the
young people were taken forcibly, and the procurers

*Tacitus is vague in his use of *sellarii* and *spintriae*, implying that they were slang words. As you might expect, they have inspired many pages of prurient scholarly conjecture. *Sellarius* must be derived from *sella*, a place to sit, a reference to public toilets and the prostitutes who frequented them, while *spintria* refers to the sphincter, and thus means a person of either sex who is skilled at anal intercourse.

satisfied their own desires with them, as if they were prisoners of war.

In his treatment of sex, too, Suetonius is compendious with anecdotes and graphic in detail. Here, he describes the *spintriae*: "On retiring to Capri, [Tiberius] devised a rural pavilion for his secret orgies, where bands of girls and male favorites who had distinguished themselves as experts in unnatural intercourse, called spintriae, copulated in triple unions in his presence, to excite his flagging lust." Some passages approach buffoonery, such as his description of groves in the garden of Villa Jovis that were fitted out as mock temples of prostitution, where the youthful talent were costumed as little Pans and nymphs. Suetonius has the irritating habit of feigning disgust at what he clearly relishes and pretending reluctance to come out and say what he is eager to tell:

> [Tiberius's] infamy proclaimed itself with even grosser depravities, so flagrant one can scarcely bear to report or hear them, or even to believe them, such as the children of the tenderest age, whom he called his little fishes, trained to swim between his thighs, licking and nibbling him as they swirled about in the water; and the babies, robust yet still unweaned, whom he brought to his penis as if it were a mother's teat, for they were surely more apt to enjoy this sort of pleasure by nature at their age.

As Suetonius concedes, difficult to believe. Yet throughout most of the nearly two thousand years since the histories of

Tacitus and Suetonius were published, the scandals were widely accepted and repeated. "Tiberius in Capri" was universal shorthand for excessive, perverted sexual license and brutal cruelty.

Gilles de Rais, the fifteenth-century serial killer who confessed to sodomizing, torturing, and murdering a large number of youths, perhaps hundreds of them, ranging in age from six to eighteen, said at his trial that he was inspired to commit the crimes after reading Suetonius's biography of Tiberius. A marshal of France who fought beside Joan of Arc, Gilles also had an element of Nero, the megalomaniac artist, in his character. He wrote a mystery play about Joan's triumph at the Siege of Orléans that was twenty thousand verses long, with 120 speaking parts and an army of extras. Gilles's homicidal rampage originated in an obsession with the occult. On one occasion, when he performed a Black Mass, the demon he was trying to summon demanded the body parts of children as the price for making an appearance. The accounts of torture and mayhem that came out at Gilles's trial make gruesome reading; the most horrible aspect of his crimes was their psychological cruelty. Like Tiberius, he delighted in feigning friendship with his victims in the beginning, treating them to gifts at a lavish banquet in order to intensify their shock when he revealed his true purpose. In his confession, he said that he would sit on the stomach of the child after he had cut his throat, for the thrill of watching him die.

Tiberius's orgy in Capri, even more than the madness of Caligula and Nero, created the paradigm of imperial wickedness. In the Renaissance, the histories of Tacitus and Suetonius were the primary sources of information about the early empire and an integral part of the curriculum at schools and colleges. In his tragedy *Sejanus, His Fall*, Ben Jonson, most learned of the Elizabethan poets, closely paraphrases Tacitus in his description of Tiberius's life in Capri:

> He hath his boys, and beauteous girls ta'en up,
> Out of the noblest houses, the best formed,
> Best nurtured, and most modest: What's their good,
> Serves to provoke his bad . . .
>   [and] dealt away
> unto his spintries, sellaries, and slaves,
> Masters of strange and new-commented lusts,
> For which wise nature hath not left a name.

Milton's readers required only a brief allusion to bring the Roman histories to mind. In *Paradise Regained*, Satan tempts Christ with earthly powers, chief among them the opportunity to expel Tiberius from his throne and restore Rome to greatness:

> This Emperor hath no son, and now is old;
> Old and lascivious: and from Rome retir'd
> To Capreae, an island small, but strong,
> On the Campanian shore, with purpose there,
> His horrid lusts in private to enjoy.

Charles Dunster, the editor of an edition of *Paradise Regained* published in 1795, footnoted this passage, "The accuracy and historical correctness, with which the character of Tiberius is here drawn, is well worth noticing," and adduced long quotations from Tacitus and Suetonius to support the assertion. Yet Dunster was already old-fashioned: skepticism about the canonical historians had taken hold in France before the Revolution.

One of the earliest works of fiction inspired by the Orgy in Capri was written by a writer who campaigned against belief in anything at all except the flesh, the Marquis de Sade, "the only writer who will never lose the power to shock us," as Francine du Plessix Gray wrote. None of his works is more shocking than his novel *Juliette*, which was published anonymously at the end of the eighteenth century, as the sequel to *Justine*. In *Justine*, subtitled *The Misfortunes of Virtue*, the heroine undergoes unspeakable torments and humiliations as a result of her virtuous behavior; in *Juliette*, Justine's wicked sister abandons every conceivable norm of human decency with joyous abandon. She and her demonic companion Clairwil go on a rampage that decants buckets of sperm and oceans of blood across Europe, and Tiberius is frequently invoked as an inspiration for their adventures. Rape, torture, infanticide, mass murder, and cannibalism are elaborated in phantasmagoric and ultimately monotonous variations. *Juliette* is not pornographic in the conventional sense; only a monster like Gilles de Rais could find the book sexually arousing. For most readers of any era, the book is a violent assault on the imagination and the gut, punctuated by philosophical digressions that anticipate the intellectual revolutions that would have respectable triumphs by the end of the nineteenth century.

Juliette and Clairwil's visit to Capri is a relatively subdued idyll, coming immediately after an orgy with Ferdinand, king of Naples, and his queen, Marie-Caroline, Marie Antoinette's sister. The latter has intercourse with a group of men as she watches the decapitation of a twelve-year-old girl she has just raped, an obscene burlesque of her sister's recent execution. As it did Tacitus, Capri inspired the Marquis de Sade to undertake an unwonted exercise in descriptive geography, a concise profile of the island's topography that appears to have been based upon his notes from a series of visits to Italy in the 1770s, after he was convicted in France and sentenced to death in absentia for poisoning prostitutes, sodomy, and other crimes.

Sade's description of the Villa Jovis has the ring of an eyewitness observation, even as it refers to a familiar passage in Suetonius: "The palace is perched on the tip of a rock rising so far above the water that the eye can barely discern the fishermen's boats moored below. That particular palace served as the theater for his most piquant lewd revels," in particular ordering children of both sexes to be flung to their deaths from the cliff "once they were of no further use to his lust." Clairwil rhapsodizes on the orgasms the emperor must have experienced as he watched his victims plummet to their deaths and makes a proposal. "Oh, dear angel," says Clairwil, hugging Juliette, "he was a voluptuous rascal, that Tiberius. What if we were to look for something to throw off this precipice as the Emperor used to do?"

As always, a perfect victim is close at hand, an innocent young goatherd who tells them that she is the sole support of her invalid mother. Clairwil is all for tossing the girl from the Salto di Tiberio straightaway, but Juliette restrains her, saying, "I am dreadfully curious to know how this child is made: health, freshness, innocence glow in her young charms: it would be ridiculous not to divert ourselves with them." Their diversion consists of collecting the girl's hymen with a pointed rock, flaying her with brambles, and finally tying her to the goat and throwing them off the precipice into the sea. Their pleasure is enhanced by the knowledge that the loss of the goat ensures that the sickly mother will soon die of starvation. "That is how I like my horrors," Juliette declares, "either make them thorough and extensive, or refrain from undertaking them at all."

Then the fiendish pair stroll down to the village and present the governor of the island with a letter from King Ferdinand commanding him to provide them with virgins to defile. The governor regretfully informs the women that they must pay: he himself enjoys an orgy from time to time, he says, but finds little opportunity for it, because Capri is ill-supplied with prostitutes "and precious few idlers or valets." So the women give him a sack of gold to procure three girls and three healthy lads, and after an all-night orgy they embark on a sightseeing cruise before their return to Naples. They stop at Herculaneum and observe the ongoing excavation of the ruins, which had begun thirty years before Sade's visit.

Doubts about the authority of Tacitus began, as many doubts did, with Voltaire, who described him as "a fanatic sparkling with wit," adept at withering abuse but deficient in facts. With the rise of skepticism about the Roman historian, Tiberius's reputation too began to rise. Some of the emperor's early advocates were scarcely more credible than boosters such as Gilles de Rais and the Marquis de Sade. In 1813, John Rendle, a mathematics don at Cambridge, published a spirited if demented defense entitled *The History of That Inimitable Monarch Tiberius*. He makes some strong arguments, starting with a detailed compendium of quotations

from authors contemporary with Tiberius's reign or immediately after it, who praise him as a wise, just monarch and
do not mention the Orgy in Capri. After the collapse of the
amphitheater at Fidenae, in A.D. 27, the deadliest stadium
disaster in ancient history, in which fifty thousand specta-
tors died (according to Tacitus), Tiberius rushed to the scene
and personally assisted in the rescue effort. At this point
Rendle goes off the rails and asserts that by the time of this
disaster Tiberius had converted to Christianity. He offers no
proof of this ridiculous claim and concludes that the principal lessons to be learned from the life of Tiberius are "that
the first Pope was an arch-impostor" and that Catholics are
"dangerous heretics."

~~~

TIBERIUS NEVER HAD a more zealous advocate than
Thomas Spencer Jerome, a lawyer from Detroit who bought
a villa in Capri on his first visit to the island, in 1899. He
lived in it until his death in 1914, laboring on a treatise that
would exonerate Tiberius of the crimes ascribed to him by
the imperial historians. In *Vestal Fire*, a satirical roman à
clef about the expatriate colony in Capri (called Sirene in the
novel), Compton Mackenzie paints an affectionately mock-
ing portrait of the eccentric American, in the character of
John Scudamore. For years, Mackenzie wrote, "foreigners
had been coming to Sirene and there been seized with a passion to prove that Suetonius and Tacitus had monstrously
slandered Tiberius. They had remained on the island for
years, some of them, working away with fanatical industry

at his whitewashing. When Scudamore arrived the time was ripe for another coat."

Jerome's plea for the emperor was passionate but based upon a wide reading of classical literature and existing critiques by skeptical German classicists and sharpened by his legal training. He directs most of his analysis against Tacitus, the revered master, and scarcely mentions Suetonius, who wrote, at least in part, to titillate his readers. Like Rendle, Jerome offers a compendious résumé of admiring reports by Tiberius's near contemporaries, such as Plutarch, who, though "possessed of much fondness for castigating vice," wrote that the monarch "passed the last seven years [*sic*] of his life on the island of Capri, and that sacred governing spirit which sways the whole universe and was inclosed as it were in his breast, never in that time changed its residence." Even Juvenal, "avid of scandal and exuberant in biting phrase," Jerome wrote, "attributes to him no worse companions than astrologers, and with tame and unaccustomed blandiloquence characterizes his later years as a 'tranquil old age.'"

Jerome's most powerful argument is the disparity, apparent to every reader of the *Annals*, between the historian's assertions of Tiberius's vicious behavior in private and the appearance of virtue in his public actions, bolstered by the uniformly admiring testimony of witnesses. Jerome's damning case in point is Tacitus's claim that Tiberius was savage and cruel in his exercise of the emperor's privilege to order the execution of his enemies, which resembled "a wave of blood through the houses of Rome, or the hand of a butcher." Yet, in Jerome's reading, "the cases on which these charges are based, and Tacitus claims to report them fully," amount to "about one execution per annum on all sorts of charges," which included the atrocious retribution against Sejanus— who was, after all, plotting a violent coup d'état and perhaps even the assassination of the emperor.

At a scholarly conference in London, in 1913, Jerome read a paper entitled "The Orgy of Tiberius on Capri," which opens with a passage from a speech that the emperor delivered to the Senate a year before his move to Capri, in reply to an embassy from Spain that sought to erect a temple in honor of himself and his mother deified. It is one of the longest extracts of Tiberius's own expression extant and suggests that if his memoirs had survived, posterity might have had a quite different impression of him. The emperor concludes,

> I declare unto you that I am no more than mortal and do but discharge the duties of a man; that it suffices me if I fill worthily the principal place among you— this I would have remembered by those who live after me. Enough, and more than enough, will they render to my memory, if they judge me to have been worthy of my ancestors, watchful of their interests, unflinching in danger, and fearless of enmities in defense of the public weal. These are the temples I would erect in your hearts, these are the fairest images and such as will best endure.

Tiberius's successors would have been incapable of such plainspoken humility, even in the service of duplicity. Like a skilled lawyer addressing the jury, Jerome uses the passage to great effect, comparing Tiberius's modest aspirations for his reputation with the posthumous infamy brought upon him by Tacitus.

Some of Jerome's arguments are not as convincing as he hopes. For example, he asserts that Tiberius's sexual adventures in Capri, as represented by Tacitus, are "a highly improbable performance for a septuagenarian to keep up for eleven years." However, the detailed descriptions of deviant sex are the work of Suetonius, not Tacitus, and none of the strenuous activities are ascribed to the emperor himself; he is a voyeur. Jerome's Latin is fallible: he offers a scornful criticism of the infamous passage from Suetonius quoted above, about the obscene weaning of babies and the bathing pool with children nibbling the imperial thighs, on account of the impossibility of "the natatory exploits of suckling infants, whose relatively large skulls however would preclude their swimming." The size of the infantile skull is just one of many reasons that babies do not swim, but in any case Suetonius clearly presents the two charges as separate, and Jerome has confused them. The "little fishes" who frolicked in the pool with the emperor, according to Suetonius, are *pueri*, children up to the age of adolescence, not babies.

What really went on at Villa Jovis? Despite his occasional lapses in scholarship and habitual excess of enthusiasm, Thomas Jerome makes a persuasive case that Tacitus's lurid tales of the paranoid, bloodthirsty monarch, driven by perverted lust, are insubstantial. Jerome's conclusions have been supported by most (though not all) modern historians, yet the legend of the orgy endures: the stories are just too sensational to die. Jerome notes with majestic, polysyllabic scorn, "As long as hypocritical pruriency demands an opportunity to glut its appetite for the lascivious under the guise of an interest in history, it needs the old story of Tiberius' Orgy, consecrated by the affection of ancestral concupiscence and fortified by the approval of contemporaneous lubricity."

The enduring image of Tiberius for contemporary English speakers is the portrait of him in Robert Graves's novel *I, Claudius*, which draws heavily on Suetonius, and the BBC adaptation of the book, with George Baker's memorable portrayal of the emperor as a weakling with putrid skin and scanty hair, always exasperated by his monstrous mother, the story's villainess. Both Graves and the BBC script, by Jack Pulman, omit the emperor's riotous years in Capri, presumably because British readers in 1934 and television viewers in 1976 were not as receptive to scenes of raunchy sex as were the readers of imperial annals in the second century.

Yet the question persists: Was Tiberius an upright moralist, as Jerome believed, or the wicked sensualist of the imperial histories? The correct answer is the unsatisfying one that applies to most controversies of antiquity: we shall never know. Even if a bombshell scroll were to turn up, it could only complicate the mystery. The admiring portraits of Tiberius are just as likely to be faulty as the salacious slanders. If the emperor in his old age, weary of the responsibilities of supreme power, and released from the need to set a moral example in his retirement in Capri, took his pleasure by watching adolescents perform sexual acrobatics, it does not strain credulity.

Thomas Jerome's life began as the pattern of elite midwestern dullness in the Gilded Age. Born into the high society of Saginaw, Michigan, he was a sickly, bookish boy. When he was an undergraduate at the university in Ann Arbor, his father was elected governor of the state. After he received his bachelor's degree, Jerome attended the university's law school and went on to earn an M.A. at Harvard. At the age of twenty-three, he set up a law practice in Detroit that did not distract him from his principal profession as a cultured bachelor, with the prospect of a leisurely lifetime of feeding and drinking at private clubs and indulging his passion for Roman history.

Then he met Charles Lang Freer, from Kingston, New York, who had made a fortune in Detroit building railway cars, which enabled him to pursue his vocation of collecting art. Freer's interests were divided between contemporary American painting, particularly the work of James McNeill Whistler, who would become a friend and confidant, and Asian art, which was almost unknown in America at that time. In his mid-forties, healthy and wealthy, Freer retired from the active management of his business affairs. The two intellectual bachelors became fast friends, and at century's end they went on a European tour together, a pair of idle-rich American aesthetes in the Old World straight out of a novel by Henry James.

When they arrived in Capri, they joined a community of effete bachelors. The preposterously bearded painter Charles Caryl Coleman, a Civil War veteran from Buffalo, was the dean of the island's expatriates. He arrived in Capri in 1870 and lived there until his death in 1928, in an extravagant mansion near the Piazzetta. Villa Narcissus united the enthusiasms of Jerome and Freer: a former convent Coleman had converted to a Moorish palace, it was cluttered with Roman marbles and mosaics, many of them dug up in the meadows of Capri, and a miscellany of Orientalia, including Chinese porcelain, Islamic textiles, and Japanese painted fans and scrolls. Coleman's paintings exploited every cliché of the Aesthetic style, conversation pieces with generic Renaissance or classical settings and decorative still lifes that imitated Japanese woodcuts, but his specialty was views of Vesuvius. He produced hundreds of pastels of the volcano, which was perfectly framed in the window of his studio. E. F. Benson, the author of the satirical Mapp and Lucia novels, a seasonal resident of the island, offered this withering assessment of Coleman in his memoir: "His pictures—picturesque corners and rugged old fishermen—had (for me) the curious quality of looking like bad copies of first-rate work, and he himself, white-bearded and rather majestic in manner, looked like a bad copy of [Frederic] Lord Leighton," the eminent society painter of classical scenes and president of the Royal Academy.

His neighbor just up the hill was a peripatetic alienist, Allan McLane Hamilton, a grandson and biographer of Alexander Hamilton. Hamilton was preparing to move to London, so his estate, Villa Castello, one of the most prestigious residences on the island, was for sale. Jerome and Freer decided to buy the house and settle down there. Inevitably, the nature of a friendship between two unmarried gentlemen, aged thirty-five (Jerome) and forty-five (Freer), who set up housekeeping together invites speculation, but their private lives are almost as elusive as that of Tiberius. Four years before they arrived in Capri, Oscar Wilde had been convicted of gross indecency and sentenced to two years' hard labor. As a result, homosexual relationships in this period were kept strictly private: the memory of Wilde's love letters to "Bosie," Lord Alfred Douglas, his "gilt and graceful boy," being read into the court record was still vivid and terrifying. We may be curious whether Jerome and Freer's relationship was a romantic friendship or a sexual affair; a recent Italian biographer has argued it was the latter, but because the issue cannot be settled, it need not detain us.

Whatever the exact nature of their relationship, Villa Castello was a romantic setting for it, set atop a hillside rising to the Malerplatte (now the Belvedere Cannone), the Painters' Plaza, so called because it was thronged by German amateur artists who went there to paint the spectacular panoramas. Hamilton wrote in his memoirs that the house, at least eight hundred years old, was built on a foundation of Cyclopean blocks of pink granite that predated the Roman era in Capri. "The rooms were lofty, and always full of fresh air, while in front was a large terrace that overlooked the entire Bay of Naples and the villages at the base of Vesuvius." The previous resident, a mediocre British painter of classical scenes named Walter Anderson, had paved the floors with antique marble from Tiberius's palaces. The garden was a pocket Eden, two acres of orange, lemon, mulberry, and fig trees and a grape arbor, shaded by feathery bamboo and parasol pines. "After I left," wrote Hamilton, "an entire Roman room with frescoes in a perfect state was opened up by Mr. Thomas Jerome, the new tenant, and I myself often picked up fragments of Greek glass, once finding a terracotta mask of Medusa."

Jerome and Freer decided to buy the estate and then went their separate ways, pledging to meet in Capri the following year. Coleman concluded the deal with Hamilton on their behalf. At home in Michigan, Jerome gave a farewell party at which he shocked his family and friends by announcing his intention to retire from the practice of law and move to Capri to write a history of Rome. He secured an appointment as the American consul at Sorrento, a post he managed to have transferred to Capri the following year. W. Somerset Maugham, who shared a fine house in the village called Villa Cercola with E. F. Benson and a ne'er-do-well dilettante named John Ellingham Brooks, wrote a fanciful short story about Jerome's magnificent midlife crisis. The story, entitled "Mayhew," also the name of the character based on Jerome, begins in Detroit:

> One evening he was sitting in his club with a group of friends and they were perhaps a little worse (or the better) for liquor. One of them had recently come from Italy and he told them of a house he had seen at Capri, a house on the hill, overlooking the Bay of Naples, with a large and shady garden. He described to them the beauty of the most beautiful island in the Mediterranean.
> "It sounds fine," said Mayhew. "Is that house for sale?"
> "Everything is for sale in Italy."
> "Let's send 'em a cable and make an offer for it."
> "What in heaven's name would you do with a house in Capri?"
> "Live in it," said Mayhew.

As so often, Maugham is writing a fable on his favorite theme of personal freedom. He states his message plainly in the opening paragraph of the story: "I am fascinated by the men, few enough in all conscience, who take life in their own hands and seem to mold it to their own liking. It may be that we have no such thing as free will, but at all events we have the illusion of it."

Maugham had met John Brooks, ten years his elder, when he was a sixteen-year-old student at Heidelberg University. Brooks was his first lover and intellectual mentor. The sexual affair had ended by 1895, when the two men came to Capri for the first time. Maugham was struggling to reckon with his homosexual inclination, as he would do all his life. Brooks and Benson were not struggling, and there was a steady traffic of local boys coming to Villa Cercola. It is unclear whether Maugham availed himself of their services, but he was impressed by the openness of his housemates. In his story, Capri represents a zone of individual liberty, outside the strictures of social conformity.

When Freer returned to Capri for his rendezvous with Jerome, a shock awaited him: Jerome had brought with him a woman from Detroit. Henrietta Sophia Rupp, known as Yetta, was ostensibly Jerome's housekeeper, but it soon became obvious that she was his mistress. At first Freer accepted this alteration in his friendship with Jerome, whatever its precise nature, but Rupp was a difficult, domineering woman who was ferociously hostile to Jerome's friends. For a vivid portrait of Yetta Rupp, we return to *Vestal Fire*, Compton Mackenzie's roman à clef. The literature of expatriate life in Capri consists of such encrypted fictional representations to a remarkable degree. Indeed, they outnumber the nonfiction accounts and are sometimes more candid than the memoirs by the same authors.

When [Scudamore, the character based on Jerome] came to Sirene, he brought with him a gypsy-faced young woman as his housekeeper, and it was as much her jealousy as his own books that kept him at home, as much her appalling Midwestern American cooking as his own late hours that made him look so wan and thin. She loved him as women like her love, with as much exasperation as passion. She could not bear to have Scudamore's "lady" friends treat her as a servant; and she made his life such a misery with her tantrums that for the sake of peace in which to work he gave way to her by inviting no woman, whatever her station, inside his house. Then she tried to keep away his men friends; and she made herself so objectionable with her insolence that fewer and fewer even of them used to visit the scholar.

The description of Rupp as "gypsy-faced" reflects frequent characterizations of her as a mulatto. That would explain one minor mystery of Jerome's life, why he would bother to carry on the masquerade that she was his servant, for by Capriote standards, relationships of any sort between unmarried men and women constituted a meager scandal. The theory that Yetta was of mixed race has been disputed on the grounds that she had previously resided in an all-white neighborhood in Detroit, which does not seem conclusive. Freer's role became that of an absent partner in the property until 1905, when he was on a visit there and had a row with Yetta Rupp, which led to Jerome's buying him out. Freer returned to America and built a grand marble museum in Washington to house his collections, which he made a gift to the nation. Many years after Jerome's death, Freer told a mutual friend of theirs from Michigan that he had "said to Jerome that he would not set foot in Villa Castello when Yetta was there. Jerome had his choice and he kept Yetta."

When he moved to Capri, Jerome's defense of Tiberius was the focus of his work, but as his researches became more intensive, he widened the scope to encompass a study of the morals of the empire from its founding. In his memoirs, Compton Mackenzie described the madness of Jerome's method: "He set to work on this magnum opus, accumulating more and more books, collecting more and more notes, finding it every year more and more presumptuous to make a beginning until he had acquired more knowledge and still more." By the time of Jerome's death, in 1914, his library was one of the most comprehensive collections of Roman history, law, and literature in the world, amounting to more than three thousand volumes, which he divided in his will between the University of Michigan and the American Academy in Rome.

Jerome never completed his treatise on Roman morals. In "Mayhew," Maugham cast Jerome's life in a tragic light: "That vast accumulation of knowledge is lost forever. Vain was that ambition, surely not an ignoble one, to set his name beside those of Gibbon and Mommsen." Maugham concludes his story on a note of patronizing optimism: "And yet to me his life was a success. The pattern is good and complete. He did what he wanted, and he died when his goal was in sight and never knew the bitterness of an end achieved."

The pattern of Thomas Jerome's life was, of course, more complex than that of Maugham's Mayhew. It is true that he never completed his big book about Roman morals, but his research was not lost. Nine years after his death, the cream of it was compiled by a professor at the University of Michigan and published under the dreary title *Aspects of the Study of*

Roman History. The principal divergence of the life of the historical Thomas Jerome from Maugham's tragic fictional synopsis of it is embodied by a book that he published a few months before he finally succumbed to an acute dyspepsia, which had made his life miserable. *Roman Memories in the Landscape Seen from Capri* is an imaginative study of the panorama the solitary scholar had contemplated for fourteen years from the terraces of Villa Castello.

Recognizing that the natural beauty of the Campania is "difficult to express without vaporous incoherence," a just damnation of the extensive literature of travelogues written by other foreign visitors to the region, Jerome proposed to view the coastline as the setting of myth and witness to history. "To make the landscape live," he wrote, "to give it an added suggestiveness, we need but to consider what has been said and done on these waters and islands, plains, and mountains, what part of the great drama of human history has had this setting for its scene, what these mountains have looked down upon, and what these waters have swallowed up."

Roman Memories was a modern book when it was published, in 1914, illustrated with well-printed photographs of the landscape by Morgan Heiskell. Jerome brings a lively, informal style to his recitals of familiar myths, which he sets on a par with the imperial histories. He credits Homer's tale of Odysseus and the Sirens with a truth more durable than that of Tacitus's account of Tiberius's Orgy in Capri. In this, his unintended magnum opus, Jerome's furious denunciation of Tacitus was refined into a worldly, polished skepticism that anticipates the conceptual approach and methods of contemporary historians.

CAPRI SURELY PROVIDES the setting for more works of fiction than any other island of its size. The finest of Capri novels, both in literary quality and for the depth and subtlety of its understanding of the island, is *South Wind*. Norman Douglas's ambitious first novel enjoyed a resounding success when it was published, in 1917, and had a flourishing afterlife, at least until mid-century. Although it sits firmly outside the innovative movements of its day, *South Wind* exerted a wide and powerful influence. Virginia Woolf, a critic not easily impressed, wrote that the book "has a distinguished ancestry, but it was born only the day before yesterday." Graham Greene, who first came to Capri to write the script for a film of the novel, which was never produced, said, "My generation was brought up on *South Wind*."

An antic romance in the style of Max Beerbohm and Ronald Firbank, the book serves Douglas as a platform for philosophical digressions and chronicles of invented history, compounded with elements of the satirical novel of manners and the murder mystery. He has more themes than he can keep track of, but paramount among them is an unyielding hostility to institutional religion; in its place, he advocates an idealistic hedonism nourished by the pagan atmosphere of the Mediterranean. From the novel's opening pages, Douglas grounds these disparate conceptual strands firmly in the limestone crags of Capri (called Nepenthe in the book), succumbing to the majestic power of the island's geography as writers had done since antiquity. When the ferry from Naples approaches Nepenthe, Douglas writes, its "comely outlines were barely suggested through a veil of fog. An air of irreality hung about the place. Could this be an island? A veritable island of rocks and vineyards and houses—this pallid apparition? It looked like some snowy sea-bird resting upon the waves; a sea-bird or a cloud; one of those lonely clouds that stray from their fellows and drift about in wayward fashion at the bidding of every breeze."

Despite this explicit claim of irreality, *South Wind* is usually called a roman à clef, perhaps from force of habit, so much does the genre dominate the fiction of Capri, and because of Douglas's close identification with the island. Nepenthe occupies Capri's geographic position in the Gulf of Naples, but it is closer in essence to the marvelous unnamed South American country in Virginia Woolf's first novel, *The Voyage Out*, published two years before, a place that English visitors find "very beautiful but also alarming and sultry." The book's characters do not correspond satisfactorily with the famous personalities resident in Capri in Douglas's era, nor are they composites, quite. The queer folk of Nepenthe exhibit traits common to expatriates throughout the Mediterranean in the early twentieth century: misfits and idlers, heiresses and remittance men in search of love and pleasure in the name of personal fulfillment.

The point of view wanders like a comet but has its center of gravity in Thomas Heard, an Anglican bishop who visits Nepenthe on his homeward voyage after a long ministry in equatorial Africa. He is stopping there to collect his cousin Mrs. Meadows and her infant child, to escort them to England to rejoin Mr. Meadows. On the ferry, Bishop Heard meets a mysterious stranger named Muhlen, "a flashy over-dressed personage" who is later revealed to be Mrs. Meadows's first husband, still her legal husband, who has come to Nepenthe to blackmail her for bigamy. In the denouement, Heard, watching through field glasses from afar, sees her murder the wretch by pushing him off a cliff, but he decides not to denounce her, the proof that he has been successfully Mediterraneanized.

Contemporary critics complained that *South Wind* lacked a plot, but Douglas responded that if his book had a narrative flaw, it was an excess of story. Denis Phipps, a dreamy undergraduate on a search for life's meaning, is besotted with love for a flirtatious maidservant in the employ of an American-born duchess, who is pursued successfully by a Jewish geologist. Meanwhile, Vesuvius erupts, blanketing Nepenthe in ash until a statue of the island's patron saint, Dodekanus, is paraded through the streets and puts a miraculous stop to the disaster. A local antiquarian sells a fake Greek bronze to an American millionaire who made his fortune in the condom trade. Another American, the dipsomaniac

Mrs. Wilberforce, turns up from time to time to undress in public. A group of lusty, red-shirted Russian vegetarians called the Little White Cows run amok when a tobacconist in the piazza sells one of them a box of matches made with animal fat. The carabinieri arrive in force to quell the melee, wielding their weapons "with such precision that four schoolchildren, seven women, eleven islanders, and twenty-six Apostles were wounded—about half of them, it was believed, mortally. Order reigned in Nepenthe."

As Denis Phipps remarks, "The canvas of Nepenthe is rather overcharged." Douglas's protestations notwithstanding, the story of *South Wind* is not the reason readers return to the book. It is a conversation novel, a minor genre that encompasses works by writers as diverse as Denis Diderot, Thomas Love Peacock, and Dave Eggers. Time and again, Douglas establishes a pastoral scene on a terrace or hillside, where his characters repose amid gorgeous descriptive prose and thrash out issues of interest to the author. The book's distinguished ancestry originates in Plato. Many passages in the book read like one of the philosopher's odder dialogues, but lacking the rational presence of Socrates.

South Wind is one of the last works of English literature that assumes a classical education. The island's name is taken from a mythical drug, mentioned in *The Odyssey*, which quiets all pain and strife, producing forgetfulness of every ill; those who have drunk nepenthe mixed with their wine will not shed a tear at the death of mother or father. A knowledge of Greek and Latin is not required to get the jokes: Douglas always explains himself, but he assumes that his readers share his interest in the esoteric margins of antiquity, and if they do not, he works hard to arouse it.

After he has introduced his principal characters and narrative threads, Douglas blithely sails into a biography of Dodekanus. In childhood, he demonstrated a precocious talent for curing lepers and raising the dead and by adolescence had made it his life's mission to convert the heathens of Africa. There, he "entered the land of the Crotalophoboi, cannibals and necromancers who dwelt in a region so hot, and with light so dazzling, that their eyes grew on the soles of their feet." After eighty years of preaching, Dodekanus converted them; to celebrate their salvation, the Crotalophoboi murdered him and cut him up into twelve pieces, provisioning a year of monthly feasts. After one of the banquets, the martyr's femur was swept up by the south wind and cast on the shore of Nepenthe, creating his cult there. The legend of Dodekanus, with its slightly mad annotations, was an inspiration to Nabokov in *Pale Fire*, another pseudo-learned excursion into manufactured history.

The story floats along with featherlight irony without ever losing sight of its message. Douglas's mouthpiece, the antiquarian Count Caloveglia, in the same conversation in which he proclaims that all the wonder of *The Odyssey* may be found in the panorama surrounding Nepenthe, declares, "We of the South, Mr. Heard, are drenched in volatile beauty. And yet one never wearies of these things! It is what you call a glamour, an interlude of witchcraft. Nature is a-tremble with the miraculous." Yet *South Wind*, for all its pagan high spirits, has a melancholy at its heart. In its painfully artificial innocence, its thundering silence about the cataclysm of blood that was engulfing Europe when it was published, the novel was in its way as much a passionate reaction to the First World War as the serious antiwar books that followed it in the 1920s. When Douglas was writing, the outcome of "the war that will end war," in H. G. Wells's phrase, was in perilous doubt. The only certainty was that the civilization that had created *The Odyssey*—and Douglas himself, for that matter—was passing away. *South Wind* was a banner floating above the citadel, a jaunty pledge of no surrender.

Like many expatriates, Douglas lacked a clearly defined nationality. Born in Thüringen, Austria, he was raised amid great wealth in Scotland, where his ancestors were barons, and educated at English boarding schools and the Karlsruhe Gymnasium, in Germany. A promising career in the British diplomatic corps was cut short after he got a woman pregnant in St. Petersburg and abandoned his post. When he returned to Britain, he married a first cousin and fathered two sons. Douglas was impoverished overnight after his brother lost the family's cotton mills in a bad business deal, so he turned to writing to make a living.

Besides *South Wind*, he found success with his travel books: *Old Calabria*, which some readers consider his best work; *Fountains in the Sand*, subtitled *Rambles Among the Oases of Tunisia*; and notably *Siren Land*, a magical-historical-mythological tour of Capri and the Sorrentine peninsula. Otherwise, his freelance career was hampered by a penchant for obscure subjects that were sure to find few readers. His bibliography includes *Birds and Beasts of the Greek Anthology, On the Herpetology of the Grand Duchy of Baden*, an essay on forestry, a collection of raunchy limericks, an aphrodisiac cookbook, and a study of children's games in London, an early classic of sociology that Joyce plundered for wordplay in *Finnegans Wake*.

Once a fixture on lists of modern classics, said to have

been the most popular title in the early catalogues of the Modern Library, *South Wind* has slipped beyond the canonical pale and arouses scant interest among scholars today. One reason for this decline, undoubtedly, is Douglas's scandalous private life. By the time he wrote *South Wind*, his sexual inclination had shifted to a mania for young boys. He divorced his wife and moved to Italy, where homosexual relations were legal and age-of-consent laws sketchy. Harold Acton wrote that by the time Douglas reached his sixties, he "could endure the society of fewer and fewer people over the age of fourteen." The exact nature of this "Nietzschean brand of naughtiness," in Paul Fussell's phrase, is irrecoverable. The charge of indecent assault that made him persona non grata in England was brought after he propositioned a sixteen-year-old schoolboy at the South Kensington tube station. Douglas was attended in his travels in Calabria by a twelve-year-old Cockney boy named Eric Wolton, with his parents' approval. In his forties, Wolton and his wife visited the elderly Douglas in Capri. A photograph of Wolton as an adult survives, inscribed "To N.D., the best pal I ever had."

Fussell theorizes that Douglas's sexuality was a relic of the decadent 1890s, before there was such a thing as the "gay lifestyle," when homosexuality (itself a freshly minted term) was routinely identified with youth worship and endowed with a specious classical pedigree based upon a vague understanding of institutionalized pederasty in ancient Greece. This tolerant attitude, which Fussell calls "an index of the pre-modern" view of homosexuality, was inextricably bound up with the Victorian class system that continued to dominate private attitudes even after it had brought down Oscar Wilde in a public disgrace. As repellent as Douglas's behavior appears in the light of contemporary morality, for his social peers in Bloomsbury a gentleman's right to do as he pleased carried more weight than any presumption of legal protection for Douglas's young working-class companions. There must have been those in Capri who disapproved of Douglas's behavior, but there is no hint of any social opprobrium in the published testimony, which always portrays him as one of the island's most popular personalities. The Capriotes, at any rate, adored him, and made him an honorary citizen of the island.

Douglas remained true to his vision of pagan hedonism to the end of his life, in 1952, at the age of eighty-three. It was a horrible death. He was tormented by erysipelas, a bright scarlet inflammation of the skin commonly known as Saint Anthony's fire, which worsened to a mysterious illness diagnosed as "a sort of consumption of the skin." Deprived of the prospect of any further pleasure from life, he hastened its end by taking an overdose of pills. As he lay dying, some German sisters of mercy came to revive him, but he waved them away. His well-attested last words were "Get those fucking nuns away from me." Douglas's funeral was an unofficial state ceremony: the shops closed and *tout* Capri, from the civic elite to fishermen and farmers he had courted when they were boys, turned out to follow the cortege to the cemetery.

T HE HISTORY OF the foreign colony in Capri is a chronicle of scandals, most of them teapot tempests by the
standards of contemporary morality, yet for that reason in-
structive about the habits and thinking of our grandparents
and great-grandparents. The Isle of Capri, as it came to be
known, was the resort of last resort for men with ready money
to pay for the rental of a villa, who typically went there for
the same reasons that Tacitus constructed to explain Tiberius's removal to the island: to avoid censure for shocking behavior and continue it beyond the strictures of home. In the
pre-electronic era, scandal control was a simpler proposition
than it is now, particularly for the highborn, who could de-
pend upon the courts, including the court of public opinion,
to take their word over that of the lower orders. Most indis-
cretions could be swept away by a modest sum of cash, so
long as the miscreant had the good sense to go on a long

holiday abroad, where such sins were tolerated or more readily forgiven.

At least until the trials of Oscar Wilde. His downfall, like that of a Greek tragic hero, was put into motion not by his deviations from conventional morality but rather by hubris, his serene belief that he was too powerful to suffer public opprobrium for his private affairs and could punish those who had the temerity to denounce him. Wilde sealed his own doom when he lodged a libel action against the Marquess of Queensberry, the father of Wilde's young lover, Lord Alfred Douglas. After all, Queensberry, bully that he was, had only spoken the truth when he accused Wilde (albeit illiterately) of being a sodomite. If Wilde had been content to disregard the accusation, his posthumous reputation as a wit for the ages would have been untarnished, and it would have been left to modern scholars to excavate the details of his romps with rent boys. Yet the indelible image of Wilde is that of a ruined man in shackles on the platform at Clapham Junction, where he was reviled and spat on by passengers as he waited for the train that would take him to Reading Gaol. After his release from prison, Wilde left Britain and never returned. He spent the wretched remainder of his life traveling throughout Europe, with occasional forays to North Africa, often incognito.

One of the stations of his martyrdom took place in Capri: for once, the island's celebrated tolerance was absent, though it was not the Capriotes' doing. Five months after his release from prison, Wilde took up residence in Naples, accompanied by Douglas. After Wilde received a windfall of ten pounds from his publisher, the pair went to Capri for a brief holiday, where they stayed at the Quisisana, the island's best hotel, which would provide the setting of many later scandals. The pathos of Wilde's ruin derives in part from his jaunty good spirits in exile. He wrote to his loyal friend Reginald Turner, "I want to lay a few simple flowers on the Tomb of Tiberius. As the Tomb is of someone else really, I shall do so with the deeper emotion." Wilde and Douglas had lunch with Axel Munthe, the island's legendary self-legendizer, at his famous villa, San Michele, in the upland village of Anacapri. In another letter, Wilde described Munthe as "a great connoisseur of Greek things" and "a wonderful personality."

Roger Peyrefitte described Wilde's public humiliation on the night of his arrival in *The Exile of Capri*, a biographical novel told from the point of view of the aristocratic French writer Jacques d'Adelswärd-Fersen, whose reckless pursuit of love and sexual adventure with adolescent boys would make him the island's most scandalous foreign resident after Tiberius. Jacques, seventeen, is traveling with Robert de Tournel, a poet his elder by some fifteen years, who is initiating him into the Uranian underworld, the earliest manifestation of what would come to be known as the gay lifestyle, though not as his lover. As the two Frenchmen peruse the dinner menu at the Quisisana,

a man, accompanied by a younger man, appeared in the doorway. The man had a powerful head, long gray hair, heavy, flaccid cheeks, and his fingers were loaded with rings; his companion was pale, carried himself insolently, and had a cane in his hand.

"Oscar Wilde," Robert muttered, "and Lord Alfred Douglas."

Jacques, overwhelmed, stared at these two personages, whom fate had thus thrown in his way on this his first visit to Capri. They were making their way towards an unoccupied table, when an Englishman summoned the *maître d'hôtel* and told him, in a loud voice, "If these gentlemen are dining here, I shall leave your restaurant at once."

Other English diners indicate that they will follow him, and the maître d' suavely refuses service to Wilde and Douglas. Jacques, his eyes "bright with tears, as Wilde's had been," in a voice "hot with indignation" demands that Robert invite the outcasts to join them at their table. His worldly friend demurs and proceeds to explain the reality of scandal to the naive young man. Wilde, he explains,

> could have continued to flaunt his tastes before the whole of society if he had been content to satisfy them among his social and intellectual equals. Whereas what his trial revealed were his relations with a pack of stable-boys, waiters, and male prostitutes. England recoiled from a man who had been so stupid as to stir up mud enough to obscure his genius, and mud, moreover, which left its mark on all England, since every Englishman had, at his public school, done what Wilde was reproached with.

In the morning, when Jacques and Robert make a pilgrimage to the ruins of Villa Jovis, Jacques stops at Villa Federico, the house where Wilde and Douglas are staying, to leave a bouquet of gladioli and tuberoses, with a note identifying himself as "a young Frenchman at the Quisisana." Wilde responds with a warm note of thanks: "You have poured the balm of your youth on the wound I received from the Pharisees . . . I shall remember Capri only for your flowers." It is a lovely fable, connecting the two martyrs in a floral symmetry, yet that's what it is, a fable. Peyrefitte's narrative of Wilde's humiliation at the Quisisana follows contemporaneous accounts of the event that survive in the record, but the only source for the presence of Jacques d'Adelswärd-Fersen at the scene is Peyrefitte's novel.

Fersen* published some twenty books of verse and fiction, most of them about the beauty of young men and the love it inspires. Some of them are charmingly written and offer points of interest, but none of them is fully satisfying as literature. Fersen's most enduring creation was Villa Lysis, the opulent mansion he built just an arrow's shot down the hill from Villa Jovis, unless one counts his life, which fulfilled the motto inscribed over the entrance to Villa Lysis: *Amori et dolori sacrum*, consecrated to love and sorrow. In his preface to *The Exile of Capri*, Jean Cocteau described Fersen as among "those beings who, incapable of creating masterpieces, try to become one in their own persons," and cruelly likened him to mad Ludwig II of Bavaria and Elisabeth of Austria, last of the Habsburg empresses, who slept one night of the week under a blanket of beefsteaks to keep her skin in good form. If Cocteau's assertion was just, and Fersen's aim was to make a masterpiece of his life, he succeeded. It was an

*He began life as Jacques d'Adelswärd and appended "Fersen" at around the age of twenty-one. In Capri, he omitted "d'Adelswärd," the name he was known by in France, and styled himself comte de Fersen. To simplify matters, I call him Fersen throughout.

anarchic tour de force, a histrionic chronicle of love fulfilled and betrayed, of ecstatic exaltation and bitter sorrow worthy of a Byronic hero.

The intense romance of Fersen's story is attributable at least in part to the fact that, like the life of Tiberius, it is shrouded in mythic shadows and mists that will never be illuminated or dispelled. Any consideration of Fersen's life presents the problem, which may be unique in modern biography, that the principal source of factual information is a work of fiction. *The Exile of Capri*, published in 1959, was based upon extensive research that cannot be verified: interviews with Fersen's friends and intimate associates, by then near the end of their lives, and documents that are lost or no longer available. The novel is a maddening literary sphinx that seamlessly mingles fact and fiction in what might be called a roman à demi-clef, a semi-nonfiction novel, or a biography enlivened with fabricated scenes of high drama. Peyrefitte identifies the major personalities by their real names, yet he gives pseudonyms to many minor actors, and some, such as Robert de Tournel, are pure invention.

Seventeen-year-old Fersen *might* have been at the Quisisana the night that Oscar Wilde was refused service; Fersen was traveling in Italy with his mother around that time, and their visit to Capri might have coincided with Wilde's. No record of the hotel's dining-room reservations exists to prove that he was not there, but if he was, his dining companion would have been his mother, and the floral tribute, and therefore Wilde's note, lie far beyond the bounds of credibility. In this instance, we may take the lack of corroborative evidence as strong grounds for doubt. Fersen, throughout his life keenly alert to the interesting pathos that it presented to the world, would surely have told the story of meeting his idol if it had occurred—and he would have kept that note.

Ostensibly a sympathetic portrait of a difficult man, *The Exile of Capri* is in fact fatally biased. Peyrefitte was an outspoken apologist for pederasty. His first novel, *Special Friendships (Les amitiés particulières)*, about a tragic love affair between schoolboys, was a succès de scandale that came near to winning the Prix Goncourt when it was published, in 1945. Yet in his subsequent career, Peyrefitte discovered that literary scandals can be as difficult to manufacture as they are to escape. His attempts to repeat the sensation of his first book fell short. He was a notable example of the sort of gay cheerleader who finds icons and martyrs everywhere he looks: not content with the usual lineup of Alexander, Hadrian, and Richard the Lionheart, Peyrefitte, guided by the principle that if no one can disprove an interesting theory, then it must be true, was ready to believe that almost any male person who made a name for himself in history was homosexual, popes in particular.

Beguiled by the witty entertainment value and confident tone of Peyrefitte's novel, many writers have overlooked its manifest untrustworthiness and turned to it as a source of historical information. Why would anyone put any credence at all in a book that begins with a forged letter by Oscar Wilde? Nonetheless, the Quisisana incident has often been repeated as fact. The cause of Fersen's death is unknown and unknowable, but many writers of nonfiction also follow Peyrefitte in making his death by an overdose of cocaine a suicide, yet contemporary testimony and circumstantial evidence would just as well support a theory of accidental death. The main reason Peyrefitte's novel has maintained its position of prestige is that it has long extracts from court records and other official dossiers that have every appearance of being genuine.

Subsequent investigators have pored over the book in search of reliable information, but the author did not provide even a rough guide to his research. In his memoirs, Peyrefitte dispensed tantalizing hints as to who's who in the book, what's real and what's not, but he took spiteful pleasure in claiming sole possession of Fersen's life. As a record of historical events, his book is a fatally alluring mirage. The novel is further complicated by its equivocal, at times malicious attitude toward its subject. Just as Tacitus had his own, republican reasons for inventing or embellishing or at least laying a heavy emphasis on Tiberius's immoral behavior in Capri, so the author of *The Exile of Capri* portrays Fersen as a feckless, pathetic victim of his own grandiosity and meager talent, in order to make him fit the pattern of the pederastic hero of a Roger Peyrefitte novel, which must trace a tragic arc.

As is often the case with expatriates, Jacques d'Adelswärd-Fersen's ancestry was cosmopolitan. The noble line of the Adelswärds is Swedish, dating to the seventeenth century; the French branch of the family began in 1806, when Baron Göran Adelswärd, fighting with the Prussians against Napoleon's army in Lübeck, was captured and imprisoned at Longwy, in northern France. There, in the comfortable circumstances of an officer in confinement during the Napoleonic Wars, he married the daughter of a local civic dignitary. According to Peyrefitte, the baron's wife was the cousin of Count Hans Axel von Fersen, a hero of the American Revolution decorated by George Washington and later the dashing lover of Marie Antoinette. This uncertain connection holds our attention only because Jacques later claimed to be a descendant of *le beau Fersen*, as he was commonly known.

The baron's son Renauld d'Adelswärd became a naturalized French citizen and got his family accepted as French aristocracy (hence the adoption of the nobiliary *de*). He created the steel industry in Longwy and with it fabulous wealth for himself and his descendants. He built a stately family seat, Château Herserange, and secured an appointment to the National Assembly. There, he became friends with Victor Hugo, a deputy representing Paris; after the coup d'état of 1851, the two men went into exile together on the Channel island of Jersey. Renauld's son Axel, Jacques's father, was a yachtsman who died on a steamship voyage en route from Marseilles to South America, under mysterious circumstances. Thus, at the age of seven, Jacques inherited a romantic family history, a barony, Protestant religion, and the promise of sole possession of a vast fortune in steel.

After his father's death, Jacques was the only male in the family; his mother, grandmother, and two younger sisters petted and spoiled him. His grandfather took an interest in him, taking the family scion on sporting holidays, though Fersen later said that he spent most of his time during these manly outdoor vacations picking flowers and chasing butterflies. On one such trip to Jersey, when he was thirteen, he formed a romantic friendship of some sort with a blond Etonian he met there. Fersen's education was remarkable for its elaborate itinerary: he attended six different lycées and collèges in Paris over the course of ten years. The cause for the frequent removals would not seem to have been poor marks, for he won several prizes. More likely he was bored by his studies and resisted school discipline. His classmates called him *fille*, a girl, and he confirmed their contempt of him when they took him to a brothel, a rite of passage he fled in horror.

When Fersen was twenty-two, he published a poem about a schoolboy much like himself neglecting his work in a study hall, which gives a vivid impression of how his twig was bent:

> Thirteen, blond, with precocious eyes
> That speak of excitement and desire,
> Lips that have a smack of mischief,
> Even something of vice about them.

The other boys are scribbling away at their essays, but he is alone in a corner, reading naughty poems by Alfred de Musset. When the prefect supervising the study hall approaches him, the boy puts away his book and presents an appearance of sedulous application to his studies. After the prefect passes, he returns to his reading. His face flushing pink, he shifts in his seat, slipping farther into the shadows.

> He runs his hands into his pockets,
> Pierced with a hole, none's the wiser,
> And languorously plays with his toy,
> A dreamer of kittenish pleasures.

In 1898, Jacques's grandfather died, making him, at eighteen, one of the richest men in Europe. Although his education was not the pressing concern it was for most of his contemporaries, he enrolled at university in Geneva, idly contemplating a career in diplomacy, in emulation of his ancestral hero Axel von Fersen. Instead, he followed Musset, his first literary hero, and became a dandy and a poet. He did not complete his studies in Geneva, but he did publish his first book there, *Love Story* (*Conte d'amour*). By 1902, the year he turned twenty-two, Fersen had published five books, which found enough readers to be reprinted several times. He followed *Conte d'amour* with two collections of verse; his first novel, *Our Lady of Dead Seas*; and a miscellany of poetry and short fiction, *Ébauches et débauches* (Sketches and debauches), which included "Arcadian Kisses," a short story that celebrated an ideal love between two fifteen-year-old shepherds in Arcady, and another story extolling the charms of "Cycladian girls, pretty Greeks who dreamed of fountains and disdained the love of men." In 1902, Fersen renewed his Swedish connection by attending the wedding of the titular head of the Adelswärd clan, in Stockholm, where King Oskar II received him in a private audience. An item in *Le Figaro* reported that he presented the minister of foreign affairs with a copy of one of his books.

One of the most marriageable bachelors in Paris, the good-looking young baron became a frequent guest at the capital's best salons. *The Exile of Capri* is packed with counts, duchesses, and princesses who welcomed him to their at-homes. At one of these soirees, he met Blanche de Maupeou, the seventeen-year-old daughter of a *vicomte* and, crucially, a Protestant. She was a passionate admirer of *Ébauches et débauches*. The book's veil of respectability was thin enough; *débauche* has the same meaning in French that it does in English, and the Arcadian kisses are plainly shared by boys (though it is possible that some of the high-flown classical references, such as "Cycladian girls," that is, girls from Lesbos, might have flown over her sheltered head). There was nothing outrageous or bold about the collection; most of the poems are conventional, addressed to feminine love objects, and Blanche might have fancied that she had inspired them. Anyway, a soupçon of homosexuality was fashionable in the salons of turn-of-the-century Paris, rather as it was for rock stars in the 1970s, endowing the male with an exciting dash of danger. It was to France, after all, that Wilde fled after his release.

Fersen advanced his career the way writers have always done, by ingratiating himself with the successful authors of his time in the hope of gaining their support. He successfully pursued two members of the Academy, José-Maria de Heredia, the Cuban-born sonneteer, and Edmond Rostand, the author of *Cyrano de Bergerac*, who wrote a brief preface for his second poetry collection, *Light Songs* (*Chansons légères*). His most notable conquest was the superbly snobbish Robert, comte de Montesquiou, the model for Jean des Esseintes, the protagonist of Joris-Karl Huysmans's prototypical Decadent novel *À rebours* (translated as *Against Nature* and *Against the Grain*). Des Esseintes embodied the fin de siècle ideal of the dandy and provided a direct link with the Uranian underworld in his fascination with liquideyed, cherry-lipped schoolboys. Fersen dedicated *Ébauches et débauches* to Montesquiou. On a visit to his estate in Neuilly, in suburban Paris, Fersen met Marcel Proust, at the time an aspiring litterateur whose artistic reputation had scarcely begun, who encouraged him in friendship.

At the rear of Villa Lysis, a marble tablet proposes an

alternative to *Amori et dolori sacrum*, the motto on the front facade, proclaiming that the house was "dédiée à la jeunesse d'amour," dedicated to the youth of love. A more appropriate wording might have been a dedication to the love of youth. Like many another exile in Capri, Fersen fled to the island to escape obloquy in his native land on account of his erotic fixation with adolescent boys. Many of his fellow outcasts in Capri came, like Wilde, from the Anglophone nations, and many more from Germany, which had equally stringent laws against homosexual relations, yet France, like Italy, had no such laws. The causes of Fersen's public disgrace were vague, arising more from middle-class outrage at aristocratic privilege than from the objects of his sexual desire. Even a century after the scandal, events are difficult to elucidate. Many documents relating to the court case are suppressed, and contemporaneous attempts to shield prominent public personalities mingle with the available facts to an extent that makes it difficult to distinguish between them.

FERSEN'S TROUBLES BEGAN as Emma Bovary's did, by reading trashy romantic fiction, specifically the novels of Achille Essebac. An admirer of Fersen's verse, Essebac sent him copies of his novels of schoolboy love. *Dédé*, his first novel, was a bestseller that was reprinted nine times. The book established the basic elements of the tragic paradigm that Roger Peyrefitte's novels would follow. When the sixteen-year-old eponym, in whose body "throbbed the naked, blond elegance of ancient Hellas," finally wins a kiss from his beloved, he dies. The novel concludes with a phantasmagoric apotheosis in grand classical style as Dédé joins the ranks of beautiful boys who died young: "Look! There they are! The ephebes* of Tiberius descend from the heights of Capri, entwined with mourning garlands of iris and hyacinth."

At the time Fersen met him, Essebac had just published *Luc*, a novel dedicated to "the little bootblacks of Marseilles, to the young flower-boys of the Spanish Steps in Rome, to the cheeky street urchins of Naples, to Pio, the little blind Florentine." *Luc* pushes the storyline to a more dangerous level by telling a story of love between an adult and a pubescent boy. The protagonist is a painter who conceives a fatal passion for a schoolboy he hires as his model for Daphnis, the shepherd beloved of Pan. The scene in which Luc poses for the first time inspires a prolonged paean to boyish beauty that struck a chord for Fersen he had never heard sounded in Alfred de Musset's muted evocations of beauteous maidens:

It was a marvel when, in the warmth and pleasing solitude of the studio, the ephebe emerged nude, a statue of polished ivory, between the wings of a folding screen covered in Venetian velvet. A strap of goatskin barely covered his dazzling loins; it encircled the rippling, satiny mother-of-pearl of his hips, and revealed, just where he was marked by the shadow of puberty, the smooth hollow of his flat belly and the

---

*Pederasts of the period often referred to the love object as an ephebe, in an attempt to burnish the pretension to a classical pedigree by suggesting a parallel with the love of Socrates for Alcibiades, that of Hadrian for Antinous, and so forth; yet it was a dishonest semantic ploy. In Attic Greek, an *ephebos* is a male who has reached the age for military service, usually eighteen. Both Alcibiades and Antinous had reached maturity by the time their famous older lovers courted them.

delicate power of his round, glossy thighs. The bright
sunlight of the studio rendered the radiance of the
robust young body luminously pale against a scarlet
background of antique drapery . . . Enormous flowers
opened their blossoms around him: roses, peonies, and
alabaster calla lilies, with their rigid phallic stamens,
blooms pale or pink, vibrant and sticky, swollen with
fragrant perfumes; yet even the supple firmness and
magnificent flesh of their petals were less perfect than
the faintly curved shoulders and pale, luminous arms
of the adolescent.

The luxurious complexity and excessive luminosity of Essebac's prose make a decorative impression, but it soon becomes
limp and tedious. It must have impressed Fersen, who would
later imitate it closely in his own effusions on the beauty of
young men in classical settings. It goes without saying that
this is a French phenomenon, which does not resemble any
thing in Greek literature.

In 1905, after Fersen had completed his compulsory
military service, he took an apartment in the eighth arron-
dissement near his mother's place, on avenue de Friedland,
close to Parc Monceau. The neighborhood is the setting of
Luc; the boys in the novel make their assignations in Parc
Monceau. Soon after he moved into his apartment, Fersen
met Louis Locré, nicknamed Loulou, a fourteen-year-old
student at Lycée Carnot. According to Peyrefitte, Fersen met
him while he was standing in front of a bookshop that displayed the novels of Achille Essebac in its window, on rue
de Berri, the street where Loulou lived. It might well be
true: the writer Paul Morand, a classmate of Loulou's who

often walked to school with him, was one of Peyrefitte's principal informants about this period of Fersen's life. Morand later confided to a friend that *The Exile of Capri* was "boring, but full of meticulous accuracy."

Fersen spoke to Loulou, who revealed that he studied at Lycée Carnot. In the days that followed, Fersen stalked him, loitering on rue de Berri and lurking by the gates of the lycée, like the menacing pedophile in a trashy thriller. After toying with his handsome, noble suitor, Loulou finally consented to come to Fersen's apartment for tea, where he gorged on cakes. Chez Fersen was decorated in high Aesthetic style, hung with silks from Liberty, a painting of Venus and nymphs by Boucher, and a photograph of Sarah Bernhardt costumed as Napoleon II in Rostand's play *L'aiglon*. It was furnished with Louis Quinze daybeds and Turkish divans, Chinese pedestal tables and Persian carpets, and lit with electrical lamps, the latest thing. The centerpiece, flanked by a harp and a piano, was a group of two bronze nudes, one male and the other female, representing "Two Loves striving for a heart fallen at their feet." The theme was one of immediate concern to the sculpture's owner, for the plans for his marriage to Blanche de Maupeou were moving forward.

One tea led to another, and soon Loulou was coming for regular worship sessions at avenue de Friedland. Fersen began giving parties for Loulou and his classmates, sometimes held within a day or two of soirees for adult aristocrats and literati, with his mother in attendance. At first the gatherings were small groups of boys with flowers entwined in their hair, who listened to Fersen reading Hugo, Baudelaire, Verlaine, and of course the host's own poems about amorous shepherds, followed by cream puffs and babas, sometimes served with small libations of champagne. As the guest list grew, the entertainments developed into amateur theatricals. Fersen staged elaborate tableaux vivants illustrating classical themes, with the guests attired in togas, enacting romantic scenes that did not require the participation of female characters, such as Pan and Daphnis, and Apollo and Hyacinth. Death scenes were often performed, which eventually dispensed with the togas: Heliogabalus, the boy-emperor of the late empire who married his favorite charioteer, a subject beloved of the Decadents; Antinous drowned amid water lilies, on a mirror to represent the Nile; Adonis on a bed of roses. An eyewitness gave a detailed description of one death scene in which a naked youth lay "on a white bearskin, his body covered with golden gauze, his forehead covered with roses and his arms resting on a skull of polished ivory." Music was introduced, written for the occasion by fashionable composers such as Reynaldo Hahn, Proust's former lover.

Fersen's tableaux vivants enjoyed a vogue among the gratin. Monocled nobles and celebrated courtesans would drop by to take in the spectacles on their way to the opera. The boys enjoyed dressing up and were thrilled by the attention from grown-ups, and might have been too young to grasp fully the implications of the louche themes. They had already been exposed to them: a master at Lycée Carnot, Albert Tozza, in collaboration with a successful pulp novelist and poetaster named Aimé Giron, had published a series of sensational novels about Antinous, Gilles de Rais, and the life of Petronius, which circulated among his students. Fersen staged a tableau based on the last theme, impersonating the author of the *Satyricon* himself to a piano accompaniment by Hahn.

It was getting out of hand, if for no other reason than that the tableaux had become a laborious proposition. The time to reform arrived when Fersen's mother concluded negotiations with the vicomte de Maupeou and his wife, and invitations were issued for a betrothal party. The date was set for July 9, the feast of Saint Blanche; although the prospective fiancée was Protestant, her family might have wanted Catholic guests to experience a sympathetic vibration. Fersen decided to put a stop to the tableaux. There was nothing overtly vicious about them, but despite the aristocratic guest list they were hardly respectable. To celebrate turning over a new leaf, he published a collection of verse with the funereal title *Processions That Have Passed* (*Les cortèges qui sont passés*), in which the references to pagan orgies and sentimental shepherds were few and muted. He composed an elegiac poem of farewell for Loulou, "The Last Kiss."

Fersen's resolution to reform came a melodramatic moment too late. On the evening of July 9, 1903, as Fersen was dressing for the fete at which his engagement would be announced, there was a knock at his door. A news story in *Le Figaro* the next day would report that the police "arrested the Baron d'A., aged twenty-three, who is accused of luring young boys to his bachelor flat in the Avenue de Friedland and there holding veritable saturnalias." In a wretched irony, the newspaper's society page ran a previously written story about a tea party at a swanky tennis club on l'Île de Puteaux, on the outskirts of Paris, where the guests included "Baronne Axel d'Adelswärd, whom everyone was congratulating on the engagement of her son, the Baron Jacques d'Adelswärd, to Mlle. Maupeou." When the police suggested to Fersen that he dress more simply for jail, he opened his wardrobe, revealing hundreds of cravats and bespoke shoes, mingled with an assortment of theatrical togas and laurel wreaths. He spent the night in a jail cell, as his mother and sisters and Blanche de Maupeou waited in vain for him to arrive at his own engagement party.

The case against him, which might have arisen from a denunciation by a disgruntled former valet, apparently supported by police surveillance of some of the Carnot boys, was thin and ambiguous. The age of consent in France at that time was thirteen. What is clear from a contemporary perspective might have been only vaguely apparent to Fersen and the court: capital-*D* Decadence was on trial more than his own behavior. It was the twentieth century, and modern times demanded men of action. The dandyish airs of men like Robert de Montesquiou were old-fashioned. In her study of Fersen's trial, the American scholar Nancy Erber summarized Fersen's legal predicament thus: "Contemporary anxiety over the presumed corrupting influence of literature and the perceived danger to the Republic of an aristocratic class seemingly exempt from the social contract converged." Fersen's unforgivable offense was the same as Wilde's, as Robert de Tournel had explained it to the fictional Jacques d'Adelswärd in the dining room of the Quisisana Hotel, in *The Exile of Capri*: it was the crime of getting caught, of making his private aberrations a public spectacle.

For five months, as Fersen idled in jail awaiting trial, the scandal owned the front pages of the newspapers, providing a pretext for screeds representing every partisan shade. The Catholic press saw in the story a proof of Protestant immorality, the anticlerical papers delighted in the abundant presence of Catholic priests, and despite the absence of Jews in the story, there were anti-Semitic critiques. Even the royalists found an angle, portraying Fersen as a victim of the nation's educational system, and when that did not stick, they presented him as a Swedish interloper. Above all, the radicals had ample material to exploit the scandal as a proof of the degeneracy of the aristocracy.

The headline, the journalistic shorthand for the scandal, derived from that skull: it was *l'affaire des Messes Noires*. The coverage spread abroad: American papers published lurid accounts of Black Masses; the Italian and German press were full of *le messe nere* and *schwarze Massen*. Although there was nothing to suggest that such a thing had occurred, Fersen was supposed to have lured innocent children to his temple of vice to invoke evil spirits, in the tradition of Gilles de Rais. Demonism was in the air. After the success of *À rebours*, Huysmans, on his tortuous path toward mystical Catholicism, had expanded that book's diabolical undercurrents into a novel on the theme of Satanism in modern France. Published in 1891, *Là-bas* (the title literally means "down there"; it has been translated as *The Damned*, though "At the Bottom" might be closer) tells the story of a medievalist who becomes obsessed with Gilles de Rais and eventually performs a Black Mass himself.

Fersen, thus identified with the Decadents, stood convicted before his trial began. He had not helped himself by having published, when the risqué tableaux were at their peak, a collection of poems entitled *The Hymnal of Adonis*, "in the style of the Marquis de Sade," a delirious evocation of a factitious Greece, "mother of perfume, gaiety, and roses." The police searched the apartment on avenue de Friedland and found the paraphernalia for the tableaux vivants, including the damning skull, and—shades of Bosie—Loulou's love letters. Fersen was charged with inciting minors to debauchery, a vague, subjective crime that was difficult to defend against. Simply reciting Baudelaire would have sufficed to sustain the charge for some right-thinking Frenchmen. A second charge of outrage to decency was dropped, perhaps for fear it might drag in aristocratic members of his audiences. Fersen had few defenders: it would have taken courage for the homosexual artists and writers he socialized with to speak out on his behalf, and some of them pusillanimously denounced him in the hope of deflecting attention from their own activities. Proust pleaded for compassion, insisting that everyone has a right to love in his own fashion, a controversial position in the reactionary atmosphere of the times. Alfred Jarry, the openly gay author of the symbolist landmark play *Ubu Roi*, also stood up for Fersen.

Fersen's mother, at great expense, hired Charles Edgar Demange, the lawyer who had defended Alfred Dreyfus. He mounted a weak defense, presenting his client as a child of privilege whose mind was debilitated by a family history of insanity, alcoholism, and epilepsy, a theory disproved by the lucid testimony of the defendant, dressed in an elegant blue suit, who quoted Plato, Virgil, and Shakespeare from memory. Loulou Locré gave a polished performance on the stand that posed no threat to the solidity of butter in his mouth. The prosecutor assumed an attitude of compassion, putting the blame for the alleged crimes on "the poison of literature."

Fersen was found guilty and sentenced to five months' time served.

The morning after his release, he tried to enlist in the French colonial army but was refused, ostensibly on the grounds of his health. The Ministry of War referred him to the Foreign Legion, but Fersen rejected the idea, fearing it would damage his reputation (though that hardly seemed possible). He moved on to his alternate plan, a thrilling beau geste in the grand Romantic tradition, a scene from Balzac rather than Huysmans. He bought a revolver and a bouquet of flowers and hired a carriage to take him to the Maupeous' country estate. When he arrived, he ordered the coachman to take the bouquet and his calling card to the door. The footman gave them to his master and swiftly brought them back with a demand that the uninvited caller leave immediately. Fersen pulled out his gun and shot himself, grazing his forehead. The vicomte de Maupeou reportedly leaned over the terrace and shouted, "Throw him out, even if he's dying."

Fersen's efforts at redemption might have had a pathetic air, but he cannot be blamed for considering himself a ruined man at twenty-three. Virtually all his friends deserted him. For the rest of his life, his name was synonymous in France with criminal debauchery. He was cruelly lampooned in a pornographic novel, *Memoirs of Baron Jacques: Damnable Lubricities of the Decadent Nobility*, a chaotic sequence of disgusting sexual exploits that were presumably intended to be in the tradition of the Marquis de Sade. Baron Jacques exhumes his mother's skeleton and rapes little boys above it; he drowns a child in semen. Years later, Paul Morand and his father encountered Fersen as they were crossing Piazza San Marco, in Venice. Morand recognized him from his schooldays at Lycée Carnot. He wrote in his memoir *Venises* that his father, a curator of painting at the Louvre, swerved aside, saying, "I don't shake hands with pederasts," prompting Morand to observe that he probably did so every day without knowing it. Fersen's family proposed that he move to Sweden, while the Swedish Adelswärds thought he should start a new life in America or Australia. He chose Capri.

<center>~~~~</center>

FERSEN'S LITERARY WORKS have been so drastically undervalued by nearly everyone who has commented on them, under the baleful influence of Roger Peyrefitte and Compton Mackenzie, that any critic with an instinct to be truthful must undertake some effort at rehabilitation. Fersen has been inaccurately portrayed as a vanity author who inflated the success of his books by publishing first editions that falsely claimed on the title page to be second or third impressions. In fact, most of his books were published by Léon Vanier, a prominent editor who also published Verlaine, Rimbaud, and Mallarmé. The assertion that he presented first editions as reprints is quickly disproved by browsing in the National Library of France. Cocteau condemned Fersen as a purveyor of "Graeco-Preraphaelitico-Modernistic bric-à-brac, at once priest and acolyte not of the Black but of the Pink Mass." Even judicious Shirley Hazzard scornfully dismissed Fersen as a "rich poetaster" in *Greene on Capri*, a memoir of her seasonal encounters with Graham Greene on the island.

His work may be derivative and uneven, but it is not the wretched pastiche and insipid doggerel denounced by writers who take as their main subject Fersen's melodramatic life and might not have read his works with care. In his verse, nuance is easily lost amid the dense classical allusions, perfumed tropes, and extravagant homages to adolescent flesh. Fersen's sin in the eyes of posterity was the same one that damned him in the eyes of the establishment of his own era: isolated in Capri, he took as his model the Decadents, a literary movement in its final decline, at a time when many of his contemporaries were inventing revolutionary modes. (Not all of them: Fersen's visions of graceful lads in bucolic settings are no more sentimental than those of A. E. Housman, among others.) Cocteau was just in his invocation of the Pre-Raphaelites but obtuse in describing Fersen's style as modernistic, for it was precisely the absence of modernist influence, conjoined with scandal, that condemned him not to a minor reputation but to no reputation at all.

In 1905, after Fersen had made his move to Capri and while his villa on Monte Tiberio was under construction, he went on a long voyage to the Orient. At his first stop, in Ceylon, he wrote an autobiographical novel that is the most original in his oeuvre. It is a problematic description of a book that is swamped by the influence of Huysmans and Wilde, but while *À rebours* and *The Picture of Dorian Gray* anticipated the gay sensibility by suggestion, *Black Masses: Lord Lyllian* is one of the first novels that openly portrayed a way of life based upon homosexual desire, and the novel is more complex than that. It narrates the life of a Scottish nobleman orphaned at seventeen who falls under the influence of a flamboyant homosexual writer named Harold Skilde, transparently based on Oscar Wilde, who plays Pygmalion and remakes him as a monstrous mixture of Narcissus and Heliogabalus. Blessed with ethereal beauty and possessed by sexual lust, Lord Lyllian engages in a series of affairs with boys and men, as well as women (one of whom commits suicide at a party when he refuses her kiss), and comes to ruin when he stages "black masses" with Parisian schoolboys.

Harold Skilde is almost the only male character who is not in some way an emanation of the author. Will Ogrino, a Dutch medieval historian who privately published a comprehensive, thoroughly researched biography of Fersen, describes the novel as "a virtually unique manifestation of narcissism." Mirrors occur in almost every scene. At fifteen, Lyllian awakes in the middle of the night, pulls off his nightshirt, and stands before the mirror. "He found himself beautiful, very desirable indeed, so that, now fully awake, exhilarated by his youth and nudity and caressing the slender body, he kissed the mirror as he would have kissed himself."

Harold Skilde seduces the young lord by writing a masque on the theme of Narcissus for him. The association of the novel's autobiographical protagonist with the myth is made literal as he carries on affairs with other characters who embody different aspects of the author's life and personality. Lyllian's first name is Renold, that of Fersen's younger brother, who died in infancy. One of his admirers is the cynical middle-aged diplomat Herserange, named after the d'Adelswärds' family seat. His most sympathetic lover is a tubercular Swedish poet named Axel Ansen, who is identified as a descendant of *le beau Fersen*, the author's own distant relation (or so he believed); Axel was his own father's name. A key difference is that Lord Lyllian is twenty, just three years older than the older boys in his entourage, whereas Fersen was twenty-three and thus unambiguously an adult at the time of his arrest.

The description of the "black masses" in the novel, told from the point of view of Lord Lyllian's servants, who are spying on him for the police, is the closest thing to a confession of his activities that Fersen ever published. The fictional description matches the court records in essential details. A naked youth lies on an altar, surrounded by white roses and black lilies, holding a skull; in the servants' naive, confused telling, Lord Lyllian brandishes a sword as he chases another boy around the room. Fersen piles on contemptuous satire of the hypocritical, philistine witnesses who testified against him: the policeman who is noting down the servants' testimony exults that he has "an excellent case of corruption of minors," with evidence of "reciting poetry and other obscenities." Fersen defends his activities in the words of Lord Lyllian, who here addresses another pederast:

> I teach these youngsters about the greatness of the love they vaguely perceive, and sometimes, after I have been entrusted with their youthful confidences, and after I have thoroughly examined their sentimental souls, as dusk falls I read to them the painful lamentations of Byron or the litanies of poor old Verlaine . . . Since they have no one to whom they can open their hearts and since school is limited to grammar and football, I encourage them to choose among themselves a kind-hearted friend with whom they will discover life, its beauty and tenderness, in the way it ought to be discovered.

Fersen is disingenuous. The court records reveal that in a few cases, particularly that of Loulou Locré, these pep talks went beyond recitations of Byron and Verlaine to include the fondling of genitals and masturbation, though there was never an accusation of intercourse, a distinction of critical importance to everyone involved.

The complexity of the novel lies in the fact that the protagonist, like the book's author at this point in his life, is bisexual, motivated by a "pure" (that is, socially sanctioned) love of women that balances his desire for men. The more outrageous Lyllian's public homosexual personality, the more punishing the guilt he feels. In the novel's denouement, he vows to renounce his dangerous dalliances with schoolboys and marry an innocent aristocratic girl. They plight their troth in a ruined Gothic chapel, kneeling before a statue of the Virgin Mary, which the beloved has strewn with roses. "Nestling against Lyllian's breast, the young fiancée, so petite and dainty, shuddered like a timid bird." Soon afterward, as he is dressing for a dinner to announce his betrothal to "his English cousin" (like many Continental Europeans, Fersen fails to observe the distinction between Scotland and England), one of his cast-off schoolboys arrives in an agitated state.

André Lazeski, whom Lyllian had previously described to one of his pederast friends as "the little seventeen-year-old Pole with pretty eyes the color of clear water," has heard the news of the engagement and angrily accuses Lyllian of breaking faith with him and his classmates. For the others, it might have been a lark, but his love, André declares, is a fathomless, undying passion. "You elevated my heart and my soul," he cries, "you changed my life." Their love, the boy tells Lyllian, "was all the more enduring because it was ethereal. How was it born, how did it grow? Do we ask such questions of the birds, of the mountains? Ah, you used to call me your 'little adored one,' do you remember?" Lyllian is moved by the boy's recollection of their former intimacy and attempts to soothe his proud, wounded heart by assuring him that his previous avowals were sincere, but now he sees that it was a delusion. He urges Lazeski to follow his new, healthy vision of love: "Abandon this way of life. Young people who, like us, believe they can replace woman's love by their own are emotionally sick . . . Today I repent and I am saved. I have suffered much, André, and I am not rejecting you. I will help you towards a speedy recovery."

Yet Lazeski's frenzy cannot be appeased. The novel's finale is a catastrophe in the style of verismo opera, which was then at the height of its popularity. The boy has a gun, there is a struggle, shots are fired, the two of them are mortally wounded. As the police clamor outside, pounding on the locked door, the forbidden love is redeemed, even as it claims the lives of its victims. They die locked in an embrace, as André's tears fall on Lyllian's face.

> "My child, my brother, my beloved," murmured
> Lyllian as if far off. "It is here . . . nearby, the peaceful
> tomb, the door that is opening onto the most beautiful
> countries . . . Oh, I am suffering! Yes, my 'little adored
> one,'" he continued, drunk with pain, "you were
> right . . . It was too easy to abandon you . . . Together
> we will embark on a long journey . . ."

André obviously symbolizes the Black Masses scandal. He descends on Lyllian while he is dressing for a festive announcement of his betrothal, just as the scandal had on Fersen. Lyllian's death at the hands of his little adored one is high camp to a modern sensibility, which obscures the bold originality, the imaginative freshness, in 1905, of a fictional scene in which two male lovers die in each other's arms. At the time Fersen wrote *Lord Lyllian*, the possibility of an openly declared love between men as equals had not yet been even distantly glimpsed.

Peyrefitte and others have cast doubts on the sincerity of Fersen's courtship of Blanche de Maupeou, suggesting that it was a pose adopted in pursuit of a respectable situation, as a cover to his homosexuality, but these cynical suspicions reveal more about the doubters' own psychology than that of their subject, which was more complex than that. The dossier of Fersen's trial at the Archives de France reveals that he sometimes dressed his boys in girls' clothing, even against their will. Until his move to Capri, at the age of twenty-four, Fersen was torn between a physical attraction to adolescent boys and an idealized love of adult women. Oscar Wilde was similarly conflicted and never disavowed his love for his wife. Wilde's feelings of guilt for her suffering as the result of his disgrace, and that of his sons, whom he never saw again after his arrest, were the crux of his martyrdom. In Fersen's case, the pederastic impulse was expressed by lust for individuals, while the love of women remained an abstraction. Lord Lyllian's fiancée is nameless, always referred to as the Young Girl, her beauty characterized in spiritual terms of purity and innocence, never as an inspiration of sexual desire.

It would be simplistic to psychoanalyze Fersen in contemporary terms as a homosexual tormented by socially implanted concepts of morality and guilt—and what use would such a distinction have been to him, anyway? Like Lyllian, he was presented with a choice between an outlaw existence as a sodomite and the hope of reform in a marriage with a sympathetic woman. No other course was open to him. His adventures with the lycée boys possessed an air of corrupt, artificial innocence; it was more about playacting and titillating dreams of antiquity than about sex. In exile, again like Wilde after his debacle, Fersen became exclusively homosexual, and it was not playacting, for a respectable heterosexual life was no longer possible for him. However earnestly he might have wished it, he could never have found a suitable match. And if a man of means wanted to chase boys, Capri was just the place for it.

～

MANY WRITERS WHO have considered Fersen's life express wonderment at his choice of Capri as the rock of his exile. Roger Peyrefitte fabricated a youthful meeting with Oscar Wilde to make it plausible. Yet it was a logical choice, almost the obvious one. In America or Australia, Fersen would have faced legal sanctions against Uranian love just as punitive as those in England, but Italy had repealed the laws against homosexual relations in 1889. In any case, Capri was under mainland control in theory only. The literary phenomenon of the Orgy of Tiberius had established Capri in the European imagination as an exotic place of escape for men (as they mostly were, until the twentieth century) who deviated from the norm in their sexual preferences. Tacitus and Suetonius were not specific about the sex of the emperor's orgy mates, but when Achille Essebac elegized the ephebes of Tiberius descending from the heights of Capri, he was following a venerable tradition that they were male.

Another attraction for Fersen was that Capri in the early twentieth century remained almost as much a sanctuary of Greek tradition as it was when Augustus visited there. Germans, most classical of Europeans, had come to the island in Greek-thirsty hordes throughout the nineteenth century. In *Recollections of an Alienist*, Allan McLane Hamilton, the early owner of Villa Castello, posted a stereotypical complaint that the Germans "overran the island: there was hardly a path that was not strewn by them with empty sardine cans and greasy papers, scraps of ham and bread, marking their daily walks; their noisy voices also penetrated everywhere."

In 1827, August von Platen-Hallermünde, like many young German men of his generation, followed in the footsteps of Goethe on a classical pilgrimage to Italy. Platen's reputation as a lyric poet of the first rank has remained secure in his homeland, but he has been only sparsely translated into English. Among his earliest works in Italy is an ode to the fishermen of Capri, which was obviously based on personal observation. Platen begins with a topographical sketch of the island, as Tacitus and the Marquis de Sade had done before him: "If you have come to Capri, this rock-girdled island, as a pilgrim, then you know how difficult it is to find a harbor for approaching ships: Only two locations are suitable." The Marina Grande is a spacious harbor open to Naples's lovely bay, while the lesser haven, the Marina

Piccola, looks out upon the sea, the "waving wilderness." From there, "you see no shore other than the one you are standing on." Above the poem's imagined pilgrim looms the Castiglione,

> a crumbling structure
> with loopholes, where there was always a watchtower
> to guard the open beach from Algeria's flags,
> come to snatch the island's virgins and young men.

Descending to the sandy gravel, "you will behold a rock low and flat, braving the surf of the waves," bare but for a fisherman's hut, the most isolated habitation on the island.

> Here, early in life, the boy tests himself dashing against
>   the waves.
> Soon he learns to take the helm and steer the rudder.
> The headstrong child caresses the curling dolphin,
> which, lured by sounds, comes rolling toward the boat.

> May a god bless you and your daily work,
> peaceful people, so close to nature and the mirror of
>   the universe! . . .

> Live! The ancient fathers of your race lived just as
>   you do,
> ever since this island was first torn from Siren's seat,
> and Augustus's daughter here bewept sweet crimes.*

---

*The final verse contains an uncharacteristic lapse in classical learning: Platen confuses Capri with Pandateria, where Julia was exiled after her adulteries were exposed.

Platen's ode, among the earliest works by a foreign poet in Capri, sounded themes that would dominate the literature associated with the island until the modern era: the island's solitude in the "waving wilderness," the desolate majesty of its landscape subjugating the human inhabitants.

Scion of an impoverished noble family, Platen was enrolled first in the Royal Cadet School, in Munich, and then at an academy for court pages, where he discovered his attraction to his own sex. Throughout his life, he was shadowed by a sense of guilt that verged on doom as a result of his sexual inclination. Platen was a master of the sonnet and cultivated archaic classical forms. German Romantic poetry often has an unhealthy dose of Weltschmerz: if things are going rapturously well with the beloved, the reader knows that tragedy will soon follow. In Platen's works, the sense of impending calamity and self-pitying grief is sometimes oppressive. It was ridiculed by his contemporaries, but his sense of martyrdom was not baseless. Heinrich Heine, for one, picked a feud with him, denouncing him as a homosexual.

Thomas Mann undertook a major rehabilitation of Platen, whose poetry was a crucial influence on *Death in Venice*. In an essay, Mann proposed that Platen's preoccupation with form was directly linked with his eros, the subject overt or covert of most of his poetical works. "The Persian *ghazal*, the Renaissance sonnet, the Pindaric ode," wrote Mann, "all knew the cult of youths and lent it literary legitimacy. Because [Platen] took them over from the past—and with what unheard-of artistic brilliance he recast them!—their emotional content could also appear borrowed, as an archaicizing convenience, impersonal and therefore possible in this world." Pederastic love was the principal theme of the *ghazal*, indeed almost its only subject. Platen did not have the Persian poet's option of addressing love poems to the living youths he admired, but by adopting the form of the *ghazal*, he invested his verses, outwardly lofty in tone, with the emotional muscle of the erotic poetry he imitated.

Platen's journey to Capri had been inspired by his close friend August Kopisch's visit there the year before. Kopisch became an instant celebrity in Germany after he claimed to have discovered the Blue Grotto, a sea cavern on the island's northwestern coast, which is illuminated by sunlight that shines through an underwater cavity and irradiates the waters with a sparkling azure glow. Kopisch swam into the cave in 1826 after his innkeeper tipped him off, and he described its weird beauty in *The Discovery of the Blue Grotto of Capri*, which was reprinted in many editions. Kopisch's claim to fame was spurious, of course; the Capriotes had always known of the grotto's existence but avoided it as an unlucky place. Yet the success of Kopisch's book soon made the Blue Grotto the island's most celebrated natural attraction, a must for every visitor.

Just fifteen years later, the choreographer August Bournonville, a principal creator of the Danish school of ballet, visited the cavern on an Italian tour, which inspired him to set an act of one of his most famous ballets there. *Napoli*, a staple of the repertory of the Royal Danish Ballet since its premiere in 1842, is the story of Gennaro and Teresina, young lovers who are shipwrecked during a moonlight cruise in the Gulf of Naples, at the end of act 1. In the second act, naiads transport Teresina's lifeless body to the Blue Grotto, where the presiding deity of the gulf holds court. He miraculously revives her and makes her a naiad in his service. Gennaro finds her there, and by the ballet's end she is restored to human form, and to him. The Blue Grotto act has long been regarded as the ballet's weakest, known as "Brønnum's akten," because after the first intermission many members of the audience would go to Brønnum's restaurant, near the theater, to have a drink and a snack and then return for the finale, an exuberant expression of the sunny southern streak in the Danish golden age, capped by a famous tarantella.

In his memoir, Bournonville is moved to a Romantic rapture by the Blue Grotto. Observing the magical transformation of his handkerchief when it is dipped in the water, he leaps overboard: "One's body glows in the water like a sulfurous flame, and each spray is a spark." He accepts Kopisch's fanciful theory that a subterranean path once led from Tiberius's palace to the cavern, which collapsed in an earthquake, "and now the imagination can have free play through the centuries during which the grotto stood forgotten and unknown," a process that, for him, resulted in act 2 of *Napoli*. "What crystalline mirrors in the sharp edges of the stone!" he effuses. "What echoes! And how mysterious is the atmosphere, which suddenly takes away the thought of everything that has delighted or offended one in the outside world."

After his visit to the grotto, in 1869, Mark Twain wrote an equally vivid yet more scientific account of the place in *The Innocents Abroad*:

> The entrance to the cave is four feet high and four feet wide, and is in the face of a lofty perpendicular cliff—the sea-wall. You enter in small boats—and a tight squeeze it is, too. You cannot go in at all when

the tide is up. Once within, you find yourself in an arched cavern about one hundred and sixty feet long, one hundred and twenty wide, and about seventy high. How deep it is no man knows. It goes down to the bottom of the ocean. The waters of this placid subterranean lake are the brightest, loveliest blue that can be imagined. They are as transparent as plate glass, and their coloring would shame the richest sky that ever bent over Italy. No tint could be more ravishing, no luster more superb. Throw a stone into the water, and the myriad of tiny bubbles that are created flash out a brilliant glare like blue theatrical fires. Dip an oar, and its blade turns to splendid frosted silver, tinted with blue. Let a man jump in, and instantly he is cased in an armor more gorgeous than ever kingly Crusader wore.

The Blue Grotto was well-known to the Romans. Kopisch found the remains of a nymphaeum, a seaside pleasure pavilion, or small temple, which might indeed have been built by Tiberius, adorned with life-size sculptures of Tritons, male sea deities, in dynamic poses suggestive of blowing on conchs. Fifty years later, John Clay MacKowen, a veteran of the American Civil War from Louisiana, conducted one of the first systematic surveys of the cavern, which he described in his guide to Capri, published in 1884. After the war, Mac-Kowen, a doctor with a practice in Rome, suffered from chronic insomnia so severe that he contemplated suicide until he visited Capri, in 1877, and found he could sleep soundly there. He met a fisherman's daughter and married her, and within two years he had fathered a child, bought a yacht, and built a house, a Gothic castle overlooking the Marina Grande, which was later converted into the first grand hotel on the harbor.

A native of East Feliciana Parish, MacKowen was studying medicine at Dartmouth College when the Civil War broke out. He returned to Louisiana immediately after the Battle of Fort Sumter and enlisted in the Confederate army. He served with distinction and was wounded at Shiloh, and by the war's end he held the rank of lieutenant colonel. He returned to New Hampshire to complete his degree in 1866, less than a year after Lee's surrender—a remarkable case of forgetting bygones on both sides. By the end of the year, he was in Paris, where he enrolled in an advanced course of medicine, but he repatriated after a debilitating nervous breakdown. He bought a ranch in Southern California, and by 1870 he had moved to San Francisco, where he served for three years as the superintendent of public schools. Yet his brief residence in Paris had captured his imagination. He wrote to his sister that "in so cosmopolitan a city as San Francisco" there was "no danger of growing narrow-minded," yet he nonetheless felt "a want of culture which makes life in Europe so agreeable . . . Ah, Europe, would that some lucky star might shine over my head in life and light the way soon to that home of all my wishes and hopes!"

A star shone, and after postgraduate training in Vienna and Munich, MacKowen was living in Rome, the choice of Italy perhaps partly the result of his enthusiasm for opera, which he had discovered in Paris. His house was in the Piazza di Spagna, where he missed being Charles Coleman's neighbor by only a few years; Coleman had occupied the house overlooking the Spanish Steps where John Keats had lived and died. In Capri, the two Civil War veterans, who had been on opposing sides of the cause, lived scarcely more than a mile from each other for some twenty years. It would have been impossible for their paths not to have crossed, but I have found no record of their meeting. Coleman was a genuine eccentric, living in an imagined chivalric past in Villa Narcissus, and MacKowen was a bluff, irritable man who lodged lawsuits as a hobby. He carried on a bitter feud with Axel Munthe (who, in a remarkable coincidence, had also rented Keats's house, where he opened a medical practice after Coleman had relocated to Capri). Munthe and Mac-Kowen were competitors in the business of digging up antiquities. According to Capri legend, the two men fell out over a marble fragment and challenged each other to a duel, which never took place because of an irreconcilable disagreement over the choice of weapons.

In 1883, MacKowen moved out of his Gothic castle on the Marina Grande and relocated to Anacapri, near the Blue Grotto. His house, now called Casa Rossa, is a little fairy-tale palace painted Pompeii red, incorporating Greek and Roman architectural fragments and stained-glass windows, crowned by a crenellated Aragonese tower. He crammed the house with a hodgepodge of medieval arms and armor, tapestries, Turkish rugs and carved furniture, ancient pottery, and porcelain figurines he collected on his travels throughout the Mediterranean. The top floor housed his library of rare books and manuscripts. Now a museum, Casa Rossa exhibits four sculptures of Tritons from the Blue Grotto, corroded by centuries of brine into menacing grotesques, which offer a plausible rationale for the Capriotes' belief that the cavern was haunted.

Parcel by parcel, MacKowen acquired the land above the Blue Grotto, and thereby made himself its owner, based on the legal principle of *usque ad inferos*, which endows the titleholder with the control of the mineral deposits as deep as one can dig or drill. He cherished a scheme of excavating an entrance to the cavern by land, a reasonable enough proposition; the Romans had built a stairway that led down to the grotto, which was subsequently buried by subsidence. Many Capriotes agreed with MacKowen's scheme, seeing in it a way of promoting Anacapri as a tourist destination to rival the Marinas Grande and Piccola. Others, led by his nemesis Munthe, feared it would disturb the nesting grounds of quail, a major export, and the boatmen who earned their livelihood by ferrying tourists to the cavern by sea were vehemently opposed. Embroiled in lawsuits, MacKowen returned to Louisiana in 1897, disgusted by the frustration of his scheme to open a terrestrial access to the grotto.

MacKowen died in 1901, in a shoot out near his home in Clinton, Louisiana. His killer was a state senator with whom he was involved in a bitter boundary dispute, who claimed that MacKowen had fired the first shot. There were no other witnesses, but everyone who knew John MacKowen believed his testimony, and the shooting was adjudged to be self-defense.

~~~

ON FERSEN'S FIRST voyage in the Far East, during his sojourn in Ceylon, he discovered the pleasures of smoking opium, which was on the room service menu in his hotel. He was soon addicted to its use, a habit that became an integral part of his life and eventually a major aspect of his damnation. From Ceylon he sailed to Singapore, then Penau, a tiny island in the Riau archipelago between Borneo and the Malay Peninsula, then onward to Hong Kong, Shanghai, and Peking, and finally to Japan. He returned to Europe via the Pacific, with a stop in Hawaii, populated by "negresses and cannibals," where, in a bantering letter to a friend, he claimed that he had to beg the local youths to be content with giving him blow jobs and nothing more. In San Francisco, he boarded the transcontinental train to embark on the sea voyage home. He arrived in Capri with "suitcases full of opium" and the manuscript of *Lord Lyllian* ready for the publisher.

The construction of Villa Lysis was progressing well. The architect of record was Édouard Chimot, a friend of Fersen's in his early twenties, who would later have success as an illustrator of frothy erotica, specializing in the "petites filles perdues" (lost little girls) of Montmartre. However, it is clear from his letters to Chimot that Fersen himself was the house's principal designer. Villa Lysis was intended to dazzle the eye, a condensed château in the neoclassical style of Louis XVI with Art Nouveau accents, such as gold mosaic insets in the grooves of the Ionic columns. The most unusual feature of the interior is a semi-subterranean opium den with short, squat pillars, overwrought with a bas-relief of chrysanthemums, and a mosaic floor with a Greek key border. In her biographical sketch of her ancestor, Viveka Adelswärd, the present baroness, describes Villa Lysis in a vivid metaphor as "a house in the sun with fantastic views, but also darkened by shadows and dangerously close to the abyss.

Take one false step and the fall is fatal. A house filled with beauty—but on the edge."

Like many foreign visitors before and after him, Fersen was enchanted by the stunning topography of Capri. In his memoir *Looking Back*, Norman Douglas wrote that a few days after Fersen's arrival there, Douglas led him to a crag near the summit of Monte Tiberio, which commanded a panoramic view of the Gulf of Naples, "a favorite spot of mine, high up, where you could dream through the summer evenings." The young lord instantly decided to build his house there. Douglas scrupulously pointed out the disadvantages: in winter, winds would lash the exposed cliffside location with rain, and the only source of water would be cisterns, which would have to be excavated from the rock, to catch rainwater. Douglas wrote that Fersen chose the location because it was spectacular: "It was remote yet conspicuous. People would be sure to enquire who could live, and build himself a palace, in such a situation; they would then learn that it was the retreat of a young and handsome French poet, who had turned his back on the world . . . He would be talked about."

Villa Lysis got its name from a dialogue by Plato. The theme of *Lysis* is the nature of friendship, but this early dialogue has an elaborate narrative context. As Socrates strolls through Athens, a group of young men hail him and strike up a conversation. One of them, Hippothales, is maddened by an infatuation with Lysis, a boy whose age is not specified but who seems to be at the threshold of puberty. Hippothales's friends chaff him for his inept attempts to woo the boy, and Socrates offers to give him some tips about how best to gain his love. The young men take the philosopher to the gymnasium, where he engages Lysis and a classmate in a philosophical discussion, while Hippothales lurks out of sight taking notes. A dispassionate discourse about friendship is the work's main subject, which is often cited in analyses of Plato's philosophy, but it is framed as a wise elder's advice to a younger man about how to seduce boys.

While Villa Lysis was under construction, a worker died (or was seriously injured; the record is conflicted) when he was struck by a falling stone. Under Italian law, Fersen as the proprietor was responsible, so he took the first of several exiles within exile and fled for the mainland under the cover of night. When he was in Rome, he met a fourteen-year-old laborer named Nino Cesarini, who was working at a construction site on the Quirinal, and took a fancy to him. Fersen picked him up and went home with him to meet his parents. He obtained their permission to hire him as his secretary, undoubtedly making them a handsome gift of cash, and carried him off to Capri.

Villa Lysis now had a muse. Fersen's attachment to Cesarini was not motivated primarily by sexual lust per se but rather by a passionate, almost idolatrous worship of youthful beauty. Their relationship was sexual, of course, as his fleeting encounters with Sinhalese and Hawaiian youths had been on his voyage and as his subsequent trysts with other Italian boys would be. But in Nino Cesarini he pursued a platonic love, in a more exact sense than the common meaning of the phrase, corresponding to Hippothales's passion for Lysis, in which possession of the body of the beloved plays an important part but is not the sole or even the principal object of the passion. Defying all expectations (including, perhaps, Fersen's own), the relationship endured to the end of Fersen's life, with no more stormy quarrels and interruptions than many long-term romantic relationships experience. Even more surprising, Cesarini, when he was old enough, took his responsibilities as secretary seriously and made himself indispensable to his scatterbrained patron. Fersen's attachment to him grew as much because of his precocious good sense as his good looks.

We have an exact impression of Cesarini's physical charms, for Villa Lysis was soon filled with paintings and sculptures of him, always in the nude and usually in classical poses. A bronze sculpture by Francesco Ierace of Cesarini riding the back of a leaping dolphin was erected on a plinth at the spot where Norman Douglas had first brought the villa's creator. Like most of the portraits of Cesarini, the sculpture was lost after Fersen's death. (However, on my visit to Capri in 2016, I heard gossip that the sculpture is now kept in a secret garden there.) The notable aspect of Cesarini's beauty is that even in early adolescence he did not look boyish but already possessed a mature body and the angular face of an adult, with prominent chin and cheekbones, and a modern Roman's canny gaze.

If anything, Fersen was the head-turning beauty, his good looks marred only by his vanity. In his memoir, Norman Douglas wrote this sketch of him: "With his childlike freshness, his blue eyes, clear complexion, and flawless figure, he could have made the impression he yearned to make, if he had not always been over-tailored." A few months after they met, in the spring of 1905, Fersen and Cesarini made their first voyage together, to Sicily, where they made a pilgrimage to the grave of August von Platen, in Syracuse, and to Taormina, to call on Baron Wilhelm von Gloeden, whose photographs of working-class boys posing in scanty togas were standard decor in the drawing rooms of pederasts. Fersen and his young consort were becoming a celebrity couple in the Uranian underground. In 1907, they set off on a long voyage to the Orient. In China, Fersen bought a collection of three hundred antique opium pipes, which were represented as having belonged to emperors.

The Capriotes were suspicious of Nino Cesarini—not on the moral grounds raised by the island's upright Christian foreign residents (by no means the majority of the expatriate community), but rather because he was a Roman interloper, elevated to a lucrative position of privilege that ought to have been given to a local. Again, however disgraceful the relationship might have been in the eyes of conventional morality, there was nothing criminal about it, even if Cesarini had barely attained the age of consent. Fersen, handsome as a matinee idol, rich beyond computation, with a rising if not quite an impressive reputation as a writer, possessed a degree of immunity to open reproach. In his early years there, he was the cynosure of the strange little world of expatriate Capri.

The cast of characters was changing. The older generation of self-romancing foreign residents, dominated by men such as Charles Coleman, John Clay MacKowen, and Axel Munthe, castle builders with a penchant for duels, was supplanted by Jazz Age socialites who gave lavish entertainments at which they could flirt and quarrel. Norman

Douglas's first bestseller, *Siren Land*, helped to stimulate the new wave of visitors by burnishing and widely disseminating Capri's reputation as a realm of magic and myth, which had begun with August Kopisch's tale of his "discovery" of the Blue Grotto. Acknowledged as the island's most learned foreign resident, Douglas was supremely sociable but a rolling stone, always running off to the mainland on expeditions in search of rare fungi and birds' nests, and too poor to entertain.

The unlikely social queens of Capri were a pair of elderly American women: Kate Perry, an only child who had been raised by her father, a colonel in the U.S. Army who commanded a fort in the American West, and her distant cousin Saidee Wolcott, whom Perry's father had adopted when she was orphaned at the age of nine. The women were devoted to each other for the rest of their lives, to the point of uniting their surnames, which gave rise to the common assumption that they were sisters (and the alternative, scandalous rumor that they were lovers). The Wolcott-Perrys' attachment to Capri followed the classic paradigm: they visited the island in the course of an Italian tour and decided on the day they arrived never to leave it. Kate sold a farm or two in Iowa and bought a house midway down the slope from the Piazzetta to the Marina Grande, which the women rebuilt in the reigning Moorish style and called Villa Torricella.

They were indefatigable hosts: their lavish dinner-dances, serving wine made from grapes produced by the vineyards surrounding the house, became the anchors of the island's social calendar. Faith Mackenzie, Compton Mackenzie's wife, sketched the parties at Villa Torricella in her memoir:

Their villa above the Grande Marina was built for gaiety: salons and loggias blazing with fairy lamps; long pergolas were lit by colored bunches of glass grapes among the vines. Till dawn they would speed the dancers, plying their band with wine, Kate fanning herself vigorously, her tall figure held upright in her lace dress till the last guest went.

"Oh, my! How I hate to have folks go!"

Soon after his move to Capri, Fersen met the Wolcott-Perrys in Rome, at the Temple of Vesta, where he conquered them with his noble good looks, polished Continental manners, and fine talk salted with classical allusions. They called him Count Jack and firmly latched onto him after they all returned to Capri. At his instigation, they built a small replica of the Temple of Vesta in their garden, which figured prominently in their entertainments and thus also in *Vestal Fire*, Compton Mackenzie's comic roman à clef.

Published in 1927, the novel takes as its main story the rustic American ladies' passionate devotion to the aristocratic dandy and their eventual disillusionment. It is at once a poignant fable of confidence betrayed and a savage satire, which paints a poisonous portrait of Fersen. His character is condemned soon after the reader meets him: "Carlyle once said that Herbert Spencer was the most unending ass in Christendom. He had not met the Count." *Vestal Fire* is crafted with precision and often brutally funny, but it falls short of its intended tragic impact because of Mackenzie's supercilious attitude toward the innocent ladies and his acidulous hostility toward the count. The principal cause of the characters' falling-out and the author's own disdain for Fersen was the Frenchman's lack of patriotism during the war. Fersen avoided military service because of a spurious medical complaint, an excuse that soon wore thin. In his memoirs, Mackenzie tells a devastating anecdote, which he repeated in his novel: "My only memory of Fersen in that year of 1918 is of meeting him one evening in the spring as he was turning into the Via Tragara and of his plucking something hastily from his buttonhole, not quickly enough, however, for me not to see that it was the ribbon of the Legion of Honor, which he had awarded to himself in some opium dream."

Compton Mackenzie came to Capri to live in 1913, prompted in part by an enthusiastic reading of *Siren Land*. At thirty, he was already a major writer, anyway a famous author. His powerful advocate was Henry James. In an essay published in 1914, James named him among the "best of the younger men," on a par with Joseph Conrad and H. G. Wells, with D. H. Lawrence lagging behind "in the dusty rear." Mackenzie's second novel, *Carnival*, was one of the bestselling books of 1912, filmed in 1916 and remade twice in the talkie era. In James's summary, the book is "all roses and sweet champagne and young love," which might explain why it has not fared as well with posterity as novels by other "younger men" on James's list. Mackenzie's next book, *Sinister Street*, a very long bildungsroman set at Oxford, had an enormous impact on the post–First World War generation. It was a succès de scandale, which dealt openly with forbidden issues such as Scottish nationalism and homosexuality. Orwell adored the book when he was the schoolboy Eric Blair, and was caned after he was caught reading it. While he was living in Capri, Mackenzie wrote *The Early Life and Adventures of Sylvia Scarlett*, a prequel to *Sinister Street*, which bolstered the author's notorious reputation by adding prostitution, cross-dressing, and atheism to his repertoire of controversial themes.

Mackenzie followed *Vestal Fire* with another comic novel set in Capri, *Extraordinary Women*, about the island's lesbian residents. In his memoir, Mackenzie claimed that his Capri books were romans à clef in the exact sense, closely based on real people and faithfully narrating events from life. One popular book about Capri has an appendix that provides a key to the true-life models for the two novels' seventy-seven characters. It is a pointed commentary on the state of Fersen studies, such as they are, that the novels of Compton Mackenzie are the most trustworthy source of information about his life, surpassing *The Exile of Capri*, for no full-length biography of him has been published.

Fersen himself wrote a roman à clef about the expatriate community in Capri, but the key is approximate. *Et le feu s'éteignit sur la mer...* (And the fire is doused in the sea . . .), "respectfully dedicated to the mademoiselles Wolcott-Perry," tells the story of Gérard Maleine, a sensitive, idealistic sculptor in Paris who falls in love with an American heiress, a Modern Woman who plays golf and goes joyriding in aeroplanes and fast motorcars. He takes her to Capri, where she models for his masterpiece, a sculpture of Psyche. He marries her there, in a pastoral wedding scene reminiscent of Mozart's *Marriage of Figaro*, and immediately experiences a disastrous disillusionment. The novel is a harmless, amusing entertainment, marred by a tragic ending that falls flat.

Fersen's evocation of Capri in the novel is affectionate if patronizing, and as accurate today as it was when the book was published. The Piazzetta, he writes, is like a little theater, thronged with people who "make extravagant gestures yet appear to be in no hurry at all, like the extras in an operetta." Debonair, mustachioed carabinieri, looking a cross between Pulcinella and Napoleon, stroll across the stage, which is wafted with the scent of frying garlic. The afternoon sun makes bright splashes on the stone staircase, its steps lined with flowerpots, that leads up to the pompous cathedral. On the right, a terrace edged with white columns overlooks the sea, with a sign indicating the entrance to the funicular. The old town clocktower looms over the scene, its powder-blue faience dial peering down at the players as if through a monocle.

The book provoked outrage in Capri when it was published, in 1909. It was condemned as a vicious roman à clef that insulted everyone in the foreign community of Capri, yet the reader searches in vain for characters that clearly target individual residents. One malicious passage, often quoted to justify the opprobrium heaped on the book, seems mild enough. If the intent was to satirize real people, it is too vague to identify them: "The people in Capri annoyed [Maleine]. It was a social cocktail with the most heterogeneous mixture: bankrupt bankers, crooked lawyers, former croupiers from the Riviera, gentlemen working at trades, newly enriched dishwashers fraternizing with virtuous old tarts, girls who were unmarriageable or too-fervent admirers of Lesbos."

The only character evidently modeled on an actual person is identified with Fersen himself: Eric Hultmann, "the little painter who lives on Monte Tiberio," who has "an unassailable bad reputation." At a dinner party, one of the guests breathlessly reports that "he lives there with a Chinaman," perhaps a conflation of Nino Cesarini and Fersen's Sinhalese servants, and "has a twenty-three-year-old male cook and statues of completely nude men." Maleine mockingly asks whether Hultmann ought to put boxer shorts on his statue of Antinous and proffers the standard Decadent defense of heterodox private affairs, echoing Proust's plea on Fersen's behalf after the Black Masses scandal: "Everyone has the right to hold his own views about life. When it comes to intimate morality, only a laundress has the right, the pleasure or the annoyance, of sticking her nose into Hultmann's dirty linen." After Maleine's bride abandons him and runs away with a former lover, Hultmann takes his brokenhearted friend on a tour of pagan Campania, endeavoring to persuade him to sample the consolations of boy love. The attempted conversion fails, and the novel ends abruptly. In Mackenzie's wicked synopsis, "following upon a tornado of invective against the falsity and lust of Woman," Maleine mutilates the sculpture of Psyche "and in pushing it over the cliff into the sea pushed himself over on top of it."

After the publication of *Et le feu*, Fersen's sterling reputation began to tarnish. His conviction in Paris had become common knowledge on the island, though the Wolcott-Perrys stopped their ears to the revelation and persevered in their belief in Fersen's hollow denials. In 1909, Nino Cesarini turned twenty, making him too old to continue to embody Fersen's erotic ideal, so Fersen imported younger talent from the mainland for sex. A hedonistic life centered on opium and sex with adolescents might raise eyebrows, but it could be overlooked if the hedonist was an aristocrat with steel shares. However, popular opinion shifted against

Fersen after another scandal brought on by his passion for amateur theatrics.

Cesarini had been called up for military service, and to celebrate his twentieth birthday, Fersen planned an elaborate spectacle in which Cesarini would be initiated into the cult of Mithras. It was performed by torchlight in the Grotto of Matermania, on the island's western coast, where the Romans had built a luxurious nymphaeum similar to the one at the Blue Grotto. Later (or perhaps simultaneously), the sea cavern was devoted to the rites of Mithras. Fersen composed a verse script for the occasion and cast himself in the part of Hypatos, the priest officiating at the rite, attended by his Sinhalese servants in skimpy togas and his maids, dressed as slave girls. The Wolcott-Perrys' obese cook took the role of Tiberius. In the middle of the night, cheered by wine and opium, the motley group packed up their ritual paraphernalia, donned coats over their costumes, and processed overland from Villa Lysis to the grotto.

Peyrefitte wrote a detailed description of the event, which might have been based on secondhand gossip that had a kernel of truth in it, or it might be a purely imaginative pastiche of scenes from Fersen's novels and desultory research into neo-Mithraic rites. It might even be true:

The two maidservants came and went, ringing
small hand bells and waving lanterns, according to
Mithraic ritual. They sprinkled the congregation
with leafy branches dipped in milk, a symbol of
fecundation, although all the loves present were sterile.
They stooped over them to administer the sacred

communion—a spoonful of honey . . . Nino hummed one of Jacques's songs, set to music by Nouguès:*

Chantez-moi doucement
La langue des amants
Solitaires . . .
Chantez-moi, voulez-vous?
Le Malheur d'être fou
Sur la terre.

[Sing to me sweetly
The language of lonely lovers . . .
Sing to me, will you?
The misfortune of being mad
Upon this earth.]

When the [Sinhalese] "boys" had called out that sunrise was near, the initiates straightened their leafy coronets and grouped themselves about the altar. Each recited invocations, and then Nino stripped off his robe. By the mingled rays of dawn and torches, he appeared in his nakedness, wearing only a belt of some creeping plant about his loins.

The Sinhalese flogged the initiate twenty lashes with a leather strap, and when sunlight struck the threshold of the cavern, Fersen as Hypatos ritually killed his lover's human incarnation, or perhaps it was the ceremonial death of his

---

*Jean Nouguès, who had recently had a success with his opera *Quo Vadis*, based on Henryk Sienkiewicz's novel set in Rome during the reign of Nero.

boyhood, by plunging a dagger (fruit knife) into his manly breast.

The young daughter of a farmer, cutting grass on the field above, heard voices and peeped into the grotto. She ran home, horrified, to report the murder of a naked Italian youth by a foreign lunatic wielding a sword. The truth must have seemed hardly less appalling to the magistrate, who issued a decree proclaiming Fersen's expulsion from Capri. Once again he was persona non grata.

THE NATURAL SETTING of Villa Lysis, perched on the island's highest cliff in the midst of a primordial forest, plays as powerful a part in its impact as the architecture does. The villa's gardens were supervised by Domenico Ruggiero, the island's leading landscape architect at the turn of the twentieth century, who had created the gardens at many of the island's grand private estates, including Villa Torricelli. In 1900, he designed the Krupp Gardens, one of the most gorgeous botanic gardens in the Mediterranean, sited on the southern edge of the village overlooking the Tyrrhenian Sea. Now known as the Gardens of Augustus, it remains a popular tourist attraction. The Mackenzies were devoted to Mimí, as he was called. In his memoir, Compton Mackenzie wrote, "Intelligence beamed from his eyes; sympathy flowed from the tips of his expressive fingers. With the manners of a diplomat, the appearance of a genial brigand in an opera," he was a genius with carnations and could cook pasta as well as anyone in Capri. Ruggiero carried on a never-ending row with Fersen, who decreed that not a twig was to be pruned from the trees on his estate, with the result that it was an impenetrable thicket.

I found it just the same on my first visit to Capri, in 2001. At that time, the villa was closed to the public, its ownership embroiled in legal controversy. On a walk through the woods up to Villa Jovis, I stopped to peer between the iron bars of the estate's high fence, longing to have a look at the lair of the infamous Count Fersen. A gap in the bars, apparently well traveled, presented itself, so I slipped inside and fought my way through the brambles and branches of the pine trees and beeches to the house, which was in a sad state of dilapidation. The golden mosaics were tarnished, and mold disfigured walls with peeling plaster. Through a broken window on the inland side I saw the ruined opium den, stacked with spindly gold chairs of the sort used for weddings. The terrace that faced the entrance, on the site where Norman Douglas brought Fersen soon after his arrival on the island, was broken and littered with evidence of illicit partying. Vines had grown over the plinth that had once supported Ierace's bronze sculpture of Nino Cesarini astride a leaping dolphin. The spectacular view of the Marina Grande far below and the Gulf of Naples stretching into the distance made me dizzy.

When I returned to Capri in the spring of 2016, the commune had established its ownership of the estate, restored the house, and opened it to the public. I arrived a few weeks before the season began. Not trusting to luck this time, I asked the commune to arrange for someone to meet me and unlock the gate.

Anita de Pascale, a slim, lively woman, looking glamorous in a clingy blue pullover and dark oversize sunglasses, greets me with a sunny smile. She is not an employee of the commune, she explains, but rather belongs to a volunteer group that has taken a curatorial interest in Villa Lysis. Anita is a founding member of Capri È Anche Mia (Capri Is Mine Too), an informal group of native Capriotes that was formed in 2014 to clean up and maintain public gardens, beaches, and plazas. The group has about fifty active members who meet on Sundays to sweep, prune, and plant flowers. Their main job, Anita says, is clearing the litter left by tourists.

The interior of the villa is clean but empty apart from some posters left over from an exhibition the year before, photographs of Fersen and Cesarini, the Wolcott-Perrys and Norman Douglas, interiors of Villa Lysis and Villa Torricelli, even a portrait of Roger Peyrefitte. The only place to sit is a sagging smelly sofa in a bay window that overlooks the gulf. Anita offers the information that the room will be refurnished before the house opens for the summer season. The bright morning sunshine and the clean, bracing smell of a fresh paint job give the opium den a strangely wholesome atmosphere. There and elsewhere, the architecture incorporates stone formations underlying the site that were left unexcavated, bringing a feeling of the outdoors inside.

The terrace at the entrance has been repaved, and the plinth now has a cute bronze of a boy wearing a leafy loincloth in the style of Peter Pan, whose torso is twisted as he looks over his shoulder to inspect his foot, which is being pinched by a crab on the base. I ask to tour the garden, but Anita doesn't have the key to unlock the padlock on the wicker gate. I propose hopping over it, which could easily be done. She counters by inviting me to return on Sunday, when Capri È Anche Mia will be working there, so I can see them in action.

Sunday is a bleak, blowy day, threatening a rain that never comes. When I arrive, at 8:00 a.m., perhaps two dozen men and women, in equal numbers, most of them in their thirties and forties, are already at work. The men are building a rustic wooden fence on the edge of the cliff, while the women are raking up mounds of dead leaves and mold. I find Anita in a crouch, cleaning a flat stone with a brush. She greets me happily and says, "Today I am an archaeologist! My great-grandfather worked here as a gardener. He laid these stepping-stones, and now I am cleaning them so they can be used again."

Anita de Pascale's great-grandfather was Mimí Ruggiero. She introduces me to her cousin Tonino Gargiulo, another descendant of Ruggiero's, who is potting geraniums to line the driveway that leads from the main gate down to the house. Tonino owns a fish market on Via le Botteghe, just off the Piazzetta. He has installed a snack bar there, in the front of the shop. Later in the week I will go there to eat crisp, tender fried calamari.

I ask the cousins what they think about devoting their Sundays to restoring the house and garden of an opium addict who took a fourteen-year-old boy as his lover. I pose the provocative question blandly, and it doesn't stop them for an instant. They shrug in unison and glance at each other.

"The past is the past," said Tonino. "I am not influenced by his way of life. I am grateful that he chose Capri as his home and built this beautiful villa." Anita picked up the thread: "In those days, he had to come here to live in freedom. Capri is the same now as it was then. Everyone has liberty to live as they want, and they are respected." They invite me to join them for lemon cake and coffee from a flask.

In a sense, Anita and Tonino are having Mimí Ruggiero's revenge on Fersen, by imposing a degree of domesticated order on the bosky wilderness that the house's master decreed must be left in its pristine, impassable state. Compton Mackenzie predicted it. When his first residency on the island came to a close and he boarded a ship in Naples, bound for Alexandria, Ruggiero woke up in the middle of the night to wave *addio* from the terrace of Mackenzie's villa when the ship cruised past. Mackenzie prophesied, "No doubt one of his family will sustain the great Ruggiero tradition."

PARADOXICALLY, FERSEN SPENT much of his final exile from Capri in Paris, where he continued to pursue his literary ambitions with unflagging energy. There, he created one of the most beautiful literary journals of the early twentieth century, *Akademos*, a "monthly review of free art and criticism." It was inspired by German periodicals devoted to the cause of homosexual equality, newly founded by Magnus Hirschfeld, but there was nothing doctrinaire about Fersen's magazine except a commitment to uphold the pagan virtues, Greek simplicity and Latin purity of expression, and a stern opposition to vulgarity, hypocrisy, and ugliness. It was launched under a cloud of tragedy: in the first issue, Fersen published his obituary of the journal's secretary, Raymond Laurent, who shot himself on the steps of Santa Maria della Salute, in Venice, in despair after he had been dumped by a lover. Just hours before he killed himself, he had made an unsuccessful pass at Jean Cocteau, then twenty years old. Laurent's body, Fersen wrote, was discovered, apparently by coincidence, by Vyvyan Holland, Oscar Wilde's son.

The roster of contributors to *Akademos* suggests that Fersen was not quite the despised litterateur manqué that Cocteau and Peyrefitte made him out to be, and commanded a measure of respect in the European literary establishment. In addition to friends with secure reputations, such as Achille Essebac, Robert de Montesquiou, and Norman Douglas, the list included such prominent writers as Colette, Anatole France, Maxim Gorky, Pierre Loti, Maurice Maeterlinck, and Filippo Tommaso Marinetti. After Marinetti proclaimed the principles of Futurism, Fersen improbably signed on to the movement, which renounced any sentimental reverence of antiquity. He wrote in Marinetti's journal *Poesia*, "If it is true that an artist has to live in nostalgia, it would be better for him to cling to the divine essence of the future than to the human materialism of the past." This fashionably modern view is difficult to reconcile with the devotion to pagan virtues extolled by *Akademos*, either a tribute to the flexibility of his convictions or an indication of their shallowness. *Akademos* was expensive to produce and found few subscribers, yet it still managed to get out twelve issues, comprising more than two thousand pages.

During the war years, Fersen's steel shares were in abeyance, forcing him to live on a reduced budget, and his avoidance of his military obligations was another blot on his reputation on the island. Nino Cesarini loyally stood by his lover and patron, and after his discharge from the army the two men were joyfully reunited and set out on a series of voyages while they awaited permission to return to Capri. They cruised first to the Cyclades and Tunisia and then embarked on another long voyage in the Orient, which concluded in Japan. In April 1913, the Italian government granted Fersen permission to return, which he celebrated with a book-length *Ode to the Promised Land*, dedicated to Prime Minister Luigi Luzzatti.

Fersen and Cesarini had arrived at a modus vivendi that followed the pattern of many gay partnerships in which the element of sexual desire, and therefore of jealousy, is unequal: Cesarini accepted his patron's incorrigible philandering, so long as his own position as consort and male chatelaine of Villa Lysis remained unchallenged. Fersen's love for Cesarini never abated, though it found expression in toxic jealousy on a few occasions, when the younger man dabbled in affairs with women his own age. Fersen's judgment was debilitated even as his libido was goaded by his narcotic habit, and he diverted more of his emotional life into casual sex with poor Italian youths, the descendants of Achille Essebac's "flower-boys of the Spanish Steps" and "cheeky street urchins of Naples" and the forebears of the hustlers championed by Pier Paolo Pasolini. Cesarini seems to have been truly bisexual by nature. His attachment to Fersen plainly arose from love, strengthened by the habit of companionship and not primarily by financial dependency.

Fersen's final years trace a pathetic trajectory of decline that followed the usual course of addiction. By the age of forty, his prodigious daily dosage of opium, thirty to forty pipes a day, had shattered his health and spoiled his good looks. He committed himself to a hospital in Naples to undergo a cure, but the horrors of detoxification were too much for him. He took to the use of cocaine, which was legally available without a prescription, to palliate the withdrawal symptoms, which had the usual result of simply transferring his addiction to the new drug. The doctors pronounced Fersen incurable, and he returned to Villa Lysis for what amounted to his own death vigil. He became increasingly isolated, though from time to time he still threw a famous party, as when Sergei Diaghilev brought the dancers of the Ballets Russes to Capri for a holiday after performances in Naples, and they emptied Fersen's wine cellar and danced on the terrace.

The rift with the Wolcott-Perrys had healed, but after Saidee's death, in 1917, Kate was inconsolable and lived in a shadowy state of widowhood. Norman Douglas had repatriated to England during the war years and came back to Capri only after his arrest for making sexual advances to a youth on the London Underground, when he jumped bail and made his exile permanent. The golden age of expatriate society in Capri, if it merits the metaphor, at any rate the era in which Fersen had distinguished himself, had come to an end. More and more often the parties at Villa Lysis had two guests now, the lord of the manor and his companion to prepare the pipe.

Even as his life force was diminishing, Fersen made one final conquest, or it might be more appropriate to say he was conquered for the last time, when he met fifteen-year-old Corrado Annicelli, the son of a notary from Sorrento, who was in Capri on a holiday with his parents. Although there could not have been much doubt about Fersen's intentions, Corrado's parents consented to their son's association with him on the grounds that he could perfect his French. For his part, Annicelli, in Will Ogrinc's analysis, "was torn between feelings of sincere love for Jacques and compassion and an intense disgust for his drug addiction." Fersen took the boy on a trip to Sicily, where they repeated the itinerary of his visit there with Cesarini, calling on Baron von Gloeden and making a pilgrimage to Platen's grave. On their return to Sorrento, Fersen was so ill that the Annicellis advised him to check into a hospital, but he was bent on going to Naples to purchase a fresh supply of opium on the black market. There, he was too weak for Corrado to care of him alone, so Nino Cesarini came and collected them at their hotel and brought them back to Capri.

Fersen died on the night of his return, of an overdose of cocaine dissolved in a glass of champagne. Peyrefitte composed an elaborate, melodramatic suicide scene, with bathetic echoes of the death of Socrates, interlocutor of Lysis. Suicide is obviously a plausible scenario; in the course of his research, Peyrefitte interviewed Corrado Annicelli, by then happily married, so he was well informed. Yet Norman Douglas wrote a different version, which was also based on contemporary testimony: "He dined, and as he was lighting his after-dinner cigarette fell forward—dead. Heart failure. Ten years' opium smoking had prepared the way: two years' cocaine sniffing finished him off." The difference in the two scenarios may not amount to much (and in any case, Fersen had smoked opium habitually for some eighteen years). One romantic detail that all accounts agree on is that on the night of Fersen's death a thunderstorm with spectacular displays of lightning struck Capri, which lasted twelve hours. He was buried in the non-Catholic cemetery in Capri, with a headstone engraved only with his name and the dates of his birth and death. His name is misspelled "Baron Jaques Adelsward Fersen," lacking the *c* in his first name, the nobiliary particle, and the umlaut in his surname.

~~~

THROUGHOUT MOST OF the twentieth century, critics and scholars, and therefore most readers, ranked writers by their claim to "greatness," a vague quality based in part upon the artistic value of their work, assessed by various systems that attempted to objectify aesthetic standards, but to a greater extent by their influence on literary history, defined in general terms by an author's stylistic originality and influence on younger writers. By the end of the century, these arbiters of taste had been supplanted by moral tribunes, who evaluate artists as phenomena of social history, judging them by their private behavior and political convictions more than by the quality of their work per se. Such ideological factors always played a significant role, notably in the aftermath of the Second World War, when many artists and writers who had supported Fascist regimes were ostracized. Yet among the academic critics who now tend the canon, there is scant leeway for artists of the past who failed to adhere to the prevalent moral standards of the present day (Norman Douglas being an egregious example).

Fersen fails by every measure. His private behavior was controversial in his lifetime and repellent by contemporary mores. Here is not the place for a discourse on evolving attitudes toward pederasty, sometimes euphemistically called intergenerational sex, in contradistinction to pedophilia, a psychiatric disorder in which adults are fixated on prepubescent children. Suffice it to say that the broad acceptance of homosexuality in Western societies in the present era has brought with it a strictly enforced prohibition against sex between adults and adolescent minors and an upward creep in the age of consent, by social convention if not in law. Anita de Pascale and Tonino Gargiulo's tolerant views about an opium addict with a passion for adolescents occupy the liberal end of the contemporary spectrum in Western democracies.

The particular interest of Fersen's works for the modern reader is the spectacle of the final decadence of Decadence, a bizarre efflorescence of hyperaesthetic attitudes of mind that shade provocatively into spiritual sickness. I have given little attention to Fersen's mature verse, but it is mostly devoted to celebrations of the beauty of youth, male youth, which found its most fervent expression in sexual jealousy. When Fersen and Nino Cesarini visited Venice on a holiday in 1907, Cesarini carried on a flirtation with a Russian woman, the daughter of Mark Antokolski, a well-known sculptor special-izing in Jewish subjects. Sacha Antokolski was smitten by Cesarini's swarthy good looks and followed him to Capri, where she seduced him. Hysterical, Fersen dashed off a col-lection of poems called *Thus Sang Marsyas*. The title refers to a mortal piper who challenged Apollo to a musical con-test. After the inevitable outcome, proud Marsyas was flayed alive, which provided Fersen with the metaphor for his suf-fering over Cesarini's betrayal, as he saw it. The poems ad-dress Nino's godlike beauty, the tragic prospect of life without him, and the treachery of Woman, a staple of Decadent lit-erature that originated in Baudelaire's angry poems de-nouncing his mistress Jeanne Duval as a vampire. Fersen's poem "She Who Crushes the Marrow" ("La fripeuse de

moelle"), which is dedicated to his rival by name, addresses
Cesarini with appalling acrimony:

> Yet perhaps one evening, embittered by remorse,
> You will remember my anguished tenderness:
> Your embrace of her will feel as icy to you
> as a swoon on the ankles of a corpse!
> And when the nauseating odor of menstruation
> Squirts its sticky vomit from the matrix,
> You will think you are seeing the overflow of an
> obscene chalice,
> Of blood coagulated deep within the sex organ of
> a gravedigger,
> Of gases evacuated by the Vampire-Eve!

Even an enthusiastic misogynist, who may derive a certain
guilty pleasure from Baudelaire's sick fancies, mellowed by
the patina of time and protected by the poet's imperishable
reputation, shrinks in horror from Fersen's disgusting vision.

His imaginative works about opium addiction, another
Baudelairean theme, embody other Decadent elements, such as
a fascination with exoticism, which had its origin in Wilde's
Salomé and, more ambiguously, *The Picture of Dorian Gray*.
"Ecstasy," a short story published in *Akademos*, is set in the
opiarium at Villa Lysis, which he describes in precise detail
as "a smoking room half underground" with a "thick archi-
trave supported by squat columns with large chrysanthemums," transposed to an island in the Indian Ocean during
a storm. Two lovers, Rama and Kali, experience a vision of
supreme euphoria. A human skull suspended above them as
decor begins to weep, inviting them to make their perfect,

ecstatic union eternal. Kali knows why the skull weeps: it is
a prediction of the day when death will part the two lovers.
He tenderly murders Rama by pressing a golden needle into
his heart, then leans down and sips the blood dripping from
the breast of his beloved.

"Ecstasy" was published in 1909, soon after Fersen had
discovered opium. Yet even when his addiction to the drug
was advanced and he was experiencing its hellish effects, he
was unable to abandon his mystical belief in the drug's mysterious power to produce visions of an alternate reality. Fersen's last book, published in 1921, was a slim collection of
verse devoted almost entirely to the subject of opium. Soaked
in exotic atmosphere, *Hei Hsiang: The Black Perfume* opens
with a worshipful paean to the drug:

Tonight I sing of opium,
Opium the unlimited, opium the vast,
Opium, hieratic son of Asia,
Who provides
The sweetness for nectar, ambrosia for peace,
Which the ten thousand tutelary genies
Have resurrected like an act of forgiveness,
The words of light since Confucius and Meng Tseu
[Mencius].

One of the poems is addressed to Baudelaire, identified
as "He who never came," a reference to Baudelaire's abortive
voyage to Asia, which terminated at Mauritius, en route to
Calcutta. Fersen's poem envisions an imaginary journey
with Baudelaire to Angkor, the prelude to a suite of poems
set in the ruins of the classical Cambodian kingdom. Angkor,

presided over by the majestic temple of Angkor Wat, exerted a fascination on the French imagination at the end of the colonial era that rivaled that of ancient Egypt and Babylon, its mystery enhanced by its remoteness at a time when steamship travel was an expensive proposition that required months or years. Apart from Peyrefitte's imaginative reconstructions of meetings with Paul Claudel and other European residents in Asia, which appear to be little more than plausible conjectures, the record of Fersen's voyages to the Orient is sparse. However, the vividness of the Angkor poems suggests that Fersen spent some time there, indulging in opium dreams. The first two stanzas of the poem to Baudelaire may be translated thus:

I would wish to live in the mystical jungle,
Guided by the fervor of your eyes of the believer,
And to fall humble, on my knees, far from this tawdry
    world,
Before the flowering of the lotus in the smiles of
    Buddhas,
O disillusioned Sovereign, O Grand Asiatic!

The Wat would reflect its unique nirvana
In your darkened soul as in these ponds.
We would climb with trembling steps
These stairways raised as an assault on the white sky
And seek the Ineffable in solemn music.

The most urgent issue in a consideration of Fersen's work is the basic one of literary quality. In his preface to *The Exile of Capri*, Cocteau dismissed Fersen with a smug phrase: "To be granted dreams but not genius must be the worst of tortures." Supercilious, very, but not altogether unjust, and Cocteau's palliative, that Fersen's life might be a masterpiece to counterbalance the light weight of his writings, also makes a strong claim. Yet some readers in Fersen's era placed a higher value on his work than Cocteau, Mackenzie, and Peyrefitte did. His most ardent advocate was Rachilde, the pen name of Marguerite Vallette-Eymery, a prominent critic and novelist of the Decadent movement. She made her name at twenty-four with a controversial novel, *Monsieur Venus*, on the theme of inverted sex roles, with the story of a woman who dresses as a man and transforms her male lover, a florist, into a submissive, dependent personality. Rachilde and her husband, Alfred Vallette, founded *Mercure de France*, one of the country's most influential literary journals. She wrote admiring reviews of many of Fersen's books in its pages, reserving her highest praise for his short novel *The Kiss of Narcissus*, which she judged worthy of the Prix Goncourt in 1907, the year it was published.

Set in ancient Babylon, it narrates the life of a youth of extraordinary beauty (needless to say) who is chosen to be a priest at the temple of Adonis-of-the-Ivory-Hands. Miles permits older men to worship him; one of them, a famous architect, in despair that he will never win the youth's love, kills himself by plunging a golden stiletto in his heart. Miles forms fleeting relationships with women his age, but they lack passion: he feels incapable of love. One of them, in a fury because Miles does not return her passion, finds a boy who is Miles's double, even younger than him and his equal in beauty, and dances with him in public to arouse Miles's jealousy. The ploy backfires when Miles falls in love with his mirror image and absconds with him. The story ends on an ambiguous, modernist note: Miles and his alter ego awaken at dawn on a dreary, deserted beach, wearing animal skins, with nothing to eat but berries. The double, disillusioned, wanders away and will not return, leaving Miles staring at his own image in a tidal pool.

The scene of Miles's initiation into the priesthood of Adonis-of-the-Ivory-Hands is a sequence of tableaux from a mural by Puvis de Chavannes, elegant and pallid, which invokes the myth of Narcissus as explicitly as *Lord Lyllian* did: "Miles asked for a mirror, and, as there was no mirror, he leaned, lovely and curious, over the basin where he had bathed. And the trembling water conveyed to him an image, or rather a shadow, but so fine and so youthful that he smiled." His attendants rub his body with precious oils and perfumes, then fasten a golden tunic at his shoulder and bedeck him with jewels. Before the assembled priests of the temple, who are all adolescent boys except the elderly head priest, Miles sings, accompanying himself on the lyre, of the life and death of Adonis, and then he dances, "slowly at first, then enlivened by the driving, lascivious rhythm, bending and twisting his chest, sliding with winged feet." Every time he spins around, "a mysterious power flung up his white arms, and the filmy golden tunic fluttered around them, framing the marvelous head, which shuddered giddily. Sometimes the little flowers scattered on the pavement rose in the vortex as the dance became more Dionysiac, as if they wished to float up to Miles's lips." At the conclusion of his performance,

with a charming, childlike gesture, he took a violet that
had fallen on his shoulder with the tips of his rosy
fingers, lifted his eyes to heaven as if to ask its protection
and to clothe him with light. Then he unhooked his
tunic and the silky cloth fell to the ground, fluttering
around him like a moth. And he remained in a pose like
that of a god, while the golden rays powdered his firm,
pearly flesh with warm light. The tapering arc of his
narrow ankles, muscular legs, slender at the knees,
like two alabaster columns, supported his supple torso,
the abdomen flat and slightly hollow, where Miles's
precocious manhood asserted itself. His head seemed a
beautiful flower blooming on the neck of this human
amphora, whose handles were formed by the two
adolescent arms, already robust.

This glorious apparition humbles the other ephebes to silence. The high priest, in an unprecedented gesture of abase-
ment, kneels to kiss Miles's knees.

For most modern readers, the scene reads simply as
camp. It is sincerely felt, a definitive requirement of camp;
the question is whether the performance falls so far short of
its mark that it is ludicrous rather than moving, as the author intended. Fersen was capable of pure camp, as here, in
the first stanza of "Distantly," a poem published in 1911:

It is in a bungalow that I would have you,
To sleep for a very long time beneath the punkah's
    lullaby.
It would be in a tropical land, a happy place:
The banana trees, for us, would ripen in the night.

The Kiss of Narcissus presents a borderline case: the description of Miles's Dionysiac dance, with the painterly image of the blossoms drawn up in the vortex toward his lips, charges the scene with mystical power, yet the metaphor of the amphora teeters on the verge of the ridiculous, with the boy's robust arms representing the tiny handles of a Greek jar, and his face a flower stuck in its neck. The description of Miles's nude body imitates Achille Essebac's ecstatic vision of the ephebe Luc, he of the satiny mother-of-pearl hips, published five years before. The principal difference is that in *The Kiss of Narcissus* Fersen attempts to evoke a dream of antiquity rather than a slice of contemporary Decadent life.

Another way of posing the issue is to put the onus on the reader. The ethos and mood of Fersen's Babylonian legend is overwrought and precious, no doubt, but any work of literature from the past requires the reader not only to suspend disbelief but also to participate willingly in the ethos of its era. We are accustomed to making this voluntary suspension of taste when, for example, we read Shakespeare: anyone who would complain that the events narrated by *Romeo and Juliet* are unbelievable, depending upon absurdly bad timing and the existence of a narcotic that mimics death, only displays a failure of the imagination. After we have read the play and seen it performed on the stage, and watched the film versions, after we have seen Gounod's opera and Prokofiev's ballet, we accept the preposterous elements of the plot with ease. To take an example more remote in the past, the erotic allure of pretty little Lysis in Plato's dialogue is simply weird, too troubling for modern readers to contemplate, so they read the dialogue for its analysis of the nature of friendship and ignore its erotic framing.

Yet *The Kiss of Narcissus* is uncomfortably close to our own era. Modern readers of the novel are aware that when Fersen wrote it, James had already published *The Turn of the Screw*, Conrad *Lord Jim*, and Gide *The Immoralist*, serious, highly original novels set in their own time that deal, in various shades of murk, with the theme of intimate relationships between males. (In the case of *The Turn of the Screw*, the character of a young boy under the unwholesome influence of an adult servant is named Miles.) The classical background of Fersen's book was conventional in its own time, its allusions to ancient Greek and Roman literature as familiar to his readers as *Romeo and Juliet* is to modern ones. Yet classical education would soon go into decline, and by the end of the twentieth century it was itself an antique. Most contemporary readers of *The Kiss of Narcissus* approach the book with little more than a vague awareness of Ovid's version of the myth.

A similar interpretive difficulty presents itself with respect to Fersen's life: for it to be a masterpiece, as Cocteau proposed, one must accept the erotic idealization of the male adolescent as a guiding aesthetic principle. It was an eccentric notion in the Decadent era, but soon it would pass into the realm of psychopathology, intolerable in even the most progressive circles of societies that place a higher value on the protection of children than any that preceded it. Pederasty was not a universal theme, but it was at least familiar to Fersen's readers, often in sublimated form. When Lord Henry Wotton, puffing on an "opium-tainted cigarette," first sees the portrait of Dorian Gray in Basil Hallward's studio, he calls him a "young Adonis, who looks as if he was made out of ivory and rose-leaves," and exclaims, "Why, my dear Basil, he is a Narcissus." Lord Henry imagines the sitter as a lovely thing, "some brainless beautiful creature who should be always here in winter when we have no flowers to look at," yet there is no clear suggestion of carnal relations. If such an idea should occur to the reader, Lord Henry offers as a defense, in what would soon become a wretched irony, "Crime belongs exclusively to the lower orders." Wilde's ruin a few years later created a panic among homosexuals, but its effects were felt throughout the society: the moral decadence of the Decadents predicted the decay of the aristocracy. Fersen's trial was a further, explicit tipping point in the process.

We may view the life of Oscar Wilde as a tragedy, with Wilde in the sympathetic role of a martyr, because he was a genius, as he himself proclaimed with immortal panache to customs agents on his arrival in New York. Yet as Cocteau gleefully pointed out, Fersen was not a genius. Fersen's vision was rooted in the Decadent literature of the fin de siècle, and his influence on younger writers was nil, but in *Lord Lyllian*, *The Kiss of Narcissus*, and other works he displays a certain boldness, even bravery, by portraying love between men (or rather males) openly, while James, Forster, and Lawrence were writing in code. The erotic fascination with doomed, beautiful youths that flickers through British poetry in the era of the First World War is acceptable because it is a muted leitmotif, merged with the modern myth of noble youths who died like Homeric heroes when their ethereal beauty was at its peak. The fleshly undertones remain safely buried.

The challenge of reading Jacques d'Adelswärd-Fersen is to appreciate the value of literature behind the curve of taste, to be moved by the pathos of a jealous, self-pitying drug addict, a cosseted aristocrat who never experienced a day of want in his life. It is a steep hill to climb. Yet those born to wealth suffer as much as poor folks do, and we cannot always be praising Homer: Fersen was both an outlier and an outcast who occupies a niche not the less interesting for its narrowness. It is more difficult to sympathize with those whose suffering is self-inflicted than with people who suffer unjustly. Yet for most of us, the victims of history and poverty remain pathetic abstractions, while we can see ourselves in fellow creatures who create their own troubles.

A T THE SAME time that Jacques d'Adelswärd-Fersen
was losing himself in amorous reveries of classical antiquity, other sojourners in Capri gloried in the present and
saw salvation in the future. "We want no part of it, the past,
we the young and strong *Futurists!*" proclaimed Filippo Tommaso Marinetti, the movement's founder, in 1909, in the first
of many manifestos. Marinetti's contribution to *Akademos*
and his reciprocal invitation to Fersen to write for his own
journal were a flirtation of convenience on both sides, arising
from the perennial pursuit of writers for markets and editors
for copy. It could never have resulted in a lasting relationship, for their essential principles were in almost diametrical
opposition.

The Futurists had no interest in slim, gilt ephebes but
rather enjoyed a lusty appetite for robust women. They despised the gentle pleasures of Arcadia and exalted the modern city. Yet imitating the flexible principles of the exiled

Bolsheviks who had preceded them there, the Futurists happily made an exception for Capri, tolerant and welcoming to visitors of any persuasion. At a conference to promote conservation on Capri, held at the Gardens of Augustus in 1922, Marinetti declared with characteristic extravagance that the island was "the refuge for indispensable disorders" and "a blow against European order and bureaucratic moral duty." He proclaimed Capri a Futurist island, in part because of its exciting, unruly landscape and in particular for its vernacular architecture, which evolved in isolation from the linear progression of historical styles—in other words, free from the tyranny of the Greek orders.

The Futurist beachhead in Capri was established in 1917 by Fortunato Depero, a student of Giacomo Balla, the first-generation Futurist painter, with whom he wrote a manifesto modestly entitled "The Futurist Reconstruction of the Universe." Depero was a guest of the visionary Swiss writer Gilbert Clavel, who had been based in Anacapri since 1910. Sergei Diaghilev had commissioned Depero, at the age of twenty-three, to design the sets and costumes for a new ballet by Stravinsky, which was never realized. It was Diaghilev's secretary, Mikhail Semenov, who introduced Depero to Clavel. Depero described his host as a "little gentleman, hunchbacked, with a nose cut like a square bracket and gold teeth, with a glassy, nasal laugh, who wore ladies' slippers. A man of strength and willpower endowed with superior cultivation, a professor of Egyptian history, a researcher and observer with the sensitivity of an artist, a writer, and a lover of people, poetry, and metaphysics."

The hunchbacked Egyptologist and the rising Futurist painter had a productive summer in 1917: Depero drew the illustrations for Clavel's philosophical novel *School for Suicide*, and they teamed up on a fairy-tale ballet for puppets. Caffè Morgano, the meeting place for expatriate artists and intellectuals in Capri, mounted one of the first exhibitions of Futurist paintings anywhere, with a small show of Depero's paintings, which included portraits of Gilbert Clavel. In 1928, Depero immigrated to New York, where he had notable success as a commercial artist and designed windows for Macy's and covers for *The New Yorker* and *Vogue*. After his return to Italy, he and Balla attempted to maintain the creative momentum of Futurism, which was now fatally identified with Fascism.

The most important Futurist visitor to Capri was Marinetti himself, the movement's glamorous leader. Among the more outrageous premises of the first manifesto was its glorification of war, "the world's only hygiene." The Futurists greeted the First World War joyfully. Marinetti led a volunteer force of bicyclists from Lombardy that fought in the mountains on the border with Austria, above Lake Garda. The horrors of combat soon dispelled the Futurists' idealistic illusions about the cleansing power of war, particularly after Umberto Boccioni, one of the movement's most talented and original artists, was killed in action in 1916. Marinetti was wounded in 1917, and at some point during or after his recovery he came to Capri with Bruno Corra, the pen name of Bruno Ginanni Corradini, whose career as a Futurist was short-lived. They collaborated on a short satirical novel, *The Island of Kisses*, published in 1918, which simultaneously presents the movement's response to the experience of war and mounts an attack on the pederasts in Capri; it also functions, perhaps more than the authors intended, as a self-satire of the Futurist mania for manifestos.

Styling itself "an erotic-social novel," *The Island of Kisses* takes a chaotic form that might be likened to the hallucinatory, quasi-journalistic fantasies of Hunter Thompson, with the authors as prankster-narrators. Marinetti and Corra recount their experience as covert observers of a meeting of a secret international society of homosexuals, the Pink Congress, which is held in the Blue Grotto. The novel begins, "Our too intense participation in the feverish life of our bellicose, revolutionary era forced us, in early August, to take fifteen days of total vacation." A Futurist holiday, it begins at a train station in Milan and proceeds to a steamship bound for Capri. After they embark in Naples, the Futurists find themselves in the company of fourteen well-dressed men, a group "linked by an incomprehensible common interest." The "mysterious tourists" are a cosmopolitan group, which includes a Russian legislator, a Rumanian baron, an Egyptian lawyer, the director of a library in Chicago, a Polish archaeologist, a Brazilian planter, and the Grand Duke Federor Cohn, an anti-Semitic English Jew who has converted to Christianity. The leader of the group is a French writer, Count Paul de Ritten, an approximation of Fersen, a required element of any fiction set in Capri: "A beautiful young man, slender, with pale blue eyes beneath wavy blond hair, which he pats into place from time to time with his thin, aristocratic hands, loaded with antique rings." De Ritten's sex-kittenish wife is the only woman in the group.

As the steamship speeds across the gulf, "the nude profile of the Isle of Capri, pearly, recumbent, useless, and absurd," looms into view. After the passengers disembark at the Marina Grande, Marinetti and Corra follow the group to the Blue Grotto Hotel. There, they meet an agent of the Italian government posing as a commercial traveler, who fills them in about what he has learned after shadowing members of the Pink Congress throughout the world for five years. Later that night, at the hotel, the de Rittens have a loud argument. After the count storms out, Marinetti sneaks into their room and comforts his wife. He makes a pass at her, which ends in a "kiss that explains nothing."

The middle bulk of the book is devoted to the polemical proceedings of the Pink Congress, which also calls itself the Physiological International, a jeering allusion to the Comintern. After the men assemble in the Blue Grotto and admire one another's bathing costumes, the congress elects Count de Ritten as president. The first order of business is to do something about the dreadful heat and mosquitoes, which are disturbing their sleep. When one member, a Swiss antiquarian and numismatist, proposes installing colossal electric fans throughout the island, de Ritten cuts him down, denouncing the proposal as "disgustingly revolutionary and Futuristic. We want nothing modern!" He calls for a crusade against electric lights and fast trains. He declares, "Down with bicycles, motorcycles, and automobiles, which deform the divine beauty of men!" and makes a counterproposal, to hire orchestras to play every night, hidden in vineyards, to fill the Capriote nights with the music of divine Beethoven and superhuman Bach.

As the debate descends into trivia, de Ritten calls on the assembly to table these proposals and get to the main business, the adoption of a platform and plan of action. He calls on Count Ricard, who is "French or Irish," round-faced, with tender blue eyes, an angelic mouth, and plump, shapely hands, to deliver a prepared speech that expounds the group's official ideology. The Futurists' ambivalence about the war is apparent in the satire: "Only the rocky cliffs of Capri have managed to resist the infamous conflagration"; only Capri, languidly lying on the sea, a neutral and international land, the tranquil mistress of twilight, opposes the ignoble brutality of war. Ricard outlines a nine-point plan of action, denouncing the wicked Germans, affirming support for the archaeological excavation of Greek ruins, condemning progressives and Futurists to death, vowing to suppress all machines and restore silence to the cities, and to expel women, so vulgar and smelly, from Capri, the capital of a new world order of elegant love, famous ruins, and manicured hands.

These dignified proceedings are brought to an abrupt halt by Madame de Ritten, who bursts into the Blue Grotto, condemns the men as pigs and pederasts who have corrupted her husband, and shoots herself. The Pink Congress is thrown into an hysterical uproar—"Women are always so stupid and melodramatic!" "What a vulgar gesture!" "Our party is ruined!"—but the Futurist interlopers admire her dead body: "The corpse was surprisingly beautiful. The head was thrown back, staring wide-eyed at the ceiling of the cavern, drenched in a rapid battle of azure reflections, which made the pupils of the eyes seem to be animated continuously by voluptuous glances." From the ruins of the corsage she was wearing "emerged the miraculous purity of the right breast, a dome with a small scarlet wound that did not drip blood." The president, unfazed by his wife's suicide, announces that on the next day her funeral will be held in Anacapri, where the Pink Congress will celebrate the symbolic death of heterosexual love.

The Futurists plan a prank to upset this solemn ritual:

they make a nocturnal run across the gulf to Naples, where they visit their favorite brothel and recruit some whores to come back with them to disrupt the funeral of Madame de Ritten. The ceremony takes place on a high crag overlooking the sea. It begins with a long speech by de Ritten, which repeats the effeminate aestheticism and misogynistic claptrap of the congress, ripe with Wagnerian allusions and inspiring maxims such as "Dress well," and declares that the supreme pleasure in life is to have your stunning ensemble praised by an intelligent friend. He promises that "our Pink Congress will save humanity" and predicts that after his wife's body has been sunk in the waters where Tiberius bathed, "the war will magically end and the new religion of distinction, elegance, refined nostalgia, and classical music will pacify the world."

Meanwhile, the Futurists and the prostitutes have sneaked up to the precipice. When de Ritten concludes his remarks and they hear the swooshing whisper ("*sussurrrrrri frussssciaaaanti*") of the coffin sliding down the cliff, Marinetti, Corra, and their Amazon warriors leap from their hiding place and attack. The whores beat the men savagely: "Broil. Indistinct gesticulation in the starry twilight. Punches, terrified yelps. Bodies collapsing on one another. The whistling rip of fabric. Body to body. Tumbles. Rolling among the stones." The women parry the insults of the sodomites and condemn them as bad for business. Echoing the slogan of a labor demonstration, the women's leader cries, "Down with unfair competition!" Then it all goes very wrong. *The Island of Kisses* concludes on an odd note of apology. "We wanted to pull off an atrocious Futurist joke and a demonstration against those who live in the past, but the wine of Capri had maddened the women. The play became tragic."Markoff, the Russian legislator, falls to his death, dragging two of the prostitutes down with him.

The Island of Kisses is an amusing jeu d'esprit, but its satire is blunted, in part because the Futurists manifestly share the Pink Congress's sentimental attachment to Capri, starting with its setting of the main action at the Blue Grotto, symbol of Capri's fabulous, unearthly beauty. The descriptions of the landscape are as rapturous as any in the conventional romantic fictions set there. After their ferry arrives at the island, the Futurists stop for lunch on the waterfront: "The warm, soft lilac twilight, suffocating in its sweetness, dampened the island's rough outlines, its green volumes of vegetation, marked by the white patches of the villas, and muffled the cries of the boatmen of the Marina Grande." The satire of the Pink Congress lacks a bitter note, the essential satiric element of animosity toward the target. Following the mainstream attitude of their age, Marinetti and Corra treat the homosexuals as spoiled milksops, ridiculous in their obsession with grooming and wardrobe, not as dangerous enemies.

Another work of Marinetti's from Capri, almost completely forgotten, which belies his self-made reputation as the nemesis of the classical past, is his translation of the *Germania* of Tacitus. The translation was commissioned by Umberto Notari, one of Italy's leading publishers, in 1928, as part of an integral collection of ancient Roman literature in Italian. The decision excited consternation at the time. Why assign the founder of Futurism to render a venerable Latin classic by Tacitus, a compendium of received knowledge about the history and ethnography of the Germanic tribes, into Italian? Notari, a witness at Marinetti's wedding to Benedetta Cappa, in 1923, might have wanted to help his old friend by offering him paid work. Marinetti explained his decision to undertake the translation in the book's preface. He wrote that when Notari made the offer, he was on a holiday in Capri, and the job gave him "a youthful way to begin days that were full of long baking in the sun in Capri, plunging headlong into the turquoise liquid sunk in the depths of sea caverns, and carrying on immense conversations with the Futurist Benedetta while she was nursing our baby."

Marinetti claimed to find an affinity between the patrician establishmentarian of the Roman Republic and Futurism, asserting that the Futurists' "passion for synthesis allows us to enjoy even Tacitus without being suffocated by the repellent dust of the past." Making a fanciful leap of logic, he proclaims that "Italian writers admire the manly conciseness of Tacitus, sister of that plastic synthesis of the Italian language we have propagated and brought about in the Futurist revolution of free speech, with the *parolibero* style." *Paroliberismo*, "liberated words," was a fundamental principle of Marinetti's writing, articulated in the "Technical Manifesto of Futurist Literature," in 1912, which ordained that the words of the text must be freed from all syntactical and grammatical principles. The narrative of the fight between the Pink Congress and the prostitutes is an exemplary passage of *paroliberismo*. Marinetti's explanation is flimsy if not absurd: Tacitus was the master of syntax, held up as a model for students of Latin prose from medieval times until Marinetti's era.

When it was published, Marinetti's translation of the *Germania* was excoriated by critics and Latin scholars. Since then, it has received scant attention in the Italian-speaking world and (for obvious reasons) none at all outside it. Another strange intersection between Marinetti and Latin literature occurred in 1924, when rumors flew in Naples that some lost volumes of Livy's *History of Rome* had been found. The discovery was attributed to Marinetti, who was in Capri at the time on another summer sojourn. The "lost decades of Livy" were soon revealed to be a hoax.

For all of Marinetti's ingenious rationalizations, the Futurists' fascination with Capri posed a glaring contradiction to every principle the movement professed. The island was as far removed from the modern, mechanized Western world as any place in Europe during the early decades of the twentieth century. Their main motive for relaxing their principles might have been economic: they were poor, and Capri was cheap. The Neapolitan critic Ugo Piscopo also discerns a geographic rationale for the Futurists' loyalty to the island. In 2001, Piscopo wrote that for the Futurists and their supporters and sympathizers Capri presented an

> epiphany of the irrepressible germination of the forces of life, plastically and dynamically renewed. The island, which looks east on a famous volcanic landscape, finds in active Vesuvius one of its fundamental reference points (volcanism being a key icon of Futurism); on the west it overlooks the open sea (and the ocean-sea is one of the central, most frequently recurring metaphors in Marinetti and his colleagues), where the Futurists discover the individual, which, as [Enrico] Prampolini says, is "a continuous variation on the theme of 'becoming

matter.'" . . . Capri is also the explosive magma of poetic vitality in its magic circle of land and water, in the unbroken flux of metamorphosis, in the excess it presents of events of light, color, smell, and sound, in the provocativeness of its allegories of simultaneity, of synthesis and synesthesia, in the states of the soul. It functions like a *parolibero* laboratory that sends circular proposals of fecundity and creative links of word-voice-color, of memory and intuition, of calculation and imagination.

The Futurists maintained a nearly continuous presence in Capri after the movement's vital force declined and petered out in the Fascist era. After the Second World War, Prampolini, one of the most prolific Futurist painters, returned to Capri, where he continued to pursue the movement's dynamic aesthetic in watercolors, palely tinted landscapes and marine paintings observed in vertiginous perspective.

B EATRICE ROMAINE GODDARD arrived in Capri in 1899 with no money, no introductions, and no plan apart from an intention to paint. The island was as hospitable to obscure and impoverished visitors as to the wealthy and fa mous; she was all of that. A few years later, after she had inherited a fortune, she returned to Capri and married John Ellingham Brooks, the feckless housemate of W. Somerset Maugham and E. F. Benson, in what might be called a marriage of inconvenience. Romaine Brooks, the name by which she was known after she found international renown as a portrait painter, would always remember her first visit to Capri as the only interlude of true happiness in her life.

In her unpublished memoir, which in some versions bears the title "No Pleasant Memories," she begins her account of her years in Capri,

At the end of the last century, Capri was still unique in character. Though only two hours by boat from Naples, it might well have been an island in the archipelago of faraway Greece, so undisturbed it was. Artists who loved color sought its beauty; intellectuals who were weary, an ideal retreat. To those who felt strange currents beneath the soil stirring them into fever, Capri was a Pagan island, and Vesuvius its burning God.

It is a concise and complete description of Capri's allure, timeless except in its characterization of the Greek archipelago, which would not remain "faraway" much longer. The sentence that follows this passage dates the author in an unflattering light, fixing her class in the late Victorian era: "The peasants were beautiful and simple children who liked the foreigner because his fever brought them gold."

Romaine's childhood, as she described it in her memoir, was a hellish vortex of suffering that surpassed the travails of Dickens's most pathetic orphans. She was born in Rome, which gave her her name, in 1874. In her memoir, Romaine portrays her mother, Ella Waterman Goddard, as a woman remarkable for her "arrogance, unusual culture, and personal elegance," who had been raised amid great wealth as the daughter of the mining magnate Isaac Waterman, in Chestnut Hill, Philadelphia. From her earliest childhood until she died, Romaine was convinced that her mother hated her. She portrayed Ella Goddard as a Satanist who conversed with invisible spirits and never exhibited "the slightest sympathy for anyone." Romaine's only solace was in drawing, which her mother forbade her to do, so she made her sketches in secrecy, on boxes and windowsills, "even with a pin on the polished wood of the piano." The memoir does not mention her father, Major Henry Goddard, a preacher's son from Philadelphia who was an alcoholic. Ella divorced him when Romaine was little. In childhood, Romaine was the caretaker of her mad elder brother, St. Mar, their mother's darling, who was given to fits of violence against everyone except her.

When Romaine was seven, while the family was living in a posh hotel in Manhattan, Ella sent her to live with a laundress, where she starved on a diet of bread and black coffee. Isaac Waterman's secretary rescued her a year later and sent her to study at St. Mary's Hall, an Episcopalian boarding school in New Jersey, where she was bullied and ostracized. When Romaine was fourteen, Ella confined her in a cruelly strict convent in Italy, where she was the only Protestant and forbidden to bathe. After five years of stiff-necked rebellion, she bolted. She eked out a bohemian life in Paris on a meager allowance from her mother by singing at a workingman's cabaret called Café Chantant, until she got pregnant. Abandoned by her wealthy lover, alone in a shabby hotel room, she gave birth to a daughter. She gave up the baby for foster care in a convent, where it died at the age of two months. Romaine fled to Rome to study art. She was the only female student in her life-drawing class, which was taken by her classmates as an indication that she was available for sex. She was harassed persistently until she took flight again, to Capri.

In her recollection, the island was a place filled with music, "rhythmic calls and responses in the vineyards, sounds of flutes from the hillsides," where shepherds clad in sheepskins played bagpipes at the Virgin's shrines, which "drew me back to the Pagan world whose music had not as yet died." Her choice of lodging was governed by price: she chose a boardinghouse that charged five lire a day, which looked out on a garden shaded by palm trees. In the first of many mysterious ailments that would torment her throughout her life, she was overcome by "a bad state of nerves. At night I would be awakened by the cries of strange birds flying over the island." She would rush to the window, where she found "all things silent in the transparent darkness of a southern sky." No one else heard the strange birds, so she did not talk about them.

Romaine did not make friends at her pension. She found the boisterous atmosphere at mealtimes intolerable, so she sat alone, in glowering silence. Loneliness turned into depression; she once stood on the edge of the cliff below Villa Castello and contemplated jumping. Her work did not go well. "All efforts to paint the peasants, who posed willingly for a few centesimi, proved a failure. I would wander about, plant my easel in some isolated pathway, and then sit before it for hours, doing nothing." Slowly she abandoned herself to the island's influence and let it mold her to its ancient form, giving her the "freedom to find the latent Pagan within oneself, or simply to live without ambition, breathing the soothing air." She made a friend, an American named Mrs. Snow, "big and blond," who had "left behind a husband in some damp and gloomy house in London." Mrs. Snow shouted at her little daughter in a loud Yankee voice, but her breezy, optimistic personality lifted Romaine from her gloom.

She decided to leave the pension, and Mrs. Snow helped her search for a suitable studio-residence. They found just the place, a deserted chapel with a redbrick floor and a high

Gothic window beside a courtyard with fig trees, enclosed by orange groves and vineyards. "The rent was only twenty lire a month, because the place was in the slums—if such a name could possibly be given to any part of Capri." The chapel was sparsely furnished, and it swarmed with lizards and "all the queer insects of the island: fat worms with padded feet that tried to crawl up the walls but whose weight pulled them down with a soft thud to the floor, and spiders the size of saucers that I had to kill and then wash away their mangled bodies." Her neighbor was an old beggar whom she always gave a few coppers. When she returned to Capri after receiving her inheritance, he was the first person she sought out. "Waving his bundle of bank-notes he danced about the courtyard with cramped-up legs, shouting 'Viva la Signorina Romana!'"

Mrs. Snow introduced Romaine to the island's other expatriate residents, starting with her compatriots, Charles Caryl Coleman, whom Romaine called Uncle Charley, and her near neighbors at Villa Castello, the bachelor couple of Thomas Spencer Jerome and Charles Lang Freer. She was also a regular visitor at Villa Cercola, shared by Maugham, who would remain a loyal friend until his death in 1965, Benson, and Brooks. Set on a knoll commanding a fine view of the sea, amid pleasant gardens with a little vineyard and an olive orchard, Villa Cercola would become her own residence when she was rich.

She discovered her artistic métier as a portraitist when the indefatigable Mrs. Snow introduced her to Thomas Burr, an American author sojourning in Capri, who paid her fifty lire to paint his likeness. "Mr. Burr's face was all beard and hair," she wrote in her memoir, "and during the sittings he became sentimental, which added to the difficulties of painting the portrait." By "sentimental," she meant that he made sexual advances toward her. "Though disappointed in me," because she did not respond to his propositions, "he was, in the end, pleased with his hairy image, which he paid for and took away." Romaine celebrated her first commission by buying a table. She arranged her library of ten books on it and would sit contentedly hours at a time, "leaning over the desk holding a pen in my hand as though about to write."

Either because he liked the painting or more likely in a desire to pursue his unrequited passion, Burr ordered a second, larger portrait. Wearing old-fashioned knee breeches, he "wanted to sit writing by the open window with the Castello seen in the distance and a pot of flowers on the window-sill." As the picture progressed, he became increasingly amorous and "more and more displeased with my resistance. Finally, disillusioned, he left the island without taking leave, and what was worse, without purchasing the almost finished portrait." He departed in a heavy sea, and the first portrait was washed overboard.

Her portraits of Mr. Burr must have been well received by the expatriate community, for they led to a second commission, from an Englishman named James Whipple, who is always called an explorer, though what or where he explored is never mentioned. Romaine wrote that Whipple was "always planning diversions somewhat too Anglo-Saxon for Capri—roller-skating on his spacious terrace, for instance." Another of Whipple's brain waves had a pagan provenance: anticipating Fersen's disastrous enactment of a Mithraic ritual to celebrate Nino Cesarini's twentieth birthday, he mounted a similar spectacle in the same place, the Grotto of Matermania. Led by Whipple and Coleman, with Charles Freer and Thomas Jerome assisting, the participants wore ivy wreaths and white kimonos that Freer had brought back from a recent collecting trip to Japan. "Walking in procession we chanted verses from the *Rubáiyát* of Omar Khayyám, which had been set to music by John Brooks, the poet and musician of the island." Romaine, the former cabaret artiste, stood on a rock altar and sang quatrain 100, "Yon rising moon that looks for us again." Then, "in propitiation, doubtless, for singing of the moon when we were worshipping the sun, Mr. Jerome pronounced a ponderous discourse on Mithras which nearly sent us all to sleep." Whipple concluded the ceremony by performing magic tricks.

Whipple agreed to pay Romaine two thousand lire for a large portrait, enough money to support her in Capri for a year. He wanted to be painted "in a smart khaki outfit with topee and leather boots, seated on a camp stool, jauntily holding a cane across his knee." She lugged easel, canvas, and paints up to Whipple's villa in Anacapri. "Finally, all was arranged and I seated [myself] before my easel, when what was to be expected happened. My sitter jumped up from his camp stool and threw himself before me in all his khaki splendor, pouring out what had been on his mind for months." She rebuffed him angrily, and after Whipple made the rounds of the island's villas lamenting her scornful rejection of his noble declaration of love, Romaine was ostracized for a brief period. One night, Uncle Charley gave a party and "invited my admirer but not me. Resting quietly in bed, listening to the music that came faintly over from his garden, I felt very relieved indeed that events had made it impossible for me to paint the khaki portrait."

The most mystifying friendship she made in Capri was the one with "the poet and musician of the island," John Brooks, her future husband. Brooks was the sort of expatriate who gives expatriates a bad name, a dilettante who lived off his friends with an unlimited sense of entitlement and not a glimmer of responsibility or gratitude. His life's work was a translation of the sonnets of Heredia, Jacques d'Adelswärd-Fersen's friend, which was never published; later in life he devoted himself to a translation of Greek epigrams. Benson, his devoted yet unsparingly frank friend, described his translations of Heredia as "frigid and labored, and had not the primary call of beauty, nor any echo of it," and declared his Greek epigrams to be "devoid of any rendered magic." Brooks diddled at the piano for hours every day, playing so badly that no one except Romaine could bear to stay in the room.

A public school boy who earned a B.A. at Peterhouse, Cambridge, Brooks was admitted at Lincoln's Inn to study law and passed the Roman law examination, but he never had any serious intention to practice. He had turned up in Capri with Maugham four years before Romaine, and when Maugham left at holiday's end, Brooks stayed on: as he would often say, "Came for lunch and stayed for life." He was among the first wave of homosexual emigrants to settle in Capri after the trials of Oscar Wilde. At that time, a taste for sex with men and boys was closer to a dangerous, exciting pastime than a way of life. Compton Mackenzie recalled meeting Brooks "coming along one day in a great flutter to say that Maugham had got himself involved with a married woman and that he was going to have to marry her." Brooks exclaimed, "I don't know what I shall do if Maugham brings a wife to the Cercola. I don't think Benson will like it at all either." Benson, who had great affection for Brooks, described him as "inexcusably indolent, he never took himself in hand, he dawdled and loitered year in year out. He never did a day's hard work, but translated his sonnets and his epigrams just as he fumbled at Beethoven's sonatas, appreciating his performance, enjoying the hideous result through a mist of self-hypnosis." Yet Brooks was not a vicious man. Soon after he met Romaine Goddard, he conquered his horror of a woman living in his house and proposed marriage to her, though she may have been the only foreigner in Capri who was poorer than himself.

A professional breakthrough of a sort came to Romaine when Charles Freer took an interest in her work. He bought a painting, a landscape of a pergola draped in vines abundant with purple grapes. The picture was pretty and competent, nothing more, but he saw something in it. The support of a major collector validated her vocation and emboldened her to take herself seriously as an artist. She grew dissatisfied with her work, which adhered to the pattern for foreign painters in Capri, emphasizing brilliant color observed in intense sunlight. Freer's encouragement brought with it an enhanced awareness of the somber-hued portraits and cityscapes of Whistler, with which her mature work is often associated. There is no evidence that Freer hung any of his Whistlers at Villa Castello, but Romaine's friendship with him enlarged her artistic imagination to encompass a conception of painting that did not rely on color for visual interest, such as *Arrangement in Gray and Black No. 1*, Whistler's familiar portrait of his mother.

Freer urged Romaine to escape the stale influence of the

mediocre artists in Capri and to study in Paris, where she could immerse herself in the old masters. In the fall of 1901 she followed his advice and enrolled in intensive painting courses at the Académie Colarossi, the fees for which nearly depleted her scanty allowance from her mother. She would have starved were it not for the kindness of a wealthy young Russian student who befriended her and brought her to her family's house for dinner. Charles Freer looked her up when he was passing through Paris. He invited her to dinner and took her to a girlie show. In Romaine's narrative, the encounter ended with a romantic proposition, which would tend to undermine the theory that he and Thomas Jerome were lovers, but the reader is permitted to take a skeptical view. In her memoir, virtually every male she met before she became involved in serious romantic relationships with women fell in love with her.

Romaine's one scheme to raise money in Paris went awry. She had brought with her the second portrait of Mr. Burr, which she had finished, and delivered it to him at his residence. He received her warmly until he noticed that she was carrying the rolled-up canvas. "He became very angry and told me frankly that he had no intention of taking it unless I became his mistress," she wrote in her memoir. The scene turned farcical: "When he tried to kiss me and I resisted, he crushed me against the wall. His manners were so rough that my only thought was to get outside the door." She escaped without her painting, and her subsequent attempts to get paid were fruitless. The portrait did, however, get the artist her first press clipping. An item in *The New York Herald*, illustrated with a small image of the painting, read, "Mr. Thomas Burr, the eminent author, now visiting the Island of Capri, has had his portrait painted by Miss R.G."

Romaine returned to Capri, where she could live on almost nothing in her Gothic chapel, because the rent had been paid in advance, and where her friends would welcome her. She found John Brooks as destitute as ever, contemplating suicide. Romaine was willing to rescue him, but she too was penniless and had no prospects, as far as she knew. When her mother agreed to give her an allowance, she had impressed upon her that by accepting the stipend, she was giving up any claim to the family fortune, a premise that proved to be false, though Ella Goddard herself might not have known it.

Romaine's return to Capri was cut short by events at home, if the word may be applied to her mother's household. She noticed this announcement in *The New York Herald*: "Mr. Henry St. Mar Goddard, the brilliant son of Mrs. Ella Waterman Goddard and Major Henry Goddard, has died at Nice of an illness that cut short a promising career." The item must have been written by Ella, a steadfast believer in her adored son's talent, for his principal occupation in the last years of his life was filling up notebooks with statistics about the cholera epidemic that was ravaging Europe at the time, copied out of stories in the newspapers. The *Herald* was the only reliable means of communication between mother and daughter, it seemed: Ella had read the item about Romaine's portrait of Mr. Burr and wrote to her, ordering her to present herself at Château Grimaldi, her opulent residence in Menton, on the outskirts of Nice. So Romaine packed up her few belongings, hid two hundred lire in a box in the chapel as an emergency fund for her eventual return, and departed for a reunion with her mother, whom she had not seen for six years.

When she arrived, Ella met her at the door. "I gazed at her spellbound," Romaine wrote. "She was untidily dressed in black; from under a blond wig that had shifted to one side, gray wisps of hair escaped. Her face which once merely quivered with madness was now a rigid mask of madness and despair." Neither woman greeted the other. Ella had transformed the gloomy mansion in Menton into a funerary monument worthy of a boy pharaoh. With no word of greeting, her mother escorted her to an unlit drawing room and said, "This room is dedicated to your brother. His spirit haunts these relics of his deathbed." In a glass case, a plaster cast of St. Mar's hand was placed upon the sheets from his deathbed. Dozens of death masks were displayed in the room. Ella handed her daughter a bouquet and said, "You are an artist. Place these flowers in an artistic way round your brother's coffin"—but there was no coffin. St. Mar's remains were in a vault at a cemetery. Ella Goddard was engaged in a protracted, ultimately unsuccessful effort to persuade the Italian government to grant her permission to inter her son in a mausoleum in the garden of Château Grimaldi. Romaine laid the flowers in the form of a cross on the empty funeral bier.

In her efforts to communicate with her dead son, Ella fell under the influence of the celebrity clairvoyant and palm reader Cheiro, who was always dressed in the formal frock coat he wore onstage. When Romaine met him, she took him for the butler. He told Romaine that as soon as his divorce decree was granted, he was going to marry her mother. Yet Ella Goddard was not only mad but dying. Romaine consulted a doctor, and after she had described her mother's symptoms, which included an unquenchable thirst, the doctor concluded that she suffered from acute diabetes. A visit from the doctor was out of the question, so Romaine brought him a urine specimen from her mother's chamber pot, which confirmed the diagnosis and indicated that the disease was too far advanced to be susceptible to treatment. It was a long, painful death, punctuated by brief periods of lucidity, which she devoted to bitter words of hatred for her daughter. "It was not delirium," Romaine wrote. "She knew she was dying and I, alive, watching. I wondered if such hate could die with death. Might it not, as earth-born *ombra* [shadow], always hover over me?" The prophecy fulfilled itself: fifty years after Ella's death, Romaine Brooks wrote in a notebook, "My dead mother gets between me and life."

Romaine was surprised to learn that she and her elder sister, Maya, would divide a great fortune. Ella's threats of disinheritance had been hollow, for she had never controlled her father's wealth. In his will, Isaac Waterman had bequeathed his entire estate to his grandchildren after the death of their mother, his only child. Ella's extravagant spending had all come from a trust fund. Romaine wrote, "From possessing almost nothing, I now had six flats in Nice alone, another in Monte Carlo, one in Dieppe, an unfurnished one in Paris, and a château near Menton." She was miserable in Château Grimaldi, where she kept finding more death masks of St. Mar in cupboards. She was firmly convinced that Ella's ghost haunted her, so she sold the place to a Russian doctor, who turned it into a laboratory to study the rejuvenating effects of monkey glands, and returned to Capri.

She decided to give up the chapel and move into lodgings more suitable to her new station in life. "When for the last time the big rusty key opened the door of the old chapel, I felt very unhappy. I knew somehow that the simple, almost monastic life so congenial to me was now over." She collected a few paintings, the library of ten books, and the two hundred lire she had hidden for her return, now superfluous, and surveyed the place with melancholy. She made handsome gifts to her old friends, the bundle of banknotes to her neighbor, the crippled beggar, and a gold chatelaine for Mrs. Snow. She made a handsome overpayment to Uncle Charley for an ugly Renaissance tapestry he claimed had once belonged to a doge of Venice; she grew to hate it and finally sent it back to him as a gift.

Romaine reserved most of her bounty for John Brooks, whom she called "my closest friend" in her memoir. His situation had declined from poverty to ruin; he had run out of friends to borrow money from and was selling his possessions one by one to pay for food. "But now it was no longer a question of more presents," she wrote. "All his debts had to be paid off and an income supplied if he was to continue living in Capri. Why I should have thought it was up to me to see this project through is now hard to understand." It is one of the most puzzling passages in a memoir full of puzzles— not for what it says, which is plain enough, but for what it omits to say: she accomplished this project by marrying him. In the typescript of her memoir in the collection of the Beinecke Library at Yale University, she never mentions her marriage to John Brooks, whom, for some reason, she calls "Mr. G." John Brooks died in 1929, before she began writing the memoir, so there was no motive of discretion.

The marriage was implausible, even irrational. When Brooks had mooted the idea just one year before, she dismissed it as absurd. Her homosexual inclination had not yet expressed itself clearly, but his had. On the surface, it might have appeared to be a marriage of convenience, in the sense of providing cover for the partners' homosexuality, a common enough arrangement at the time. The marriage was undoubtedly a convenient one for Brooks, for financial reasons, but Romaine, after her experiences as the only female student in her life-drawing classes, had long since given up any interest in satisfying the expectation of proper behavior for ladies in Edwardian society.

Perhaps she wanted the immunity from the unwelcome advances of men like groping Mr. Burr that the estate of marriage would confer, but the simplest explanation, that she felt an emotional attachment to Brooks, has much to recommend it. His personal charm was warmly attested by all who knew him, even those who despised his sense of entitlement. The Cambridge graduate and the heiress from Philadelphia were well enough matched socially, and they held similar, aristocratic views about Capri and its inhabitants. In 1903, a few months after the marriage unraveled, John Brooks (signing himself Ellingham Brooks) published a sonnet, preceded by a couplet in French, which summarized the ideal of the island as a pagan paradise in terms that closely resemble those in Romaine's memoir. His theme is the feast of San Costanzo, Capri's patron, one of the island's principal festivals. "Festival of San Costanzo—an Island Carnival," published by a British ladies' magazine called *The Gentlewoman*, is one of the few works Brooks managed to publish:

Paganisme immortel, es tu mort? On le dit
Mais Pan, tout bas, s'en moque et la Sirène en rit.*

What mean these flower-strewn lanes, these banners
    gay,
These blue-veined maidens in this fair attire,
These gossips come to see and to admire,
These ruddy youths, who make such a brave display,

A long procession files in slow array,
Aloft, a silver image gleams like fire,
Borne shoulder-high, amid a white-robed choir,
The patron saint moves on his festal way.

Great Pan is dead? Ah, No! he lives. 'Tis we
Blind with the scales of centuries on our eyes,
Have lost belief and thus the power to see.

These humble folk, in their simplicity,
Perceive the glory which around them lies
And commune with their Gods perpetually.

Somerset Maugham wrote several stories set in Capri;
the most lyrical of them, virtually a parable extolling the island's beauty, is "The Lotus Eater," which is transparently
based on the life of John Brooks. Maugham's wise and worldly
narrator, on a visit to the island, meets an Englishman named

*"Immortal paganism, are you dead? So we say, / But Pan mocks in a whis-
per, and the Siren laughs." Brooks's usage of *Sirène* in the singular is unusual, and anticipates the name of Compton Mackenzie's fictional Capri.

Wilson, who came to Capri on a holiday in midlife and decided to stay there to the end of his days. When he arrived, a joyous festival resembling that of San Costanzo was being celebrated in the village, and in the evening he strolled down in the moonlight to see the Faraglioni, Capri's iconic stone stacks rising from the sea, painted a thousand times and encapsulated in countless souvenir snow globes. Wilson cashes out his bit of capital in London and lives an idle, modest existence in Capri for twenty-five years, wandering the hills, reading, and playing the piano badly. When his money runs out, he goes to pieces and ends up living off the charity of the Capriote woman who had been his maid. Finally, Wilson's body is discovered on a hillside. "From where he lay he had been able to see those two great rocks called the Faraglioni, which stand out of the sea. It was a full moon, and he must have gone to see them by moonlight. Perhaps he died of the beauty of that night." It is not a portrait lifted precisely from life, like "Mayhew," Maugham's story about Thomas Jerome: Wilson is a middle-class bank manager, and there is no fortunate marriage to a rich lesbian. Yet Maugham clearly has his old housemate in mind in this neatly turned appraisal of Wilson: "You may say that it was a grossly selfish existence. It was. He was of no use to anybody, but on the other hand he did nobody any harm."

Brooks's uselessness would not have deterred Romaine; she was happy to be the one doing things. Dispelling any notion that she married him to create an appearance of what would come to be known as heteronormativity, soon after the wedding she began to experiment with gender presentation. "I decided to forgo the many hateful prerogatives of my sex," she wrote, "the complexity of female clothes, for instance." She dreamed of living the simple life, "garbed solely in male sport attire." She planned a rural walking tour, "burdened only with knapsack and sketchbook." On a visit to London, she "spent many hours in Our Boys Shop, so as to be sure of ordering myself a genuine sport outfit." When she appeared before her husband wearing baggy trousers and hiking shoes, with her hair chopped short, "ready for what I hoped would be my future life," he was horrified, declaring that in her company "his reputation would be forever damaged." Romaine's vision of the relationship anticipated that of the protagonist of Radclyffe Hall's landmark lesbian novel, *The Well of Loneliness*, who forms her first overt attachment in adulthood to a young sportsman who shares her love of the outdoors and horseback riding, and is bitterly disillusioned when he proposes a conventional marriage, with sex. Romaine was looking for a male chum with whom she could pursue traditionally masculine activities.

She could hardly have made a worse choice. In the first place, John Brooks was much too lazy for country walks. His ideas about marriage proved to be utterly conventional. He wanted his wealthy wife to buy a mansion on a square in London and preside over dinners for his friends; he wanted to be invited to join the right clubs. Conventional, with a hypocritical Edwardian twist: his prenuptial boyfriend was hanging around the house, casting baleful looks at his new feminine rival. It was an insupportable situation. Romaine rented a house of her own, with a tower, where she could paint and sleep alone. Brooks responded fretfully, "But what on earth will the people in Capri say?," a remark that must have elicited her contempt. When he began to drop heavy hints that Romaine should make a will to ensure the transfer of the Waterman millions to him after her death, she pursued the strategy of her years of poverty: she bolted, for London.

A year after it began, the marriage was finished, though there is no evidence of a divorce decree. Uncle Charley wrote to Charles Freer in September 1904, "Mrs. Brooks has returned to London. Brooks is not with her and was not when she was here. *They are parted forever.*" She gave Brooks a stingy annual pension of three hundred pounds (in the words of Alan Searle, Somerset Maugham's secretary and companion in the writer's later years, "Enough for meat, but not enough for pickles") and reneged on her promise to send him her address in London for an eventual reunion.

She arrived a few months after the death of James Whistler, the master of shades of gray, and bought a studio on the same block of Tite Street where he had lived. "Of all the painters of that period," she wrote, "I of course admired Whistler more." Yet her admiration was complicated and far from adulatory: "I wondered at the magic subtlety of his tones, but thought his 'symphonies' lacked in corresponding subtlety of expression. There was no surprise, no paradox, no complexity." Another famous American painter, John Singer Sargent, the city's reigning society portraitist, lived in a house opposite hers on Tite Street, yet, she wrote, "as his work did not interest me I never sought to know him." One of her motives in marrying John Brooks might have been simply to put her life as a Goddard behind her. "I was born an artist," she wrote. "*Née* an artist, not *née* Goddard." The only thing of value she got from her husband was his name.

When she began her career as a painter in earnest, and for the rest of her life, she was Romaine Brooks.

EVERY RESORT GIVES rise to a community of artists to paint views for visitors to buy as souvenirs. In Capri, the market developed soon after August Kopisch's *Discovery of the Blue Grotto* put the island on the international tourist's itinerary. By mid-century, there were scores of industrious hack painters active in Capri, mostly Neapolitan and a few from abroad. Casa Rossa, John MacKowen's toy castle in Anacapri, is crowded with views of the island's famous topographical features, with fishermen at work or rustic maidens at rest in the foreground. The municipal collection includes just one work by a native Capriote, a fine seascape in moonlight by Michele Federico (1884–1966). Charles Coleman's studio was virtually a factory for pretty pastels of the Gulf of Naples, with Vesuvius, the burning god, as the pictorial focus. The American symbolist Elihu Vedder, best known as a book illustrator, was frequently Coleman's guest at Villa Narcissus. After Vedder scored a smashing success with his edition of Edward FitzGerald's translation of the *Rubáiyát* of Omar Khayyám, in 1884, he designed and built a villa of his own in Capri, called Villa Quattro Venti, which was sited atop a high saddle of land exposed on every side. Vedder produced some competent genre paintings of island life during his tenure in Capri, but he relocated to the mainland after he discovered that his house was all too aptly named and was uninhabitable when the winds blew, as they almost always did.

The first painter with an international reputation to visit Capri was Camille Corot, who arrived in 1828, almost immediately after the publication of Kopisch's book. He made a brief call there during an Italian tour, early in his career, and painted a fine picture of Monte Solaro, the great rock outcropping on the island's western side, with Capri village in the middle ground. A complex, carefully composed exercise in coloristic harmony, it bears the hallmarks of Corot's mature work, yet it is indistinguishable from the paintings he produced on the mainland, exhibiting no discernible sense of place.

Capri exercised a potent influence on John Singer Sargent, who made a sojourn there in the summer of 1878, when his career was just beginning. Like Brooks an American painter primarily known for portraits of women, also born in Italy (Florence, in 1856), Sargent spent his youth in the doting company of his parents and sisters. His mother was a hypochondriac who roamed Europe in search of warm winters and cool summers, avoiding the major cities and glamorous watering holes, and his father, a taciturn eye surgeon from Philadelphia, docilely followed her. The family rarely stayed in one place long enough to make friends. As a result of this nomadic life, John received only a smattering of education outside the home until he was accepted as a student at the atelier of the portraitist Carolus-Duran, in Paris, when he was eighteen. Carolus Duran taught a radical approach to painting, which eschewed preliminary sketches in favor of drawing directly on the canvas with color. A devotee of Velázquez, he wandered through the atelier chanting the Spanish master's name like a mantra.

Sargent was an adolescent prodigy, accepted by the École

des Beaux-Arts on his first try, less than a year after his formal studies with Carolus-Duran had commenced. He exhibited his first painting at the Salon, a portrait of a young woman, the following year. Henry James, an enthusiastic booster of rising young men, wrote that the painter's early work presented "the slightly 'uncanny' spectacle of a talent which on the very threshold of its career has nothing more to learn." Sargent had had little experience with hot weather, and he hated it. Soon after he arrived in Capri, he wrote to a friend, "One generally feels used up" by the heat, and complained that he could not sleep for the mosquitoes and fleas. Things looked up after he met an English artist named Frank Hyde, who invited him to share his studio at the monastery of Santa Teresa, in Anacapri. More important, Hyde introduced him to his model, Rosina Ferrara, who became one of Sargent's favorite subjects. Evan Edward Charteris, Sargent's first biographer, described Ferrara as "an Anacapri girl, a magnificent type, about seventeen years of age, her complexion a rich nut brown, with a mass of blue-black hair, very beautiful, and of an Arab type."

Sargent could not get enough of Ferrara: he painted her in olive groves, in domestic genre scenes, dancing the tarantella, and a famous portrait with her head in profile, like a Roman medallion. In his paintings and drawings of Ferrara, Sargent gave free expression to a sensuous exoticism, a crucial element of the legacy of Velázquez, which remained an important theme throughout a career that was otherwise devoted to commissioned portraits of powerful men with mustaches and, more often, their handsome, vivacious wives. Rosina Ferrara was a rare case of a model who found a fame that equaled and even exceeded that of most of the artists who painted her. She was able to hold a pose for hours without a twitch, a minor talent but one that is highly esteemed by artists. Charles Coleman painted her often and hired her as his housekeeper; she might have been his lover. Years after Sargent had left Capri, Rosina Ferrara modeled for an American decorative painter named George Randolph Barse, who had studied at the academic atelier of Alexandre Cabanel, a rival of Carolus-Duran's. Barse married her and brought her home to Katonah, New York, forty miles north of Manhattan, where she lived as a society matron until her death in 1934.

Among the most talented artists who lived in Capri for an extended period and made the life of the island his principal subject was Christian Wilhelm Allers. Born in Hamburg in 1857, he studied art at the Karlsruhe Gymnasium, Norman Douglas's alma mater, and made a name for himself as a portraitist. Allers was one of Bismarck's favorite artists and became a personal friend. One of his portraits of the chancellor was reproduced in lithographs that were distributed widely in Germany. Allers had made a little fortune for himself by his early thirties and built a showy mansion in Capri. Like every artistic sojourner of the era, he attached himself to Charles Coleman. Villa Allers imitated the pseudo-medieval style of Coleman's Villa Narcissus and was similarly stocked with tapestries, armor, and antiquities, updated with relics of Bismarck.

Allers was an accomplished painter in oils, but his principal gift was as a draftsman. He produced hundreds of fine pencil drawings in Capri, executed with a crisp, fluid line. Allers went far afield from the usual generic subjects in detailed, realistic snapshots of the festival of San Costanzo, quail hunts, prankish children, and buffoonish tourists. He published two books of engravings, in 1892 and 1893, which did as much to arouse interest in Capri in Germany as Kopisch's book had done half a century before. Allers's stay on the island came to an abrupt close, for the usual reason: his lustful pursuit of the local adolescent boys he hired as models attracted the notice of the police in Naples. Donna Lucia Morgano, the owner with her husband, Giuseppe Morgano, of the café that served as the informal clubhouse of the foreign residents in Capri, got wind of it and tipped him off, and even hired a boat for his escape. After his flight from Capri, Allers continued his artistic and pederastic careers in German Samoa.

The charge of pederasty brought against Allers was a direct result of the disgrace of Friedrich Alfred Krupp, the most spectacular of all Capri scandals after Tiberius. The *Fall Krupp*, as the affair is known in Germany, was as disastrous for the German homosexual underground as Oscar Wilde's conviction had been for its counterpart in the English-speaking world. Krupp, Europe's leading manufacturer of steel and weapons, and reputedly the richest man in Germany, came to Capri in 1898 to indulge his passion for marine biology. He outfitted yachts for marine exploration and developed an improved diving apparatus for the use of Anton Dohrn, a German zoologist based in Naples, which resulted in the discovery of thirty-three new species of oceanic fauna in the Gulfs of Naples and Salerno. Krupp was a generous patron in Capri: he purchased paintings from local artists at inflated prices, made liberal donations to charities, and commissioned Mimí Ruggiero to design the botanic garden named after himself, now the Gardens of Augustus.

Krupp paid for a major renovation of the Quisisana, motivated primarily by a desire to enhance his own comfort in the floor of the hotel he reserved for his own use year-round. He built the serpentine Via Krupp, the first direct overland road from the village to the Marina Piccola, where he anchored his yacht.

In Capri, Krupp developed a passion for the island's young men. He threw lavish, noisy entertainments for his favorites at the Quisisana; later he moved his parties to the Grotto of Fra' Felice, near the Marina Piccola. He was reasonably discreet, and there is no evidence that he had sexual relations with minors, but he was naively oblivious to the perils of patronage and got himself entangled in local rivalries. Ferdinando Gamboni, a schoolmaster who felt snubbed because Krupp took Italian lessons from another teacher, got in league with Manfredi Pagano, the owner of the Quisisana's main competitor, and fed salacious gossip about wanton sexual orgies to an unscrupulous Neapolitan journalist. The Marxist press in Germany picked up the story as a part of its anti-imperialist and therefore anti-Krupp mission, precipitating the *Fall Krupp*. When his wife received anonymous letters with the inflammatory newspaper clippings enclosed, she went straight to Kaiser Wilhelm II and demanded that he take action against her husband's enemies. The kaiser, as appalled by Frau Krupp's boldness as he was by the outrageous stories about her husband, had her locked up in an insane asylum. Krupp was left to choose between acquiescing in his wife's unjust confinement and owning up to the charge of homosexuality. A few days later he was found dead, apparently by suicide. No autopsy was performed, and he was buried in a sealed casket.

There appears to be little doubt about the essential veracity of the main accusation against Krupp, but Gamboni's tales of sexual depravity, as reported in the newspapers, were probably embellished by a process similar to that in Tacitus's accounts of the Orgy of Tiberius. The details are just too exciting. After he moved his entertainments to the Grotto of Fra' Felice, it was alleged, Krupp choreographed spectacles of sexual acrobatics, performed by good-looking porters, waiters, and barbers to an orchestral accompaniment, with orgasms celebrated by fireworks: a fanciful narrative that could have been inspired by Tacitus's reports of Tiberius's sexual acrobats, the *sellarii* and *spintriae*. Gamboni was a far from credible informant: a native of the Sorrentine peninsula, he had been discharged from his post as a schoolteacher there on the grounds of improper conduct with his charges, including violent disciplinary methods. Before he came to Capri, he had lived for a while in New York City, where he busked as an organ-grinder. Much was made of the golden pins Krupp gave his young friends, in the shape of artillery shells or crossed forks, which, it was hinted, were awarded for heroic sexual feats, yet such tokens were standard party favors at Krupp's dinners in Germany.

As with the Orgy of Tiberius and Jacques d'Adelswärd-Fersen's cream-puff teas for the schoolboys of Lycée Carnot, what exactly happened at Krupp's parties is irrecoverable. Not much may be inferred with certainty from his suicide, given the extreme opprobrium attached to homosexuality in Germany at the turn of the twentieth century, where it was treated as criminal immorality and punished with a severity equivalent to that of British law. It seems as certain that these revelries had some element of sexual activity as it is unlikely that they were spectacular orgies of mass buggery, but the record does not offer a reliable scenario of what went on behind closed doors at the Quisisana Hotel and in the Grotto of Fra' Felice.

AFTER SHE LEFT Capri to avoid her husband, Romaine Brooks quickly matured as an artist. During her years in England, she discovered and honed the nearly colorless palette that would become her signature as a painter. Yet after Capri, she found the damp climate intolerable. "It was one thing to wish to paint gray effects," she wrote in her memoir, "and another to have to breathe the thick gray of a London fog even within one's own home." Brooks declared her house in Tite Street "decidedly depressing," and that went for the stiff, stuffy servants as well. To relieve her nostalgia for Capri, she wrote to her gardener there, asking him to send his young son to come work for her. At her bidding, little Giovanni wore a Capriote fisherman's costume, a dark blue jersey and trousers with a scarlet sash. "There was of course an incongruous background of wainscoting and Jacobean furniture, but this failed to detract from memories of the blue seas and skies of Italy," she wrote. Giovanni, of course, fell in love with her. When he was found hiding in a corridor with a knife, "about to waylay the new French maid of whom he was inordinately jealous," Brooks was forced to discharge him.

She became listlessly involved in society, the inevitable

result of her newly acquired wealth. Her aversion to the empty pursuits of the idle rich, *"gens du monde* ever seeking diversion and trouble," who came to her for advice about "such things as lampshades and cushions," only made her more interesting to them. In fact, most of Brooks's new friends, indeed nearly all, came from the ranks of the peerage and royalty. Her first major romantic entanglement after her marriage failed was a public flirtation with Lord Alfred Douglas, Oscar Wilde's beloved Bosie, whom she met at the home of Robbie Ross, Wilde's first male lover and lifelong defender. Brooks was surprised by Douglas's youthful appearance: "Blond and boyish, his face showed no signs of recent upheaval, no dropping lines of bitterness." The attraction, or the affectation of one, appears to have been mostly on Douglas's side. "Bosie would often say, 'How is it that we never met when I was in Capri?'" He presented her with a copy of *The City of the Soul*, a book of poetry he had published five years before, inscribed "To Romaine from Bosie, *Nous avons souvent dit d'impérissables choses* (We have often spoken of imperishable things)." Whatever the things were, they perished before there was any risk of a consummated love affair. By the time she wrote her memoir, Brooks said that the only emotion that survived her friendship with Douglas was a "definite feeling of guilt for having abandoned my work for even so short an interlude."

A penchant for permanently youthful gay men threatened to become a pattern until she met Princesse Edmonde de Polignac, the former Winnaretta Singer, of Yonkers, New York, the daughter of the inventor of the sewing machine. "She was a good musician," wrote Brooks, "and her forcible character and dry American wit went to form a personality which had little in common with the title she bore." Like Brooks, she was in a *mariage blanc* with a gay man whom she supported with an American fortune. Singer made a deal with Prince Edmond de Polignac, an amateur composer: she consented to the match on the condition that he never set foot in her bedroom, and in return she paid for the performances of his music. Brooks's fascination with Princesse de Polignac was her only escape from the tedium of Edwardian society, the "fairy tale of life wherein only Queens, Princesses, Duchesses, and a few witches had the right to parade about, while such small fry as geniuses, artists, musicians, and the like were called in solely to entertain these higher beings."

For someone who professed a bitter aversion to the haut monde, Brooks enjoyed a sensational success as a social climber, ascending to the loftiest peak. As a result of what she called "my obsession for my American friend," she met the eponym of Edwardian society, Himself the King, at a tea party in Marienbad. When he allotted her her five minutes of royal face time and learned that she was an artist, he asked her what she thought of the Royal Watercolour Society. She had never heard of it, "but rising to the occasion I said that I considered it ranked very highly indeed." The king was pleased to hear it and expressed a wish to see her next exhibition in London. It was a lively chat by regal standards.

Brooks had reached a creative impasse in her painting. "I was accustomed to the vivid colors of Southern Italy," she wrote, "and I now found that my palette lacked range and subtlety of tones. This was a defect that had to be remedied." She decided on a change of scene and left London to take up residency in St. Ives, on the bleak, stormy Cornish coast, "the very place where one could study an ever-changing opalescent sea." The isolated fishing village was just beginning to be known as an art colony, primarily attracting amateurs, the idle rich, and the pensioned. In St. Ives, Brooks "spent many hours training my eyes to detect and my hands to note down an endless gamut of grays," an exercise that eventually enabled her "to isolate tones of gray so refined as to approach imperceptibility." An early self-portrait is a study in dark grays that compete in their approach to absolute blackness. The figure is wearing a hat bigger than the head, hung with a heavy veil, an early Brooks hallmark. The gaunt face gazes dimly at the viewer with a flicker of suspicion or even fear, on the threshold of invisibility.

When she returned to London, she found the house on Tite Street more intolerable than ever. The front rooms resounded with the cries of sick children at the hospital across the street, and the rear rooms echoed with doleful hymns from a Protestant chapel at the other end of the garden. After a neighbor sent her the third black-edged announcement of a death in the family, she started packing. "When at last the all-pervading gloom drove me away from Tite Street, it was to Paris that I again proceeded." Another motive for the move might have been that Princesse de Polignac lived there.

Brooks's public career as an artist was successfully launched in 1910 with an exhibition at the Galerie Durand-Ruel, one of the most influential venues in Paris. In the same year, the gallery exhibited paintings by Cézanne, Manet, Monet, Pissarro, and Renoir; at his gallery in London, Paul Durand-Ruel had represented Whistler. Imitating her compatriot, Brooks covered the gallery's red walls with a beige fabric to harmonize with her paintings, as Whistler had repainted the walls gray to suit his. For her debut, Brooks chose thirteen canvases she had painted at St. Ives, studies of women and young girls dressed in the extravagant fashions of the era, observed with a mild satirical eye. Only two of the pictures were formal portraits that identified the sitter by name, but the artist's gift for psychological penetration was evident in every work. The reviews were triumphant: Robert de Montesquiou, who had previously patronized Baron Fersen, wrote in *Le Figaro*, "These pensive portraits, these severe yet penetrating harmonies, reveal a genuine originality and emerge with much charm." He singled out the portrait of his close friend Madame Cloton Legrand as a masterpiece and bought it. He called Brooks "the Thief of Souls" for her uncanny gift of psychological insight, a nickname that stuck.

Brooks's apartment, on the avenue du Trocadéro, was furnished in a style as distinctive as that of her paintings and reflected their grisaille palette. An interview with her in *Le Figaro*, the first of many newspaper stories to publish a detailed description of her interior designs, reported that pale gray dominated in the wall coverings and carpet, with black accents. The sparse intrusions of color came from old master paintings and Oriental ceramics (again, the influence of Whistler). The furnishings mixed antiques and chairs covered in black mohair. The apartment's most distinctive feature was the roof garden, which was enclosed by plate glass. At the rear, Brooks painted a trompe l'oeil mural depicting a crowd of people on a balcony, strolling through a pergola hung with billowing black drapery into a garden. Dramatic displays of white flowers lightened the pervading darkness.

As in London, Brooks was sought out by the *gens du monde* in Paris, but she instinctively fled their attention. "I had neither friends nor pleasant outside relaxations of any kind," she wrote of her life in Paris. "What I called grown-up games, such as teas, dinners, receptions, and such like, bored me intensely. As time went on I even stopped going out in the evenings altogether. I would draw the curtains at the close of day and retire to my library. There for hours at a time I read and studied and tried to be as happy as I had once been in Capri." So she said, yet it is difficult to square her description of herself as a solitary recluse with the lengthy catalogue of her new friends and acquaintances, many of whom sat for portraits.

In 1912, she painted a portrait of Jean Cocteau at twenty-three as a dandy, lounging limply on a balcony, with the Eiffel Tower, the subject of one of his poems, looming in the background. The tower was still new enough to be controversial. In her memoir, Brooks wrote that people asked her how she could paint anything so hideous, and she explained, "This colossal steel structure had ushered in the machine age and was now boldly defying a city of low uniform lines." The tower, she said, was "a rebel that fascinated me." The portrait of Cocteau cost her Montesquiou's friendship. Notoriously jealous, the count coveted the distinction of being the subject of a Romaine Brooks portrait and despised the vain, ambitious young poet, who had perfected a devastating mimicry of his mincing airs, behind his back. Brooks wrote, "It was the *'lettré,'* the aristocrat, versus the clever, ultra-modern young *arriviste.*" The painting originally included a pair of women on the balcony, standing apart from Cocteau;

she cut the painting in half, making the Eiffel Tower the focus of the composition. Brooks would later delight in quoting Maugham, who predicted when the painting was first exhibited that Jean Cocteau would be remembered only because of Romaine Brooks's portrait of him.

Isaac Waterman's millions, in addition to making her financially independent, also gave her an unusual degree of independence from the subjects of her portraits. Indeed, she was usually richer than the sitter and was thus freed from any need to please him or, more often, her. Brooks nearly always kept the finished painting for herself, having learned that "to give a portrait to a sitter is a sure way of making an enemy." Many of her subjects were lesbian artists and writers and their entourage, some of whom Brooks had affairs with. Her portraits were not unflattering so much as merciless, making no concession at all to the sitter's self-image. Her notorious portrait of Una, Lady Troubridge amounts to a subtly wicked caricature. The wife of an admiral and the public lover of Radclyffe Hall, Una in her portrait wears male formal attire, the starched shirt flat as a crepe, and a monocle on a black velvet ribbon, which glints opaquely. She poses with her dachshunds, clenching a riding crop in her right hand. Una pronounced herself pleased, though she asked her friends, "Am I really like that?" Yet it was obvious to most of the people who saw the painting when it was exhibited in New York, Chicago, London, and Paris that Brooks's real subject was the sitter's absurd air of self-possession.

From the 1920s on, Romaine Brooks was publicly identified as a prominent member of the international lesbian elite, particularly after her fourth, prolonged stay in Capri, but she rebelled against this group, with its suffocating atmosphere of smug self-satisfaction, as much as she had done against the haut monde that sought her advice about lampshades and cushions. (Of course, the two sets often overlapped.) Radclyffe Hall, who called herself John, was the unofficial doyenne of lesbian society in Europe, having earned the credentials of martyrdom after a British court, in 1928, declared *The Well of Loneliness* obscene, despite the absence of any sex scenes, and banned its sale. The novel narrates the life of Stephen Gordon, a horsey aristocratic Englishwoman whose sexual inversion is apparent in childhood and follows the pattern described by the most advanced psychological theorists of the day, such as Richard von Krafft-Ebing, who described lesbianism as "the masculine soul heaving in the female bosom, [which] finds pleasure in the pursuit of manly sports." Havelock Ellis, another prominent sexologist of the era, wrote an introduction to the first edition. Brooks despised the novel, calling it "a ridiculous book, trite, superficial, as was to be expected," and described Hall as "a digger-up of worms with the pretension of a distinguished archaeologist."

Nonetheless, Brooks was fond of Lady Troubridge and maintained a loyal public friendship with her and John. She invited them to visit her in Capri when she returned there, after the war. In 1924, the year that Brooks's portrait of Una was exhibited, Hall returned the favor in her second novel, *The Forge*, with a glamorous literary portrait of the artist, *à clef*. Here, the character modeled after Brooks is pointed out to Susan Brent, a young English artist, a graduate of the Slade art school, at the Bal Bullier, a chic ballroom in Paris:

Venetia Ford! So that was Venetia Ford, the strange, erratic, brilliant genius of whom she had heard so much in the old days at the Slade. A fellow student of hers had known Venetia Ford in Paris, and the girl had fallen under the spell of this woman's charm, as did most people whom she admitted to her intimacy . . . The girl told her that Venetia hated color, that her pictures were all grays and whites and neutral tones—masterly things, subdued and powerful. She had said that Venetia had been begged to sell them over and over again, but had always refused. It was a crank of hers. One portrait, that of an Italian poet, she had parted with to the Luxembourg Gallery . . .

Susan remembered other things about Venetia Ford, her American parentage, her wealth that had come to her unexpectedly after years of work and starvation. The girl had told her of innumerable and very ruthless love affairs, on which it was said that Venetia fed her genius. By all accounts, she gave short shrift to love! And now here she was at a Bal Bullier: Venetia Ford, the artistic ideal.

The key fits the lock exactly, a concise thumbnail biography of Romaine Brooks more than a fictional impression of her, with the possible exception of its characterization of the love affairs, which is difficult to confirm. The record of Brooks's private life is vague: the main source is her memoir, which is discreet more than secretive. She refers to every one of her female lovers as "my friend."

Hall omits to mention that the Italian poet who was the

subject of the portrait bought by the Musée du Luxembourg was Gabriele D'Annunzio, with whom Brooks carried on an intense love affair. A reader with no other source of information than Brooks's memoir would conclude that he was the great love of her life. Several writers have been called the last Romantic, but D'Annunzio's claim to the distinction is stronger than most, both because of the florid exuberance of his poetry and his novels of doomed love and specifically because of his parallel career as a man of revolutionary action, in the mold of Byron. Today, D'Annunzio may be just as well-known as the most successful Don Juan of his day, with a catalogue of conquests to rival the canonical 1,003 of Mozart's Don Giovanni, as for his literary works; yet at the time that Romaine Brooks succumbed to his charms, D'Annunzio was the most influential Italian poet of his era. His intensely romantic novels were international bestsellers, and his historical stage plays, such as *La gioconda* and *Francesca da Rimini*, were acclaimed as masterpieces and rapturously received by the public. His posthumous reputation has suffered in part because of his sexual mania, in part because he did not follow the modernist orthodoxy, and in particular because Mussolini embraced him as the national poet of the Fascists.

The potency of D'Annunzio's seductive charm was all the more remarkable because his person was, by all accounts, repellent. Liane de Pougy, a celebrated courtesan who eluded his grasp, described him as "a frightful gnome with red-rimmed eyes and no eyelashes, no hair, greenish teeth, bad breath, [and] the manners of a mountebank." Brooks met him at a lunch given by the Italian artist Leonetto Cappiello, where she saw in him "the great *lapidé* of our times."

One of the principal themes of Brooks's memoir is her sympathy and identification with heroic individuals who are stoned (*lapidé*) by the Philistine mob, martyrs for art. "His true personality was all but eclipsed by his notorious reputation," she wrote of D'Annunzio. "Stoned out of his own country, he was to face even more stoning in Paris."

Her admiration for D'Annunzio was electrified when they first met, by a chance remark. Cappiello's vibrantly colorful posters for Cinzano and Campari were plastered all over Paris, and when he showed his guests some new designs, D'Annunzio whispered in Brooks's ear, "And to think how much can be expressed without any color at all." Impulsively, she invited him to come see her paintings. "When he entered the studio," she wrote, "D'Annunzio, paying scant attention to me, went straight up to my pictures, and after contemplating them he began improvising aloud a *dédicace* to each in turn. So began my great friendship and admiration for Gabriele D'Annunzio. He changed the world about me and lifted me from a state of deep despondency." In her letters to him, Brooks expressed her love with an ardent passion untouched by the sardonic wit that dominates her memoir, written many years later. As the relationship was ending, she wrote to him, "I am angry that you never understood my real love for you, how I adored you, how much tenderness I had for you, how much I wanted to protect you. I wanted to serve you with all my strength."

She found herself in the unaccustomed position of being the pursuer, with the added humiliation of a rival. When Brooks decided to paint his portrait, they were living near each other in rented villas in Arcachon, a village overlooking a small bay on France's southwestern coast. She invited him to move in with her while she worked on the painting. While he was trying on costumes for the first sitting, Brooks's chauffeur, Bird, burst into the room and said that a woman was at the gate, clamoring to be admitted. It was Nathalie de Goloubeff, a wealthy married woman who had been D'Annunzio's mistress for two years, before Brooks supplanted her in the position. Brooks described her as "a beautiful statue whose emotional ego had been quickened by a careless Pygmalion," so maddened by love "that she emulated successfully the tortured heroines of his books." D'Annunzio delighted in torturing Madame de Goloubeff. After he dismissed her, she kept a nocturnal vigil on his doorstep, waiting for him to return from assignations with other women, to beg him to take her back. Brooks called her Niobe, because she was always weeping in public about her lost love. Goloubeff was reputed to carry a pistol in her bag, so Brooks ordered Bird to keep her out. "To be killed by a Niobe," wrote Brooks, "would be too ridiculous."

Meanwhile, D'Annunzio came downstairs wearing a hunting costume, a pink coat, riding breeches, and boots. Brooks told him what was going on outside, but he paid her no heed: "He had come down on purpose to be admired; nothing else mattered. To show himself off, he began pirouetting about the room." Bird returned to say that he had expelled the visitor "and that he had been obliged to detach her hands from the bars when she tried to climb over the gate." Finally alert to the gravity of the situation, D'Annunzio collapsed on a sofa and remained silent for a long time. Brooks bolted for Paris, motivated, she explained later, by pity for the wretched Niobe.

Brooks's portrait of D'Annunzio was not painted until

two years later, after the affair had ended. When she exhibited the painting at her studio in the Trocadéro, it was acclaimed as her finest work. *Gabriele D'Annunzio, the Poet in Exile*, as she called it, poses the subject standing before a stormy sea, with a black cape thrown over a somber vested suit. He lifts his eyes wearily to the gray sky, pressing his lips together in what came to be known as a *pli amer*, a bitter crease. As ever, the artist makes no concession to the sitter's vanity: the nearly colorless palette is paler than usual, making the poet look wan, as if the blood has been drained from his body. Nonetheless, it is a profoundly sympathetic portrait. The artist's intention to portray D'Annunzio as a martyr is radiantly apparent; a pearlescent glow hovers faintly in the sky around his head, like a martyr's aureole. The Musée du Luxembourg's purchase of the picture, which is now in the collection of the Centre Pompidou, confirmed Brooks in the first rank of the artists of her day. D'Annunzio wrote a long, effusive essay about Brooks for the Italian magazine *Illustrazione*, in which he called her "the most profound and wise orchestrator of grays in modern painting." He gave her the manuscript of the piece, which she kept to the end of her life in a carved wooden box, locked by a golden key.

Around the time of the disaster in Arcachon, while Brooks's affair with D'Annunzio was at its volatile peak, it became even more turbulent after Brooks met Ida Rubinstein, creating a new love triangle. Rubinstein was a principal ballerina with the Ballets Russes at a time when the roster included Nijinsky and Pavlova. She was not in their league as a pure dancer, for she was much too tall, but her stage presence exerted a potent magnetism equaling that of any performer of her day, Bernhardt included. Born to vast wealth (like all of D'Annunzio's lovers, and most of Brooks's) and raised in the Jewish enclave of St. Petersburg, Rubinstein moved in a nimbus of glamour, dressed in fabulous frocks from the House of Worth that she was supposed to have worn just once each, and bedecked with jewels. Robert de Montesquiou was a worshipful admirer. He introduced her to D'Annunzio, who was likewise dazzled. When he asked Montesquiou what could possibly be done with her, the dandy commanded the poet, "Write a tragedy for her!"

So he did: in 1911, D'Annunzio cast Rubinstein in the title role of *The Martyrdom of Saint Sebastian*, a mystery play he wrote while he was staying with Brooks at Arcachon. It was an experimental, gender- and genre-bending drama, five hours long, that blended poetry and dance, set to a score by Debussy (which Rubinstein commissioned), with choreography by Fokine and sets and costumes by Léon Bakst. The piece had a chorus of two hundred singers. In one scene, Rubinstein appeared almost completely nude, a remarkable coup de théâtre for a female performer: pantless in a pants role. After the play's premiere, at the Théâtre du Châtelet, Montesquiou wrote in his review, "I have seen many things, many beautiful things, but in my experience I have never seen anything to compare in beauty with what this artist disclosed to our gaze." He exalted Rubinstein's "ivory face with gemlike eyes capable of looking into our hearts, and locks of hair which seem to be the expression of the poet's phrase 'cluster of pain.'"

D'Annunzio's drama follows standard church hagiographies, infused with the perverse eroticism of pagan myth. Sebastian was a Roman soldier in the third century, conventionally portrayed as a beautiful, epicene youth who secretly practiced Christianity and made many covert conversions. After he was exposed, he was bound to a stake (or tree) and shot with arrows. The scene was a favorite subject of Italian Renaissance painters, because the binding of the saint presented an opportunity to present the male figure in torsion. Partly for that reason, and also because his martyrdom resulted from a secret life, Sebastian has long been identified as the unofficial patron saint of homosexuals. The painting of him often used in church literature is that by Il Sodoma, the Sodomite, the nickname of Giovanni Bazzi, in the collection of the Uffizi. In *Death in Venice*, published a year after D'Annunzio's play was staged, Thomas Mann proclaimed that "the figure of Sebastian is the most beautiful symbol" of the spiritual heroism extolled in the writings of his protagonist, Gustave von Aschenbach: "Forbearance of the fact of fate, beauty constant under torture, are not merely passive. They are a positive achievement, an explicit triumph." Mann's exaltation of forbearance is an approximate definition of Romaine Brooks's ideal of the *lapidé*, the source of her devotion to D'Annunzio.

The reader of Brooks's memoir must take care to distinguish her serious intentions from her sarcastic wit, which sometimes gets the better of her: in her farcical narrative of Nathalie de Goloubeff's siege of the villa at Arcachon, Brooks's description of her lover pirouetting in his hunting costume makes him appear buffoonish, yet there is no doubt that D'Annunzio aroused in her a profound intellectual admiration. The best explanation for the lesbian artist's passion for the ill-favored poet may be that he seduced her with ideas. Those long summer evenings in Arcachon were not all devoted to playing dress-up: at the same time that

D'Annunzio was writing *The Martyrdom of Saint Sebastian*, Brooks painted one of her most unusual canvases. *The Masked Archer* depicts a pale, slender woman bound to a stake; facing her, a dwarf in the costume of a medieval jester, standing on a platform, aims an arrow at her with his bow. The female figure is not a portrait of Ida Rubinstein, yet it is plainly she. The link between the painting and the play is clear. In her catalogue of a comprehensive Romaine Brooks exhibition at the National Museum of Women in the Arts, in 2000, the art historian Whitney Chadwick wrote, "The violent transformation of Sebastian from warrior to martyr at the hands of ignorant believers and from male to female in D'Annunzio's imagination is perfectly expressed in Brooks's cult of the *lapidé*."

The Masked Archer might have been inspired by an incident in Arcachon. When Ida Rubinstein came to visit D'Annunzio, as they were walking in the forest, the sight of pine trees that had been gashed to release their resin reminded him of the paintings of Saint Sebastian he had studied in his research for the tragedy. He asked Rubinstein to shoot the trees with arrows. Sebastian's speech in the finale of the play resonates with Romaine Brooks's art: "I come, I ascend. I have wings. All is white. My blood is the manna which whitens sins." In her drawings, Brooks had adopted as her iconic signature a schematic image of a wing bound by a chain that forms the letter *R*, analogous to Whistler's famous butterfly monogram.

Readers of Brooks's memoir must also bring a skeptical eye to the chronology it presents of her life. In the Beinecke typescript, she states that she first met Ida Rubinstein after the premiere of *Saint Sebastian*, yet she exhibited *The Masked*

Archer at her studio ten days before the play opened. It might have been a lapse of memory, or perhaps Brooks was away when Rubinstein visited D'Annunzio in Arcachon. Whenever it was that they met, Brooks was moved by Rubinstein's spectral appearance as much as D'Annunzio and Montesquiou had been. Rubinstein, she wrote, "seemed to me more beautiful when off the stage, like some heraldic bird knit together by the finest of bone structure." She recalled walking with Rubinstein one snowy morning at the Longchamp Racecourse, in the Bois de Boulogne:

> Everything was white, and Ida wore a long ermine coat. It was open and exposed the fragile bare chest and slender neck which emerged from a white feathery garment. Her face sharply out with long golden eyes and a delicate birdlike nose; her partly veiled head with dark hair moving gracefully from the temples as though the wind were smoothing it back. When she first came to Paris she possessed what is now so rarely spoken of—mystery.

The elements of the triangular psychodrama, which possessed all the libidinal complexity of a play by Arthur Schnitzler, were now in place. Each of the artists was in love with the other two, but in the dominant emotional scenario that emerged, Rubinstein was besotted with Brooks, who was utterly devoted to D'Annunzio, who was consumed by lust for Rubinstein. It was obviously an unstable dynamic, which ended, inevitably, in chaotic disillusionment, but not before Brooks had painted some of her finest works, with Ida Rubinstein as the nude model. In a series of large oil paintings, portraits and allegorical subjects that celebrate Rubinstein's extraordinary physique, Brooks captures the sense of mystery that had fascinated her.

The last of them, *La Venus triste* (translated as *The Weeping Venus*), was painted in the winter of 1916, during a dark period of the First World War. Brooks wrote in her memoir, "Who other than Ida Rubinstein, with her fragile and androgynous beauty, could suggest the passing away of familiar gods?" Venus's pose in the painting is identical to that of the figure in *The Masked Archer*, rotated from a standing to a reclining position. The painting takes a star turn in *The Forge*. Radclyffe Hall describes it in precise detail as a work by Venetia Ford. When Susan Brent sees the painting in the artist's studio, it has a transformative effect on her: "The Venus lay on a somber couch with a moonlit sky as background. One arm was flung above her head, the other dropped by her side. Susan got the impression of a body languid with too much pleasure, emaciated by too much suffering. Tears fell from under the closed eyelids, and the face seemed to hold the suffering of all the world." The painting moves Susan to leave her husband and study with Venetia Ford.

Brooks's plan to paint Rubinstein in the studio was thwarted by the model's habitual twitchiness, so she worked from photographs. In the finished work, the legs of the figure are remarkably long, to such an extent that the viewer might conclude that the artist exaggerated their length to enhance the visual impact, in the manner of El Greco. Yet after Brooks's death, a series of photographs of Rubinstein in the pose of Venus were discovered among her effects, which revealed that the painting accurately reflected the model's unusual proportions. Whitney Chadwick discerns a revolutionary intent in *The Weeping Venus* quite distinct from the modernist movements that ruled Paris at the time: "For the first time in depicting the body of a female lover, Brooks links death and eroticism under the sign of a new, female image of the androgyne. Fusing a pictorial style derived from decadent and symbolist representations with a body type stressing slenderness, small breasts, and sexual ambiguity, she appears to move toward a new, more fully realized representation of the lesbian body."

By this point in her life, despite the pleasure and intellectual stimulation she got from the company of sensitive, artistic men, Brooks firmly identified as lesbian. After the stressful relationship with Gabriele D'Annunzio ended, she confined her amours to her own sex. Her homosexual orientation was confirmed when she met the woman who would be her great love, the American poet and *salonnière* Natalie Barney. Brooks's memoir is much vaguer in its terse account of this relationship than in the many pages devoted to D'Annunzio. She does not mention the date of their first meeting, but it must have taken place by late 1916, when Brooks painted *The Weeping Venus*, because Barney wrote a poem about the picture. It begins,

THE WEEPING VENUS
(by Romaine)

Laid out as dead in moonlight shroud
Beneath a derelict cloud:
A double wreckage safe from flight
High-cagèd as grief, in prisoned night.

Brooks's memoir is also elliptical about the nature of the relationship; throughout the text, Barney is referred to as "my friend." It might seem logical to entertain the possibility that Brooks is more candid about her relationship with D'Annunzio than that with Barney because she wished to conceal her homosexuality, or to veil it in euphemism, but that would be a misreading. The authorial reticence is in part simply a function of Brooks's old-fashioned ideas about good manners, and it might also have had a mild erotic motive. In her fine recent biography of the artist, Cassandra Langer writes that Brooks "believed that sensuality flourished best in secret, so she tells us very little about love and lovers." Brooks might have made an exception in the case of D'Annunzio because his death, in 1938, had conferred upon him the retroactive exemption from blame often granted dead lovers and because he could no longer make mischief. Brooks's recollection of her affair with D'Annunzio had mellowed with a nostalgic patina, but in her later life she became increasingly irascible, collecting quarrels with Barney and everyone else. In the memoir, she begins her account of her relationship with Barney on an acerbic note: "Friendship came to me again, bringing me its compensations but also demanding its toll."

Natalie Clifford Barney was born in Dayton, Ohio, in 1876. Her father was the heir to a railway fortune, and her mother, Alice Pike Barney, was a painter who studied with Carolus-Duran and Whistler. Natalie met Oscar Wilde when she was a little girl, on a family holiday in Long Island, while he was on his triumphant American lecture tour. She was being chased down the boardwalk by little boys who pelted her with candy cherries that got stuck in her flaming-

In this small fresco from
Pompeii, Odysseus sails past
the Sirens, who play pipes
and horns to lure his ship
to destruction. Skeletons of
previous victims litter
the shore.

A sardonyx cameo of Augustus
deified, carved soon after the
emperor's death

Engraving of Tiberius,
by Balthasar Moncornet
(ca. 1600–1668)

Bust of Tiberius
at the Louvre

The ruins of Villa Jovis, Tiberius's palace atop Capri's highest cliff

A fanciful reconstruction of the palace by the German
antiquarian C.F.W. Weichardt, 1900

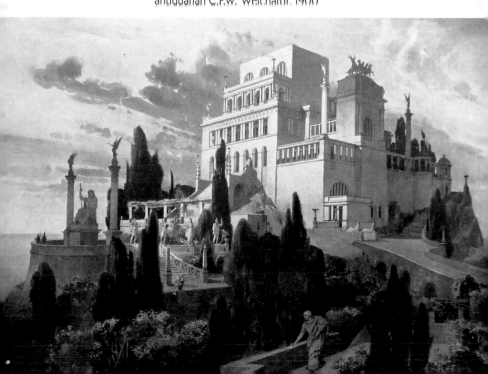

Jacques d'Adelswärd Fersen
at twenty

Villa Lysis, Fersen's
mansion in Capri,
"dédiée à la jeunesse
d'amour," dedicated to
the youth of love

FACING PAGE: Thomas Spencer Jerome and
Charles Freer in the garden of Villa Castello

Salon of Villa Lysis

The terrace, overlooking the Marina Grande

Period photograph of the salon of Villa Lysis

Period photograph of a bronze sculpture of Nino Cesarini riding a dolphin,
by Francesco Ierace, now presumed lost

Mimì Ruggiero, Capri's
master gardener

Baron Jacques at forty

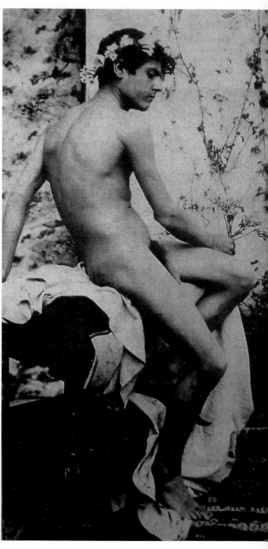

Nino Cesarini in a classical pose,
photograph by Wilhelm von Plüschow

Casa Rossa, home of John Clay MacKowen, in Anacapri,
which now houses the municipal art collection

Coastline of Capri near the White Grotto, oil painting by Michele Federico
(1884–1966), the only native Capriote artist represented in the collection

Studio portrait of
Romaine Brooks,
circa 1915

At the Seashore
(*In riva al mare*),
self-portrait by
Romaine Brooks,
oil on canvas,
1914

Romaine Brooks at Villa Cercola, circa 1920

Photograph of Villa Cercola around the time
that Romaine Brooks lived there

Gabriele D'Annunzio, le poète en exil, oil painting
by Romaine Brooks, 1912

Portrait of Ida Rubinstein, by Romaine Brooks, 1917

Allers at Home Again (*Allers Wieder daheim*), self-portrait of the artist in Capri, by Christian Wilhelm Allers, 1898

Rosina Ferrara, Head of a Capri Girl, oil on cardboard, by John Singer Sargent, 1878

Zum Kater Hiddigeigei café, meeting place for foreign
travelers in Capri, circa 1880

FACING PAGE: Villa Discopoli, residence
of Rainer Maria Rilke in Capri. Oil painting
by Giuseppe Ferrarini (Parma, 1846–?)

Maxim Gorky
in Capri village,
around the time
of his meeting
with Rilke

Villa Behring, Gorky's
residence after 1909,
where Lenin, Feodor
Chaliapin, and Ivan
Bunin stayed as
houseguests

red hair when she ran into Wilde, who lifted her up and rescued her from her tormentors. She gratefully sat on his knee, and Wilde told her a fairy tale.

In her early twenties, Barney made a permanent move to Paris, where she published collections of Sapphic verse, in French, which attracted little attention. In 1910, a slim volume of epigrams, *Éparpillements* (Scatterings), caught the eye of Remy de Gourmont, the influential critic and philosopher. He had become extremely reclusive after he contracted lupus, but he made an exception for Barney. They formed a bond of friendship that deepened on his part into a hopeless romantic infatuation. Gourmont published their conversations in *Mercure de France*, addressing her as *l'Amazone*, because she frequently came to him after horse riding in the Bois de Boulogne dressed in equestrian attire, the only socially acceptable costume that permitted women to wear trousers. Barney used the nickname to the end of her life. Brooks's portrait of her is called *L'Amazone*; it is an unusually subdued, opaque likeness, with a bronze horse on a tabletop in front of the sitter.

By the time she met Brooks, Barney had launched the salon at her mansion at 20 rue Jacob, in the Latin Quarter, which held an eminent position for more than sixty years, spanning the eras of Marcel Proust and Truman Capote. It would be easier to name the handful of major writers in Paris who did not attend her salon than to compile a list of those who did, which constitutes a nearly comprehensive census of modernist literature. An invitation to her Friday soirees was even more sought after than one to Saturdays chez Gertrude Stein, with whom, inevitably, Barney is often compared. She laid on a more lavish spread and had a Barnumesque flair for spectacle: Mata Hari once rode into the garden on rue Jacob as Lady Godiva, naked on a horse with a turquoise cloisonné harness.

Natalie Barney resembled Gabriele D'Annunzio in one important respect: she was compulsively promiscuous in her pursuit of sex and love. By the time she met Brooks, around the age of forty, she had had many intense romantic relationships, all of them with women, which brought her a notoriety that eclipsed the attention given her literary works. Among her lovers were Liane de Pougy, one of the few women who rejected D'Annunzio, the "frightful gnome"; Olive Custance, the future wife of Lord Alfred Douglas; and Renée Vivien, born Pauline Tarn, a British poet whose mother was from Michigan. When she was courting Vivien, Barney enlisted the aid of Emma Calvé, the reigning mezzo-soprano at the Paris Opéra, to serenade her from the street. When Vivien opened her window, Barney tossed up a bouquet of flowers with a love poem attached. Barney, who had written a play early in her career about the life of Sappho, studied the poet's fragments with Vivien. The two women traveled together to Mytilene, ancient Lesbos, with the intention of founding an art colony there for women.

Near the end of Renée Vivien's brief, unhappy life, when she was depressed and living in seclusion, she fell in love with Romaine Brooks and pursued her with pathetic perseverance. Here, Brooks recalls their first meeting, at Vivien's flat, near the Place de l'Étoile:

There comes before me the dark heavily curtained room, overreaching itself in lugubrious effects: grim life-sized Oriental figures sitting propped up on chairs, phosphorescent Buddhas glowing dimly in the folds of black draperies. The air is heavy with perfumed incense. A curtain draws aside and Renée Vivien stands before us dressed in Louis XVI male costume. Her straight blond hair falls to her shoulders, her flowerlike face is bent down . . . We lunch seated on the floor Oriental fashion, and scant food is served on ancient Damascus ware, cracked and stained. During the meal Renée Vivien leaves us to bring in from the garden her pet frogs and a serpent, which she twines round her wrist.

Brooks was impervious to the calculated drama of the scene and remained obdurate to Vivien's desperate demands for love in the ensuing friendship. Vivien died a few months later of self-starvation, complicated by an addiction to chloral hydrate.

Soon after they met, Barney became Brooks's deepest emotional attachment, but it was a complicated relationship. Barney adored Brooks, but she was still in love with a woman she had met seven years before, Élisabeth de Gramont, the duchesse de Clermont-Tonnerre, known as Lily. Gramont's mother was a princess of the blood, and she was descended on her father's side from a mistress of Henri IV's. She was trapped in a wretched marriage with an abusive aristocrat, Philibert, duc de Clermont-Tonnerre, who demanded abject obedience from his wife and beat her often, for trivial reasons. She suffered two miscarriages as a result of his brutality. When she met Natalie Barney, Gramont was consumed by a passion that lasted to the end of her life. In Barney, she discovered affectionate love and sexual excitement and through them a salvation from her *mariage noir*. When the duke divined what his wife was getting up to, he confined her and their two daughters in a rural château, a scenario that might have been lifted from the Marquis de Sade. Gramont escaped and sought refuge with her new love at the mansion on rue Jacob. Impoverished by this declaration of independence, Gramont sold a few antiques she had inherited and bought a house in suburban Passy. A close friend and confidante of Proust's, she made a tiny income as a writer and eked out a modest middle-class life with "loans" from Barney.

By the time Barney and Brooks met, Lily de Gramont had embraced an open lesbian identity—or more properly, she was playing a major role in the creation of the emerging paradigm. She was said to be the first lesbian in Paris to crop her hair short, a style that Gertrude Stein imitated. When Gramont became aware that she had a serious rival in Brooks, she was just as defiant as she had been with her ducal husband and broke off the relationship with Barney, imperiling her new life as boldly as she had her old one. In a letter redolent of fine scorn, with a bitchy dig at her lover's new coiffure, she wrote to Barney, "I am a cynic, and I find that pleasure is perhaps the only certainty apart from beauty. You look charming, of course, with your new haircut à la Brooks—the blonde and the brunette—an excellent pair—and I wonder if I am right to want to put asunder what the world has joined together?" Chastened, perhaps even panicked at the prospect of losing the woman she adored, Barney responded with a remarkable scheme: she proposed marriage.

In 2004, in his biography of Élisabeth de Gramont, Francesco Rapazzini revealed the existence of a contract between Barney and Gramont that gave a semblance of legal form to their relationship. Drafted by Barney on the stationery of the Hôtel d'Europe, in Aix-les-Bains, the document is a curious blend of romance and lawyerly boilerplate. If it had had any legal force, it would have made Gramont a bigamist, for the duc de Clermont-Tonnerre did not divorce her until two years later. The contract declares that "one is indispensable to the other" and states, "No one union shall be so strong as this union, nor another joining so tender—nor relationship so lasting." The document concedes that "adultery is inevitable in these relationships where there is no prejudice, no religion other than feelings, no laws other than desire, incapable of vain sacrifices that seem to be the negation of life." The women consecrated their symbolic marriage in 1918, a few months before the end of the First World War, and celebrated it with a honeymoon in America, where they called on Barney's mother and followed tradition with a trip to Niagara Falls.

However Barney, Gramont, and Brooks worked out their relationships, the arrangement endured until Gramont's death, in 1954. Cassandra Langer asserts that "Lily, Natalie, and Romaine were mapping new territory and building a model that simply did not have a name. This is not to imply that the relationship was always harmonious and without contradictions, but it was one of mutual respect and dependency within an open architecture of independence." Barney, who was able to maintain and stabilize her relationships with both her lovers, was the most obvious beneficiary of the tripartite alliance, but it also suited Brooks, the most independent tenant of the open architecture. The record offers no evidence that Brooks and Gramont were ever lovers, though Barney nurtured a hope that they would be.

Brooks might not have been as promiscuous as Barney, but she was equally averse to the bonds of a monogamous union. Her commitment to Natalie Barney was the only romantic partnership she entered into, unless one includes her marriage to John Brooks, and it remained strong almost to the end of her life, in 1970, more than half a century after the two women met. It was an attraction of opposites, which might have played a part in the durability of the relationship. Natalie Barney was a warmly affectionate woman, always demonstrating her love, whereas Brooks, a loner since childhood, became ever more misanthropic in later life. She seemed to be almost incapable of feeling jealousy and as a rule took scant interest in Barney's perpetual philandering. Brooks inspired hot passions but experienced them herself rarely after the affair with Gabriele D'Annunzio.

Brooks had no interest in establishing a flamboyant public identity as a lesbian, as Lily de Gramont had done, and shunned the company of lesbians who campaigned for social acceptance, such as Radclyffe Hall, the "digger-up of worms." Natalie Barney did not campaign for gay rights, but she had been open about her sexuality since girlhood. Her outrageous gestures arose from an enlightened idealism that may appear naive to a contemporary eye, yet it anticipates late twentieth-century feminism in a classical mode that verges on camp. Barney dedicated a Doric "Temple of Friendship" in her garden, where she and her devotees dressed in white robes and recited Sapphic verse as they strummed tortoiseshell lyres. In

1927, she established an Académie des Femmes to honor French women writers, fifty-three years before Marguerite Yourcenar, an habitué of Barney's salon, became the first woman to be elected to the French Academy.

If male homosexuality in the early decades of the twentieth century was poorly understood, a subject for lawyers and judges more than doctors and scientists of the mind, its female counterpart was all but unknown. The principle underlying the legend that Queen Victoria asked Parliament to strike a proposed law forbidding sexual activity between women, on the grounds that "women do not do such things," might apply just as well to the medical establishment of the day. One of the pioneers of the scientific study of female homosexuality was Allan McLane Hamilton, the alienist who lived in Villa Castello until he sold it to Thomas Jerome and Charles Freer. In 1896, he published an article in *The American Journal of Insanity*, which applied to lesbians the prevailing classification of male homosexuals into active predators and passive victims: "The offender was usually of a masculine type . . . and she nearly always lacked the ordinary modesty and retirement of her sex. The passive agent was, as a rule, decidedly feminine, with little power of resistance, unusually sentimental or unnecessarily prudish."

From a modern perspective, it is difficult to accept that Hamilton was among the more enlightened early investigators of the phenomenon, despite the asperity of his terminology, simply by raising the subject. In his article, he complained that gathering data about lesbians was difficult because the "mental perversion was not of a recognized kind." The tale of Queen Victoria's intervention in the British criminal code is apocryphal, but it is true that sex between women was not prohibited by law. While male homosexuals lived in a perilous social penumbra, lesbians occupied a nonexistent terrain, which freed them to live as openly as they dared. Radclyffe Hall and Lady Troubridge claimed martyrdom because people whispered and sneered behind their backs when they came to the opera dressed in tuxedoes, but sneers and whispers were the worst they could expect at a time when gay men were being led to prisons and workhouses in shackles.

AS THE CATASTROPHIC war was grinding to a close, in 1918, Romaine Brooks returned to Capri and took up residence at Villa Cercola, where her husband was living with Maugham and Benson when she first met him. It was one of the best houses in the village, built at the end of the nineteenth century in plain boxy island style, with an interior space of six hundred square meters. The principal attraction of the villa was its garden, nearly an acre in extent, including an olive orchard and a pergola hung with grapevines. It was a sentimental choice: Brooks painted her early picture of a pergola in fruit, which she sold to Charles Freer, at Cercola. The house had three inconspicuous entrances on the footpaths winding up to Tiberius's palace. The marble doorstep of the upper gate was engraved with the Latin motto *Cave hominem* (Beware of the man!), a learned joke that had John Brooks's classical fingerprints on it, playing on the familiar injunction *Cave canem* (Beware of the dog), a warning to intruders, which was the subject of a famous mosaic at Pompeii.

The house had six bedrooms, two dining rooms, two bathrooms, and at the rear, most enticing for Romaine Brooks, a long studio with a northern exposure, which looked out on a terrace and beyond to the Gulf of Naples. When Brooks took the house over, it had a ballroom with a wooden dance floor, one of just two on the island. In *Final Edition: Informal Autobiography*, Benson wrote that in 1913 he "moved into a most delightful house," which he had long coveted. "A plumbago ramped up the whitewashed rough-cast of the house wall. From the terrace ran out a short vine-covered pergola over the cistern for rain water, and in the garden, lying rather steeply down the hillside, grew a great stone-pine which whispered to the slightest breeze and roared when sirocco blew." A tangle of passionflower and morning glory hung over the garden wall. Benson's description of his life with John Brooks at Villa Cercola in the summer before the First World War is a lyrical evocation of Capri's sirenic allure, which may not seem overripe to those who have experienced it. "Long mornings of swimming through translucent waters interspersed with baskings in the sun, siestas, fresh figs, walks up to the top of Monte Solaro, homecomings in the glowing twilight, dinner under the vine pergola, games of piquet in the café, strolling on to the piazza at night to look at the lights of Naples lying like a string of diamonds along the main, with the sultry glow of Vesuvius behind."

Villa Cercola today remains just as it was in Benson's description. The present owner is Nicolino Morgano, the proprietor of the Quisisana and other hotels in Capri. He invited me to have a look at the house on a morning in early spring, just a week after the hotel had reopened from its winter hibernation. We enter by the lowest of the three gates, which presents a view of the house at the top of the knoll, with beds of flowering shrubs descending in lazy terraces. Gardeners kneel by the paths, replanting the floral borders. As we ascend to the house, Morgano explains, "I bought Villa Cercola because I felt a responsibility. My family is one of the oldest in Capri, and I was afraid what someone from the outside might do if they bought it."

He is being tactful: the remark is an indirect jab at the previous owner of the house, the fashion designer Valentino Garavani, who entertained the jet set here in extravagant style in the 1960s and 1970s, including famous clients such as Audrey Hepburn, who made Capri pants a worldwide staple of women's leisure attire, and Jacqueline Onassis. As we wander through the garden, Morgano confides, "The house was in terrible condition when I bought it from Valentino. The electrical wiring was no good—there was no electricity in the house at all." When I ask how Valentino lit the house for his famous parties, Morgano responds with an eloquent shrug and says, "The house had been empty for a long time. It was full of candles."

When Morgano took over the place, he made no changes apart from the repairs needed to make it habitable. "No changes at all," he says. "We just painted it." The exterior of the house is now a foggy shade of gray, very Romaine Brooks. He points out the old-fashioned rectangular swimming pool, a novelty in Capri when it was built, and the pergola, where, he says, Norman Douglas used to sit and write. I think he means Somerset Maugham, but I don't say anything. Douglas was a frequent visitor and must have sat there often, and he undoubtedly wrote there sometimes as well.

Morgano leads me inside. His wife, Carmen, makes a striking entrance, wearing a smartly tailored tweed suit with black leather trim. Looking elegant and tall in stiletto heels, she greets me warmly. One relic of Valentino's tenancy that the Morganos have retained is a decorative mural in the smaller dining room, which is painted with a trompe l'oeil mural of vines in lush foliage, giving the room the feeling of a rustic bower. The weather is too warm to take coffee outdoors, so Signora Morgano serves it in the living room. She explains that Villa Cercola is not the family's main residence, yet it is nonetheless decorated in a homely style. Where Andy Warhol's portrait of Valentino used to hang, there are now family snapshots. She has kept a few mementos of the villa's past; she hands me a framed photograph of Richard Burton and Elizabeth Taylor lounging by the pool with a panting sheepdog.

Affable and mild mannered, Morgano speaks softly yet exudes the self-confidence of a man born to leadership. "Tourism and hospitality were born a hundred and fifty years ago in Capri with the Morgano family," he says proudly. "My great-grandmother Donna Lucia Morgano was the patron of the cultural world. I represent the fourth generation."

In the last decade of the nineteenth century, Giuseppe and Lucia Morgano took over an existing café that catered to German tourists called Zum Kater Hiddigeigei ("The Tomcat Hiddigeigei," a cynical feline in popular satirical poems by Joseph Viktor von Scheffel, a literary antecedent of George Herriman's Krazy Kat). Caffè Morgano became the hub of expatriate life in Capri, purveying, in addition to coffee and cocktails, goods that were otherwise hard to find, such as bathing suits and foreign newspapers, and providing invaluable services, which included tipping off their regulars when the carabinieri were after them, as Donna Lucia did for Christian Wilhelm Allers. When foreign friends ended up in jail, she helped them find a lawyer and sent over hot meals. Compton Mackenzie wrote, "Receiving a glass of vermouth from the hands of the Lady Lucia Morgano is like drinking from the miraculous breast of Mother Earth." In 1934, Giuseppe and Lucia's grandson Mario opened the Morgano Tiberio Palace, the family's first hotel, which aimed to rival the Quisisana in luxury. Fifty years later, Mario bought the Quisisana, just around the corner from Caffè Morgano, which maintains its reputation as *la grande dame*, the island's most prestigious hotel.

Although he is in the prime of life, Nicolino Morgano as a native Capriote has seen enormous changes in the island. When I take my leave, as he escorts me to the upper gate, he recalls, "The big change in Capri came in the late nineties, when they started to have regular ferry service at night. Before that, there were only three or four boats a day, so not so many people could come, like now." As a hotelier, of course, he does not complain about the volume of tourism; every visitor is a potential guest, and hospitality is in his blood. He swings the door open for me and says, with a genial smile, "Watch your step!" He points with his toe to the inscription carved on the doorstep: *Cave hominem.*

~~~

ROMAINE BROOKS'S RETURN to Capri at the end of the war was motivated in part by nostalgia, a desire to return to the place she had been happiest, where she had escaped the demands of her crazy mother before she inherited the responsibilities of wealth. John Brooks stayed on in Villa Cercola long after Maugham and Benson had left Capri, and spent the war years there. When he learned that his wife was arriving to take possession of the house, he vacated the premises, in accordance with his undertaking to stay clear of her, a requirement for his meat-but-no-pickles pension, and moved into a one-bedroom cottage at a discreet distance. Romaine adored the house and took an unwonted interest in the garden, digging and replanting it with her own hands.

She gloried in her solitary situation at Villa Cercola and immersed herself in her work. She confided in a letter to D'Annunzio, "I shut myself up for months without seeing a soul, and give shape in my paintings to my visions of sad and gray shadows." Yet as with her self-description as a misanthropic recluse in Paris, it is hard to reconcile this claim of months of solitude with the tally of her social calendar in Capri, which appears to have been a busy one. The island was more thickly populated by foreign visitors now than it had been on her previous visits, and it is possible that her social life seemed to her a lonely one by comparison with the never-ending round of dinner parties and picnics and *thés dansants* that the other foreign residents pursued; more likely, it is an attempt to make herself appear interesting to her former lover. Soon after her arrival, Faith Mackenzie paid her a welcoming call and wrote this romantic picture of the hermit of Villa Cercola: "A heat wave, hot even for Capri in August, sent temperatures up. Feverish bouquets of exhausted blooms lay about the big studio, letters and invites strewed her desk, ignored for the most part, while she, wrapped in her cloak, would wander down to the town as the evening cooled and sit in the darkest corner of Morgano's Café terrace, maddeningly remote and provocative."

Now a woman of substance, wealthy and established as an artist with an international reputation, Brooks no longer needed to fend off gropers like the sentimental Mr. Burr. If there were any lingering doubts about her identity as a lesbian, in Capri she devoted herself almost entirely to the company of women. Nonetheless, Norman Douglas took a great liking to her, and she called on Fersen from time to time to have a look at a portrait of herself that hung at Villa Lysis. The artist and the present whereabouts of the painting are unknown. According to Faith Mackenzie, the portrait presented Brooks seated, wearing black knee breeches, with one white-cuffed hand dangling, and full, challenging eyes.

Reconstructing Romaine Brooks's life in Capri in 1918 presents the same difficulty that faces Jacques d'Adelswärd-Fersen's biographers: the manuscript of her memoir dwindles to an inconclusive end before reaching this period of her life, and the principal account of events is a work of fiction. *Extraordinary Women*, Compton Mackenzie's novel about Capri's lesbian community, is in many ways a better book than *Vestal Fire*, his roman à clef about Fersen and the Wolcott-Perrys. He gathered much of the intimate background from Faith, who was Romaine Brooks's confidante.

Mackenzie wrote that "every one of the characters in *Extraordinary Women* is an exact portrait" (with one insignificant exception), but it is a misleading claim. Olimpia Leigh, the character that is supposed to be based on Romaine Brooks, diverges from its model in significant ways. In appearance, Olimpia Leigh is "small and dark"; Brooks was neither. The author puts her up not at Villa Cercola but rather at Charles Coleman's Villa Narcissus, thinly disguised, with the disadvantageous site of Elihu Vedder's Villa Quattro Venti added for comic interest. Olimpia Leigh's mother was "a Swedish mathematician who had also been a musician and a scholar of Greek," very different from Ella Goddard. Leigh composes lyrical music, which might be a workable substitute for painting, but her work is devoted to Sappho, and she frequently drops ancient Greek into her conversation. The Sapphic theme, perhaps borrowed from Natalie Barney and grafted onto Brooks, is an egregious misrepresentation, for Brooks took no interest in her partner's efforts to find a classical pedigree for lesbianism in ancient Lesbos.

In *Extraordinary Women*, Mackenzie's habitual irony takes on a sarcastic edge that may be attributable to the fact that his wife had a lesbian affair while they were living in Capri. He treats the loves of those women as inherently ridiculous: neither more nor less so than love between men and women, and that between men, but the distinction is easily lost. Most readers of *The Well of Loneliness* are impressed (not often favorably) by Hall's earnestness, but if *Extraordinary Women* was Mackenzie's attempt to correct the discourse, he overcompensated. Nonetheless, his book, which came out immediately after *The Well of Loneliness* was published and banned by the censor, earned the distinction of being the first novel about lesbian lives that was permitted to be sold in British bookshops.

Taken on its own terms, his novel is a learned, amusing fictional frolic, which resembles E. F. Benson's ironical satires of quarrelsome provincial ladies, with an even stronger dose of venom and enlivened by a bracing dash of classical erudition. Mackenzie's narrative skill as he unwinds a tangled skein of plots and subplots is deft and sure. One of the principal threads is a triangle, or rather a trapezoid, that involves Rory Freemantle, a female fight promoter who favors men's suits, in furious pursuit of Rosalba Donsante, a capricious, conceited beauty, slim and graceful, who resembles Benson's "Lucia," Emmeline Lucas, more than a little. Rosalba in turn vies with Olimpia Leigh for the conquest of an American heiress. Rosalba gives a dinner party, narrated in a passage that exposes the misogynistic edge to Mackenzie's view of lesbian love:

> These dinner-parties of Rosalba's had little in common with that form of entertainment as it is usually practiced in civilized communities. They partook more of the nature of séances at which everybody is wrought up to a pitch of nervous tension and expectation. The mere passing of the salt or pepper involved as much expense of emotion as an elegy of Propertius. All life's fever was in the salad bowl. A heart bled when a glass filled with wine. We know what an atmosphere can be created at a dinner by one jealous woman. At Rosalba's parties there were often eight women, the palpitations of whose hidden jealousies, baffled desires, and wounded vanities was in its influence upon the ambient air as the dreadful muttering of subterranean fires before an eruption.

Mackenzie balances his contempt with occasional flashes of sympathy for the emotional pain his characters inflict upon each other. When Rosalba appears to have shifted her affections to Olimpia Leigh, Rory Freemantle ponders whether the dignified response would be to offer her successful rival the villa she had built for her true love: "When the dusty road was behind her and she was in that cool and white seclusion, when she saw once again the azure sea through the colonnades and heard the bamboos whispering and walked past the cypresses to lean over the marble parapet and gaze upon the enameled floor of the bay, she hesitated to forsake all this for another woman. Why *should* Olimpia have it? Why should she withdraw in favor of a woman who had already enjoyed all that life could give?"

In its ingenious plot construction, *Extraordinary Women* resembles Clare Boothe's comedy *The Women*, a hit on Broadway in 1936 subsequently filmed by George Cukor, in which all the characters are female (including the children) and much of the action takes place in a couturier's dressing room, a beauty salon, and an exercise class. Men are only talked about. In *Extraordinary Women*, the male characters are sketchy and usually nameless. One of the few male characters in the novel, in the comic bit part of the misguided suitor who fails to comprehend that the girl he fancies prefers her own sex, is described only as "a young Neapolitan neither more nor less good-looking than innumerable other young Neapolitans who were screaming at one another all over the island night and day, to the perpetual astonishment of elderly Englishmen who could not understand why they were not in the trenches."

Natalie Barney came to visit Brooks in Capri on several occasions, but never for long; Barney preferred city life and disliked travel generally. Their partnership thrived upon separation, though Brooks thrived on it more than Barney did. While Brooks was living at Villa Cercola, Barney wrote to her from Paris, "I know that you have not bathed without everyone on that hot island desiring you—that they could follow the glimmer of your perfect form to the end of the earth." In the same letter, Barney predicts the potential result of Brooks's love of solitude: "I fear, I suppose, that relentless quality I've seen at times in you, that getting-rid-of-everything quality," and declares that if it is ever directed against her, "I must change into some dumb devoted pitiable animal."

This effusion of jealousy was provoked by an affair Brooks was carrying on with the concert pianist Renata Borgatti. "I am alone and you are with her," wrote Barney. The portrait Brooks painted of Borgatti in Capri is among her finest works. In it, the theme of the androgynous female martyr to art ventures beyond the lissome, boyish figure epitomized by Ida Rubinstein and takes on a powerful female "warrior," an artist with a male-like physique and habits. Borgatti was the daughter of the renowned tenor Giuseppe Borgatti, the leading Wagnerian Heldentenor of his time, under the patronage of Arturo Toscanini. Renata began her musical career by accompanying her father on concert tours and later found success as a solo recitalist, specializing in programs of Debussy (which presumably would have included his sparkling Prelude No. 5, Book 1, "The Hills of Anacapri," which he composed on a visit to the island). She resembled her father not only in her blunt facial features but also in her husky build. Contemporary memoirists describe Borgatti as a woman inhabiting a man's body, the embodiment of theories about the "third sex" espoused by Havelock

Ellis and Magnus Hirschfeld. When John Singer Sargent saw her perform in London, he was so struck by her extraordinary appearance that he asked her to sit for him.

Borgatti made many other conquests in Capri besides Brooks—including Faith Mackenzie. Compton, perhaps expressing a hope about his wife's temperament more than an objective appraisal of Borgatti's personality, wrote of the pianist in his memoir, "The masculine side of her nature was so dominant that she sought women as she found them, without waiting for those who were temperamentally akin to herself." Borgatti appears to have blundered from one fleeting affair to the next, at the mercy of her libido, like a female Don Juan. Later, she had a romantic relationship with Princesse Edmonde de Polignac, the former Winnaretta Singer, one of Brooks's first lovers.

It is difficult to form a reliable conjecture as to whether Brooks was sleeping with Renata Borgatti when she painted her, nor does it matter. When Brooks painted a portrait, she approached the subject with the scientific precision of a surgeon, allied with a timeless grace. The composition of her portrait resembles an early painting by Whistler, *At the Piano* (1858–59), in which the figure of the pianist, rapt in her playing, is balanced by a graceful young girl in petticoats, leaning against the instrument. Brooks's portrayal of Borgatti's face in profile catches a resemblance to Franz Liszt that was noted by contemporary observers. The painting takes as its principal subject the absolute dedication of the player, her life absorbed by music. The face is somber, with a waxy pallor lit from within by a spiritual or intellectual glow, like a melancholy prelude by Debussy in a minor key.

Borgatti never attained great prominence as a pianist. For all their passion, her performances had too many wrong notes, for she did not practice enough. But her private recitals at her studio on the Punta Tragara, the majestic massif that overlooks the Faraglioni, and at the Mackenzies' villa were a legend in Capri. Faith Mackenzie, who had given up a promising career as a pianist when she married, wrote, "I want to cry: Ah, but you should have heard her at the Punta Tragara, playing music because she loved it, with divine irresponsibility." Mackenzie's admiration of Borgatti's musicianship must have been warmed by her emotional attachment to the musician: "You should have seen that silhouette swaying to the music in the candlelight which flickered because outside the wind was booming from the southwest. You can't tell unless you hear her like that, what an artist Borgatti is!"

The portrait Brooks painted of Marchesa Luisa Casati in Capri, in 1920, was unknown, or completely forgotten, until it was found after the artist's death, wrapped up and stored beneath her bed. Casati was a unique figure in the history of modernist art and performance in Europe. She is often called a muse, to (among many others) the Futurists and Gabriele D'Annunzio, with whom she carried on a long-term love affair, but the label falls short of the mark. She might more aptly be described by the concept of the artist who makes his life the work, as Cocteau remarked of Fersen. Casati did not make durable art objects or perform on theatrical stages; reality was her medium. She presented an inhuman appearance, often assuming personae demonic or divine. For D'Annunzio, she was Coré (a feminine form of "kouros," the idealized figure of a youth in archaic Greek sculpture), "the destroyer of mediocrity." Casati commissioned more than 130 portraits of herself, including major works by Léon Bakst, Giacomo Balla, Giovanni Boldini, Kees van Dongen, Jacob Epstein, Augustus John, and Man Ray.

Casati dyed her hair a flaming red to match her vermilioned lips, rimmed her large green eyes with kohl and dilated the pupils with belladonna, and framed them with extraordinarily long false eyelashes. She wore extravagant gowns, some of them created for her by couturiers such as Mariano Fortuny and Paul Poiret, others of her own design, sometimes accessorized with a living snake coiled around her arms. Casati's sensational appearances at balls in Venice and Paris, accompanied by a pair of leashed cheetahs wearing diamond-studded collars, were frequently appropriated by illustrators and filmmakers. The femme fatale in the first Futurist film, *Thaïs*, directed by Anton Giulio Bragaglia, is plainly based on her.* Marinetti called her "one of our most original national products," who succeeded "in sensationally beating in eccentric elegance and astounding creation of bizarre oddity and dandyism all that Paris has to offer in terms of originality, elegance, eccentricity, and dandyism." Casati collected palaces, including the Palazzo dei Leoni, on the Grand Canal in Venice, which Peggy Guggenheim later bought to exhibit her art collection.

*Released in 1917, the film is not based on Anatole France's novel, which inspired Jules Massenet's opera. The scenario, by Bragaglia and Riccardo Cassano, is a conventional deadly-diva thriller with a contemporary setting, about a diabolical seductress who wreaks havoc in her fast aristocratic set and dies inhaling deadly perfumes in a secret chamber of horrors in her bizarre mansion. The film was believed lost until a unique print was discovered, miscatalogued, at the Cinémathèque Française and screened at the Palazzo Grassi, Venice, in 1970.

Brooks's portrait of Casati came about by a process that reversed the usual dynamic: it was the sitter's idea. Ordinarily, when friends asked Brooks to paint their portrait, she resisted. She turned the marchesa down when she first suggested the idea, perhaps fearful of unflattering comparisons with the artists who had preceded her. "I should like to paint a chef d'oeuvre," she wrote in her memoir, "but also hesitate before the ordeal." Yet Casati was not to be denied. Brooks extemporized: she said that she had no canvas, then Uncle Charley loaned her some. She made the conditions ever more demanding: she announced that she would not come to Anacapri, and Casati agreed to come to Villa Cercola. Finally, Brooks insisted that she pose in the nude, something Casati had never done before. When she agreed to that, Brooks felt compelled to paint the picture.

The result is exceptionally dramatic, one of the few paintings from Brooks's maturity that employs vivid color, a loud orange for the subject's hair, which writhes and coils like serpents. Daniela Ferretti, director of the Palazzo Fortuny, in Venice, wrote this imaginative description of the painting in an essay for the catalogue of *La Divina Marchesa*, a landmark exhibition that reconstructed Casati's career, at the Fortuny in 2014: "Her Mephistophelean gaze, Medusa-like hair, feet transformed into claws, and androgynous body standing out against a rocky background, make her a proud creature of the night, a haughty fallen angel." The portrait is visually striking but has little of the psychological penetration characteristic of "the Thief of Souls." The artist is receiving and transmitting the Casati legend in its lurid glory and misses the sitter's complexity, her vulnerability and emotional neediness. Brooks hated the picture and refused all offers to buy it, including Casati's. "It isn't me," Brooks wrote.

By the time of her first visit to Capri, three years before, Marchesa Casati was well established as the Futurists' muse, the embodiment of their concept of Eternal Woman, the temptress and avenging sorceress. When Marinetti gave her a portrait that Carlo Carrà had painted of him, he inscribed it "To the great Futurist Marchesa Casati, with the slow eyes of a jaguar digesting the steel cage it has devoured in the sun." On her visit to Capri in 1917, after Casati had checked in at the Quisisana, Fortunato Depero, the painter in residence at Gilbert Clavel's villa in Anacapri, left a card at the desk inviting her to visit him at his studio there. By day's end, Depero wrote, she arrived "accompanied by a Neapolitan prince and a white greyhound as elastic as a feather. She wore shoes with mother-of-pearl heels and proved friendly and very intelligent." She bought a painting from Depero (now lost), "a vision of Capri with Clavel's villa in the center. Stretched out on top of it, as red as a little devil, and surrounded by figures, flora, and views of the island, the poet was like a little king asleep amongst his fabulous belongings." Casati created one of the best collections of Futurist art in the world. In 1930, her entire collection, including the portraits of herself and her jewels, was sold at auction, in partial satisfaction of a personal debt of some twenty-five million dollars.

On her visit to Capri in 1920, when Romaine Brooks painted her portrait, Casati stayed as the guest of Axel Munthe. She had asked to rent San Michele, the villa he built in

Anacapri adjoining the restored ruins of a medieval chapel, but he refused her. Casati, never deterred, disembarked at the Marina Grande amid mountains of luggage and sent a message to San Michele announcing her imminent arrival. Even the Capriotes, accustomed to eccentric visitors, were astounded by the apparition she presented. In Compton Mackenzie's account, "She wore an astrologer's hat, from which depended long veils enveloping her person. Her face was plastered like a mountebank's, her eyes surrounded by large black circles, and her hair was red. She wore bells in her ears."

Once installed in San Michele, she turned the place upside down. Mackenzie's memoir continued, "The walls were hung with black draperies and the stone floors covered with black carpets. She herself wore black, with black pearls and jet rings. Her hair, which had been red at first and later green, was now likewise black." Mackenzie writes that when he arrived for tea one afternoon, she received him completely naked, lying on a black bearskin in front of the fireplace. In Capri, Casati was attended by a servant Mackenzie describes as a "buck negro," whom she had stripped naked and gilded from head to toe. The man collapsed and would have died had not a local doctor come in time and scraped the gold leaf from his skin. An avid opium smoker, she often visited Fersen at Villa Lysis.

Casati became a popular fixture in Capri, for despite her bizarre affectations she was a kind, generous friend and hostess. Munthe's hope that his hellish houseguest would leave at summer's end was dashed, as it turned into an indefinite stay. A pugnacious advocate of animal rights, Munthe complained about Casati's use of snakes, big cats, and greyhounds (dyed to match her outfits) as props and personal adornments. He had a point: she once created a thrill at the Paris Opéra when she arrived with one bare arm dripping the blood of a chicken she had had beheaded for the occasion.

Any consideration of the expatriate community in Capri must reckon with Axel Munthe, the Swedish doctor who made himself the island's most famous resident. *The Story of San Michele*, his memoir, is the bestselling book about Capri ever published, translated into more than thirty languages. Indeed, it is reputed to be one of the bestselling books of the twentieth century, though like much of the book's contents, that may be an exaggeration. In its pages, Munthe portrays himself as a healer of miraculous powers, the most admired and sought-after physician first in Paris and then in Rome, where he set up his practice in Keats's house on the Spanish Steps; a brave humanitarian who brought an end to a cholera epidemic in Naples; a lover of celebrated beauties to rival Gabriele D'Annunzio; and the esteemed friend of the powerful and famous, particularly royals. The Swedish queen, Victoria, was devoted to him. The author's egotism is only made the plainer by his fulsome self-deprecations.

The Story of San Michele perfects the cliché of the Capriotes as carefree, childlike peasants, whom Munthe watches over like a loving patriarch. He was more passionate in his devotion to the island's quail and campaigned indefatigably for laws to protect their breeding grounds, regardless of the havoc wrought on the livelihood of many of the Capriotes he claimed to care for so tenderly. Curzio Malaparte, the political gadfly who built a villa in Capri that became as famous as San Michele, wrote a brutal description of Munthe in *Kaputt*, his semi-fictional memoir of the Second World War. In old age, nearly mad from loneliness, Munthe was "a prey to his black whims shut up day after day in his tower, stripped bare and like an old bone gnawed by the sharp teeth of the southwest wind." When Malaparte called on him, Munthe "stood there stiff, wooden, sulky; an old green cloak over his shoulders, a little hat perched crossways on his ruffled hair, his lively mischievous eyes hidden behind dark glasses, which gave him something of that mysterious and menacing air that belongs to the blind." Querulously, Munthe said, "I hope that you have not come to talk about the war." Nonetheless, he asked whether the Germans were killing birds. Malaparte replied, "They have no time to bother with birds. They have just time enough to bother with human beings. They butcher Jews, workers, peasants. They set fire to towns and villages with savage fury, but they do not kill birds." Munthe removed his dark glasses and smiled. "At least the Germans do not kill birds," he said. "I am really happy that they do not kill birds."

Munthe possessed a potent personal charm, enhanced by a ruthless disregard for speaking truth. Compton Mackenzie, who delighted in the role of tattletale, recorded a classic example of Munthe's habitual mendacity. When the Mackenzies visited Munthe, San Michele was still under construction, and he was living in a Saracen tower at Materita, about a mile away. When the carillon at Materita rang Angelus, Faith noted the particular beauty of the third bell. Munthe responded, "You are quite right, Mrs. Mackenzie. I had never noticed what a beautiful note that bell has.

You have a wonderful ear." Two weeks later, Faith came again to Materita for tea, with a baroness whose name and nationality Mackenzie suppresses in his memoir. When the carillon played the Ave Maria, Munthe pointed out to the baroness the sonorous beauty of the third bell. She responded on cue and exclaimed at its exquisite timbre. "I will tell you an interesting story about that bell," he said, and proceeded to spin an inspirational fairy story, with himself as the dauntless hero.

When he was visiting Florence, he told her, he heard the golden peal of that bell and conceived an irresistible desire to possess it. He awoke in the dark for matins, listened for the bell at midday and at every canonical hour, and finally found where it was, a nunnery in the Lung'Arno. He pounded on the convent's door and said, "I am the physician of her majesty the Queen of Sweden, and I must speak urgently to the Reverend Mother Superior." He persuaded the mother superior to sell him the bell, "and that is why you have heard that beautiful bell, Baroness, when Ave Maria rang at six o'clock." Munthe's brass to tell this story in the presence of Faith Mackenzie, who had pointed out the sonorous beauty of the bell's voice to him for the first time just two weeks before, was a proof that he had mastered the art of lying, which requires the liar to believe implicitly in the veracity of any yarn that pops into his head.

AFTER ROMAINE BROOKS'S residency in Capri came to an end, as she visited France more often and for longer stays, her artistic activity declined sharply. She continued to paint almost to the end of her life, but infrequently, as the desire to paint a masterpiece was thwarted more and more by self-doubt. By the mid-1920s, Brooks had painted most of the pictures that her posthumous reputation depends upon. Her grisaille palette became a habit, a trademark, lacking in the rigor of her self-schooling at St. Ives, where she trained her eyes to detect "an endless gamut of grays."

After quitting Capri, she lived first in Paris, in an apartment in Passy, but she was a constant presence at Natalie Barney's house on the rue Jacob when Barney's salon was at its height of influence. Brooks was a forbidding fixture at her partner's Fridays, more than a co-host, averse to meeting newcomers and cantankerous with people she knew. In Paris, she painted portraits of her friends, who were mostly lesbians, and a few male friends, including a fine likeness of Paul Morand, Loulou Locré's classmate, looking characteristically smug. The portrait of Una, Lady Troubridge, dates to this period. A process of masculinization similar to that painting is evident in a self-portrait from 1923 in which the artist wears a riding coat, gloves, and a top hat that shadows her eyes. The only spots of color are traces of scarlet lipstick (also the only unambiguous indicator of the subject's sex) and the tiny red ribbon of her Legion of Honor, pinned to the lapel.

In the 1930s, Brooks lived in New York, first in the penthouse of the Waldorf Astoria and then in the Hotel des Artistes, on West Sixty-Seventh Street, and rented a studio above Carnegie Hall. When Gertrude Stein and Alice B. Toklas came to town, Brooks took them for dinner at the Tavern on the Green. She adored Central Park by night, which she said reminded her of a Japanese garden, but by day it looked like "an abandoned farmyard."

The only constant in her emotional life was her profound, affectionate attachment to Natalie Barney. The women managed to stay together by not living together, in obedience to Brooks's growing need for solitude. They quarreled, of course; the relationship nearly foundered over Barney's infatuation with Dolly Wilde, the dissolute daughter of Oscar's dissolute older brother, Willie. Brooks had tolerated most of Barney's affairs, but this one went on for far too long. Finally, she wrote Barney a letter of farewell, a definitive dismissal. As usual, Barney responded with abject surrender. She proclaimed that her friendship with Brooks was "the most important thing in my life" and swore, "I shall always serve under your near or distant banner all the days or years of my life that remain, Romaine!"

In the postwar years, Brooks devoted more and more time to her memoir, obsessively revising and polishing it. Excerpts pertaining to her childhood with St. Mar were published in 1938, in a British journal called *Life and Letters To-day*, and twenty years later Brooks was still laboring over the manuscript. The version in the Beinecke collection, quoted here, is witty and filled with keen psychological insights about her friends and enemies, but as a memoir it is deeply flawed. She devotes many pages to trivial spats with people she barely knew yet fails to mention that she married John Brooks. Barney makes only a fleeting appearance, as a nice and interesting friend. A more serious problem is that there is good reason to believe that some passages are invented or heavily embellished. The author's martyrdom is presented in language that at times approaches hysteria; her suffering, particularly in childhood, attains a degree of wretchedness that defies belief. Throughout her life, she meets an incredible number of hunchbacks.

The remaining twenty-five years of Brooks's life were a pathetic decline into misanthropic isolation. One after another, she picked feuds with her old friends. By the end, Willy Maugham and Paul Morand were almost the only friends who remained loyal to her. She made one final friendship, with Marchese Uberto Strozzi, who lived the life of a Renaissance prince in a palace on the Piazza del Duomo. In 1961, at the age of eighty-seven, Brooks painted his portrait. She converted a room of the house in Fiesole where she was living into a studio, installing a glass panel in the roof with a complicated system of black curtains on pulleys to maintain precisely the lighting she required. She made the marchese, nearly as old as herself, pose for long hours in a hot, airless room, sitting in a black velvet armchair. The result is a fine portrait of the nobleman in repose, looking as though he might leap to his feet at any moment, a painting on a par with her best work from forty years before.

In the last decade of Brooks's life, her mental decay accelerated. She retreated to one of the houses in Nice she had inherited from Ella Goddard, where she lived among ghosts and nurtured imaginary ailments, particularly that of losing her eyesight. She was possessed by an irrational fear of being poisoned. Another quarrel with Natalie Barney, over another young rival, led to the final break, which Barney refused to accept but could not repair. At the age of ninety-two, she undertook the journey from Paris to Nice, uninvited. When she turned up on Brooks's doorstep, she was refused admittance. Marchese Uberto was the last friend to be dismissed. They had continued to chat by telephone after she moved to Nice, but eventually she stopped taking his calls. Finally, when he asked the servant if he had given Madame his message, the man replied that yes, he had, and her reply was "What's the use?"

IN THE AUTUMN of 1904, after Joseph Conrad had published *Nostromo* to disappointing reviews, and with his always precarious financial situation vitiated by an operation for his wife, Jessie, he abandoned England to spend the winter in Capri, motivated by thrift and the hope that the climate would conduce to her recuperation. He met Norman Douglas soon after his arrival, and they became fast friends. Conrad wrote to H. G. Wells that he had met "a Scot (born in Austria) once in diplomatic service, [which] he threw up I fancy in sheer intellectual disgust. A man who can not only think but write." The purpose of the letter was to enlist Wells's aid in getting Douglas published. To soften him up, Conrad added that he, Douglas, and Thomas Jerome had discussed Wells's visionary novel *A Modern Utopia*, which was then being serialized in *The Fortnightly Review*, and they agreed that Wells was "the one honest thinker of the day."

Capri disappointed Conrad, for reasons cited by many

visitors before and after him. In a letter to his friend and collaborator Ford Madox Ford, he reported,

> I've done nothing. And if it were not that Jessie profited so remarkably I would call the whole expedition a disaster. This climate what between tramontana and sirocco has half killed me in a not unpleasant languorous melting way. I am sunk in a vaguely uneasy dream of visions—of innumerable tales that float in an atmosphere of voluptuously aching bones . . . The scandals of Capri—atrocious, unspeakable, amusing scandals, international, cosmopolitan, and biblical flavored with Yankee twang and the French phrases of the *gens du monde* mingle with the tinkering of guitars in the barber's shops . . . All this is a sort of blue nightmare traversed by stinks and perfumes, full of flat roofs, vineyards, vaulted passages, enormous sheer rocks, pergolas, with a mad gallop of German tourists *lâché à travers tout cela* [loosed amid all this] in white Capri shoes over the slippery Capri stones, kodaks, floating veils, strangely waving whiskers, grotesque hats, streaming, tumbling, rushing, ebbing from the top of Monte Solaro (where the clouds hang) to the amazing rocky chasms of the Arco Naturale—where the lager beer bottles go pop.

Although Capri did not prove to be a good place to work, it provided the raw material for a brilliant short story, a genre that Conrad undertook infrequently in its pure, Chekhovian form. His near neighbor in Capri was a Polish compatriot,

Count Zygmunt Szembek, who told him about an unpleasant incident he had experienced in Naples. "Il Conde," subtitled "A Pathetic Tale," is told by a classic Conradian narrator,
chatty and confidential, an honest but unreliable informant.
On a visit to Naples, he meets an elderly Bohemian aristocrat, "a good European," an "intelligent man of the world, a
perfectly unaffected gentleman." They are staying at the same
hotel, where they become dining companions. The Count, a
widower, is elegantly dressed in a dinner jacket and evening
waistcoat "of very good cut, not new—just as these things
should be." He reveals that he is a regular visitor to the Gulf
of Naples, where he stays at hotels in Sorrento or rents a villa
in Capri, for relief of a painful and dangerous rheumatic af-
fliction. When the narrator leaves for a few days in Taormina,
to look after a sick friend, the Count sees him off at the train
station.

When the narrator returns, he finds the Count a changed
man. After dinner, over cigars, the Count tells him about an
"abominable adventure" that occurred in a public park in
Naples. He went to hear a musical concert, he says, where
he encountered a well-dressed young man of a certain type,
"with colorless, clear complexion, red lips, jet-black little
moustache, and liquid black eyes, so wonderfully effective in
leering or scowling." They shared a table without speaking.
Soon after, the Count strolled near the bandstand and saw
the young man again, and they exchanged glances. When
the music began, the Count wandered down a poorly lit alley,
where he once more encountered the young man, who asked
him for a light for his cigarette. When the Count reached for
his matches, the youth put a stiletto to his chest and demanded his money. The Count tells the narrator that he felt

powerless to call for help, because the robber could have thrown down the knife and claimed that he was the victim. "He might have said I attacked him" or "bring some dishonoring charge against me." The Count handed over what little money he had but refused to give up his rings, one a gift from his wife and the other a legacy from his father. The robber melted into the night.

Shaken, the Count stopped at a café in Galleria Umberto to eat a risotto. After he sat down, he saw the cutthroat sitting at the end of the banquette. A cigar seller informed him that he was "a young Cavaliere of a very good family" and a capo of the Camorra. After the Count paid his bill with a gold coin he kept hidden for such an emergency, the hoodlum menaced him for the last time: "Ah! So you had some gold on you—you old liar." He called him a rascal and a villain, and concluded, "You are not done with me yet." The Count decides that he must leave Italy at once and never return, which the narrator calls the equivalent of a death sentence. He sees the Count off at the station and ends his story with the maxim *"Vedi Napoli e poi mori"*: See Naples and die.

"Il Conde" has excited as many critical theories as some of Conrad's novels. The story anticipates the themes of anarchy and nihilism that he elaborates at length in *The Secret Agent*, which he was writing at the same time, and the novel that followed, *Under Western Eyes*. Modern critics have been attracted to the story because of its homosexual subtext, rare in Conrad's work. Jim's affectionate friendship with his native sidekick, in *Lord Jim*, possesses a sentimental edge, but the textual justification for a sexual charge is flimsy there and absent elsewhere in the novels. In "Il Conde," however, the homosexual element is scarcely submerged. From the start, the hints are plentiful. The narrator and the Count, both men traveling alone, first meet at the National Archaeological Museum when they are standing next to each other contemplating the bronze sculpture of a nude ephebe from Herculaneum, known as the Resting Hermes. Even before they meet, the Count attracts the narrator's notice when he leaves a yellow silk parasol behind at the hotel's dining room and a "lift boy" chases after him to return it.

The Count's narrative of his abominable adventure is transparent. He sits at the young man's table, they exchange glances in the crowd, he strolls past him as he sits alone in a dark alley. It is a classic description of what would come to be known as cruising, which culminates in asking for a light, the clichéd opening for a homosexual proposition. There is scant ambiguity, too, in the phrase "dishonoring charge"—what could it be, given the Count's age and social position, apart from a sexual advance? Yet the narrator of "Il Conde" portrays the Count not only in a positive light but affectionately. The gay reading of the story got support from Count Zygmunt Szembek's grandson, who told Conrad's Polish biographer that his grandfather was in fact homosexual. He also contributed a Pole's insight that the plebeian Conrad might have been impressed by the real Count's aristocratic polish, his air of instinctive cultivation, and even the discreet elegance of his wardrobe.

A more interesting issue than speculation about the elusive fictional "truth," whether the Count went to the concert in search of a young man for sex, is the perennial question in Conrad of the relationship between the narrator and his tale. Does the Count suppress important information telling his story to a naive, credulous confidant? Or is the narrator himself a player in the game, who intends his story to be a cautionary tale, lightly coded, to other homosexuals? The latter approach might not have occurred to Conrad: although he was friends with several writers who were gay, he appears to have been oblivious or indifferent to their private lives and might have been naive about the phenomenon, as most of his contemporaries were. Perhaps he simply took a story-teller's passing interest in the subject after meeting the charming, urbane Count Szembek and the intellectually brilliant Norman Douglas, who belied the stereotype of the predatory pederast, which resulted in this unique work.

~

FIFTEEN YEARS LATER, another modern master of the novel came to Capri for a longish stay and wrote a small-scale tour de force that was distinctly unlike his best-known works. D. H. Lawrence met Norman Douglas in London when Douglas was working at *The English Review*, edited by Ford Madox Ford, where Lawrence launched his literary career. In November 1919, when Lawrence decided to leave England to live abroad, beginning in Italy, he wrote to Douglas, who was then living in Florence, to ask him to recommend a cheap lodging there. Douglas put him up at the same flophouse where he was staying with an American journalist named Maurice Magnus, previously an artist's agent who had represented Isadora Duncan. The three penniless writers passed a few strange days together eating, drinking, and bickering until Lawrence departed for Capri for a rendezvous with his wife, Frieda, and Magnus, for obscure reasons, left to take up residence at Monte Cassino, a Benedictine monastery eighty miles southeast of Rome. Lawrence transformed these encounters into *Memoir of Maurice Magnus*. Barely a full-length book, it is now all but forgotten, yet Lawrence himself later called it "the best single piece of writing, as *writing*," he had done.

He is at his trenchant best in his account of bumping into the two men by the Ponte Vecchio immediately after his arrival in Florence, while he was looking for the hotel. In his observation, they are a music-hall comedy team: "Douglas tall and portly, the other man rather short and strutting," the former "decidedly shabby and a gentleman, with his wicked red face and tufted eyebrows," and Magnus "very pink-faced, and very clean, very spruce, very alert, like a sparrow painted to resemble a tom-tit." Lawrence pours on his contempt for Magnus. For all his bewhiskered apparatus of bohemianism, Lawrence was middle-class in his soul, "determined to keep a few pounds between me and the world," as he put it, whereas Magnus lived beyond his means, cadging handouts from friends to pay for first-class train tickets.

In this memoir, Lawrence's scorn is complicated by contempt for his new friend's effeminacy. When he calls on him in his room, Magnus "minced about in demi-toilette," looking "like a little pontiff in a blue kimono." Even at this dingy boardinghouse, everything was "expensive and finicking," with silver-studded suitcases and ivory-backed hairbrushes. "On his dressing-table stood many cut-glass bottles and silver-topped bottles with essences and pomades and powders." In Lawrence's observation, Magnus was "queer and sensitive as a woman with Douglas," while his idol treated him disdainfully and even seemed to despise him. Yet, of a piece with Lawrence's lifelong ambivalence toward homosexuality in principle and in particulars, he found himself charmed by the painted sparrow and promised to come visit him at the monastery.

Lawrence was even more acidulous about Capri than Conrad had been. He and Frieda soon became regulars in the island's quarrelsome social scene, yet he held himself aloof, calling Capri "a gossipy, villa-stricken, two-humped chunk of limestone, a microcosm that does heaven much credit, but mankind none at all." Soon after he had settled in, Lawrence received a wistful note from Magnus. He asked for nothing, but Lawrence intuited that it was an appeal for help. He made a fatal misstep: having just received a windfall from an American journal, he posted off a check for five pounds. Magnus wrote back immediately, overjoyed, reiterating his invitation to come for a visit at Monte Cassino. At this point, Lawrence's memoir begins to resemble James Hogg's *Confessions of a Justified Sinner,* about a man pursued by a familiar spirit, a grinning demon who turns up in his path everywhere he goes.

The narrative of his visit to Monte Cassino is a bravura performance of travel writing in a gloomy, gothic key. Lawrence's journey begins in Capri, waking

> in the black dark of the January morning, and making a little coffee on the spirit-lamp, and watching the clock, the big-faced, blue old clock on the campanile in the piazza in Capri, to see I wasn't late. The electric light in the piazza lit up the face of the campanile. And we were there, a stone's throw away, high in the

Palazzo Ferraro, opposite the bubbly roof of the little duomo. Strange dark winter morning, with the open sea beyond the roofs, seen through the side window, and the thin line of the lights of Naples twinkling far, far off.

Lawrence arrives at the monastery, icy cold in January, and finds Magnus living in a sumptuous, well-furnished room with a dressing table for the pomades and powders. The monks appear to share Lawrence's disdain for Magnus's lordly pretensions and to have accepted him as a guest as an act of charity. Magnus lends Lawrence a luxurious overcoat lined in sealskin, made for him, he says, by one of the best tailors in New York, and takes him on a tour of the monastery. The monks are at their evening prayers, so "we went by our two secret little selves into the tall dense nearly-darkness of the church." Magnus shows him the pillars and pavements, "all colored marbles, yellow and gray and rose and green and lily-white, veined and mottled and splashed," and mosaics of trees and birds glinting with gold and lapis lazuli. "We tiptoed about the dark church stealthily, from altar to altar, and Magnus whispered ecstasies in my ear."

Lawrence's final encounter with Magnus was in Malta, an island he hated even more than Capri. There, he found him sponging off a pair of innocent locals who owned small businesses in the port. When the police came to arrest Magnus for bad debts, he bolted the door and killed himself by drinking poison.

At Monte Cassino, before Lawrence's return to Capri, Magnus gave him the manuscript of a gritty narrative he had written about his service in the French Foreign Legion in Algeria, entitled *Dregs*. Lawrence found it "vague and diffuse," not very good, "yet there was something in it that made me want it done properly," so he undertook to edit it. After Magnus's death, Lawrence wrote *Memoir of Maurice Magnus* as a long introduction for the book and set about trying to publish it, in order, he said, to pay off its author's debts in Malta. Lawrence persuaded Martin Secker to publish it in London, in 1924, under the dull title *Memoirs of the Foreign Legion*. Magnus's only book is dreary and unpleasant, with lurid accounts of the legionnaires' murderous vendettas and vicious abuse of Arab boys kept for sex in conditions near slavery. Lawrence asserts that the narrative is "alive and interesting" but warns that "it should be read only by those who have the stomach. Ugly, foul—alas, it is no uglier and no fouler than reality."

In a bitter, feverish conclusion, Lawrence excoriates Magnus as a parasite, a "common little bounder," and a hypocrite who paid poor youths for sex with a pseudo-gentility that offends him even more than the legionnaires' brutish exploitation. The peroration spirals into a turbid rant that reveals much more about the confusion of Lawrence's mind than it does about Maurice Magnus. Lawrence identifies him with the "hideous depravity" of the war just concluded, "a purulent smallpox of the spirit," yet on the next page he declares that "in the great spirit of human consciousness he was a hero, little, quaking, and heroic," and even finds that he can admire Magnus as "a courageous, isolated little devil, facing his risks, and like a good rat, *determined* not to be trapped."

Douglas responded with a furious pamphlet with the insipid title "A Plea for Better Manners." His defense of Magnus falls flat through an excess of sentiment, with a testimonial to his subject's saintly generosity to the poor when he had the means to indulge it. Yet his principal complaint, that Lawrence is novelizing when he portrays Douglas as despising Magnus, is just. Exasperation with a friend who is fussing over one hardly amounts to despising, and for a third party to describe it so in print is an ethical breach. Douglas charges that Lawrence was a hypocrite for portraying himself as being nobly motivated to repay Magnus's Maltese debts, when in fact he was seeking to recoup his own paltry losses. After it was published in a collection of essays, Lawrence responded with a public letter in *The New Statesman* that is just as petty. He wrote, "Certainly Magnus was generous with his money when he had any; who knew that better than Douglas?" It is astonishing that a notorious literary feud should have arisen from such small sums of money. In his "Plea," Douglas emphatically asserts that Magnus's debts never exceeded a hundred pounds: "Apart from what he got from Lawrence, who has recouped himself many times over by the sale of [*Memoirs of the Foreign Legion*], he borrowed fifty-five: neither more nor less."

Soon after he published his letter in *The New Statesman*, Lawrence had a falling-out with Compton Mackenzie. The Lawrences and the Mackenzies had been constant companions when they were living in Capri. Mackenzie had lent Lawrence his ancient typewriter, of which only the red half of the ribbon was still usable, the same machine on which Faith Mackenzie had typed the manuscripts of *South Wind* and her husband's own *Sylvia Scarlett*, and which Somerset Maugham had borrowed to type the script of his stage play *Our Betters*. (In a curious coincidence, George Cukor directed the film versions of *Our Betters*, in 1933, and two years later *Sylvia Scarlett*, starring Katharine Hepburn and Cary Grant.) Yet Monty, as Compton Mackenzie was called by his friends, wrote in his memoir that he wished the Lawrences "would sometimes say a good word for somebody." Lawrence complained about the gossip in Capri, calling the island "a cat Cranford," referring to Elizabeth Gaskell's novel set in a gossip-ridden English village; however, Mackenzie wrote, "if Lawrence and Frieda had not themselves always encouraged that gossip, they would not have taken it so seriously, and, let it be added, contributed so much to it."

On a later visit to Capri on his own, Lawrence called on the Mackenzies and found that Faith, too, was alone. She told him that Monty was away at Herm and Jethou, tiny Channel Islands he had leased from the Crown. The two dined tête-à-tête. Faith wrote in her memoir, "Warmed by Capri wine, and the sensitive understanding and the glow of kindness in his deep eyes, I gave him some of the secrets of my heart." A few months later, an American magazine published Lawrence's short story "Two Blue Birds," which begins, "There was a woman who loved her husband, but she could not live with him." In Faith Mackenzie's view, the story was "a malicious caricature of Monty and a monstrous perversion of facts." The worst was yet to come, in one of Lawrence's best stories.

At that fateful dinner warmed by Capri wine, Faith had told Lawrence about Monty's attempt to establish a self-sufficient working community on Herm. After the experiment failed, he sold out and moved to the nearby, much smaller isle of Jethou, formerly a place for burning witches and hanging pirates. Later, Mackenzie wrote to Lawrence inviting him to come on a cruise to Barra, in the Outer Hebrides, which he had just bought. From these isolated glimpses of Mackenzie's islomania, Lawrence confected "The Man Who Loved Islands," a story in three short chapters, which begins, "There was a man who loved islands. He was born on one, but it didn't suit him, as there were too many other people on it, besides himself." The story's narrative bones follow Mackenzie's life, but the protagonist has the shadowy, emblematic quality of a character in a parable, the genre that best describes this delicately crafted story on the theme of the tragic consequences of failed idealism. It is rich in philosophical subtlety and psychological penetration, the very qualities that Douglas had airily pronounced to be lacking in Lawrence's fiction.

Mackenzie had made no protest over "Two Blue Birds," despite Faith's bitter objection to the portrayal of her as a fretful, jealous wife, but "The Man Who Loved Islands" enraged him. He informed Martin Secker, who published both writers, that he would lodge a lawsuit if Secker published the story in Lawrence's forthcoming collection, *The Woman Who Rode Away.* The contretemps brought out the peevish in both men. Mackenzie complained that Lawrence had covered "a granite island in the Channel with cowslips; he should know that cowslips favor lime." Lawrence, for his part, angrily protested Mackenzie's interference and insisted that the story be included in the book. In one letter to Secker, he struck a positively juvenile note: "What idiotic self-importance! If it's like him, he ought to feel flattered, for it's very much nicer than he is . . . What does he think he is, anyhow—the one perfect man on earth?"

I N THE FALL of 1906, Rainer Maria Rilke found himself stranded in Berlin, a city he despised, after a row with Auguste Rodin, who had employed him as his secretary, forced him to leave Paris. Unable to find a sponsor for a projected pilgrimage to Greece, he reluctantly accepted an invitation from his loyal patron Alice Faehndrich to spend the winter at her villa in Capri. She installed him in comfort at Villa Discopoli, on the Via Tragara, and left him very much on his own. The conditions were ideal, and he stayed for six months, but Rilke was never at a loss for things to complain about. In his letters from Capri, most of them addressed to his wife, he continually lamented that he was not in Paris, where he could see Manet's *Déjeuner sur l'herbe* whenever he pleased, and he whined about the sirocco, like one of the querulous old ladies in *South Wind*.

He even contrived a grievance with the island's beauty: "Always I grow really melancholy in such beauty-spots as these, faced with this obvious, praise-ridden, incontestable loveliness." To seal his case that Capri is a "monstrosity," he likens the island to Dante's *Paradiso*, "stuffed full of beatitudes all hopelessly heaped together, without form, with no gradation of light, full of repetitions, composed, as it were, of simpering, seraphic vacuity." Yet amid the irritating hyper-refinement and self-pity, Rilke captures the essence of Capri's eternal fascination to minds formed by classical ideals: "Where the few stony paths stop, there is the sea once more, or rather another sea, a sea through which Odysseus might come again, at any moment." Anticipating Norman Douglas (whom he did not meet), he declares, "This *is* Greece, without the art-objects of the Grecian world but almost as though before their creation . . . as though even the gods had still to be born who called forth the torrent of ecstasy that was Greece."

Rilke's most substantial work on Capri was his translation of Elizabeth Browning's *Sonnets from the Portuguese*, which he described as "crystals of feeling, so clear, so right, shiningly mysterious." The same phrases may be applied to a sonnet he wrote in Capri, "Song of the Sea." Subtitled "Capri, Piccola Marina," the poem brings us back to the cove where August von Platen set his ode to the island's fishermen, and, like Platen, Rilke is moved by the sublime majesty of the island's geography. It is a slight work, a breath of pure poetry at once sharp and soft, thoughtful yet unencumbered by heavy ideas. The American poet Louise Bogan described it as a poem that "rises and subsides like a wordless cry," one "whose subtlety should warn off any translator from an attempt on it." At my request, Matthew Gurewitsch came up with this rendering, as literal as possible, he said, apart from the occasional leap of faith:

Ancient breath off the sea,
wind of the sea by night:
you come here for no human;
if someone is watching,
then he must see how he
may endure you:
ancient breath off the sea,
which blows
as if only for primal rock,
space all aroar
tearing in from afar . . .
Oh, how the fig tree feels your power,
heavy with fruit
up in the moonshine.

When he was in Capri, Rilke held himself aloof from the foreign artists and writers resident there, with their scandals and quarrels and romans à clef—with one exception. He set as a major goal of his sojourn on the island to meet Maxim Gorky, who was living in exile in a villa on the outskirts of the village with his common-law wife, Maria Fyodorovna Andreyeva, formerly a leading actress at the Moscow Art Theater. The encounter took place just days before Rilke left for Paris.

Born in Prague and educated in Austria, Rainer Maria Rilke cultivated an identity as a man without a country. As if to prove the point, he declared after his first visit to Russia, in 1899, that it was his spiritual homeland. He was under the powerful influence of Lou Andreas-Salomé, Nietzsche's former lover and one of the most remarkable intellectuals in Europe at the time. She took Rilke as her protégé and lover when he was twenty-two and she was thirty-seven, apparently with the consent of her husband, Friedrich Andreas, an Orientalist, with whom she lived in a white marriage, in Berlin. A native of St. Petersburg, she taught Rilke Russian, and by the time of the inspirational visit to Moscow he was reading Pushkin and Tolstoy. In a letter to Andreas-Salomé in 1903, Rilke wrote, "The fact that Russia is my homeland is one of the great and mysterious certainties by which I live." Very mysterious: in another letter, he called Moscow "the city of my oldest and deepest memories." Yet there must have been some grounds for the fantasy; when he met Tolstoy, who knew about such things, the novelist proclaimed Rilke to be "the eternal Russian."

It would be hard to imagine two men more different in background and temperament than Rainer Maria Rilke and Alexei Maximovich Gorky: the dreamy, cultured German poet, who lived the life of the mind in isolation from the social turmoil of his times, immersed in dreams of antiquity, and the unpretentious self-educated author of gritty plays and stories about the wretched of the earth, a man at the vortex of Russian revolutionary politics, for whom history existed only as a cautionary guide to the glorious, classless future of mankind. When Rilke made his desire to meet him known, Gorky, always happy to meet anyone, invited him to drop by. At Gorky's house, just below the Krupp Gardens, the two writers sat and talked shop for an hour or two. The meeting went no better than might have been expected.

One of the few surviving eyewitness reports of Gorky's activities in Capri is that by Vasily Alexeyevich Desnitsky, a revolutionary literary critic. In an untranslated reminiscence, he wrote that Gorky delighted in his compatriots' roughhousing at an unidentified inn (certainly not Morgano's café). "Alexei Maximovich laughed to tears as one of the entertainers jumped up and down with a paper tail tied to his coat," Desnitsky wrote. "We onlookers tried to light the tail with a match." It is easy to imagine the revulsion that Rilke, the refined, mystical poet, suffering acutely from the excessive, Dantean loveliness of Capri, would have experienced witnessing this low manifestation of the great Russian soul that he laid claim to. The writers' meeting was cordial but pointless except to give them the satisfaction of having met, to check each other off a list, a matter of much greater importance to the caller than to his host.

Three weeks afterward, in a letter to Karl von der Heydt, a banker who dabbled in literature, Rilke wrote, "I have seen Gorky. One evening I sat with him at a round table. The melancholy lamplight fell upon everything equally without picking out anybody in particular: him, his present wife, and a couple of morose Russian men who took no notice of me." The colloquy began in Russian, but Rilke's side of the conversation was halting, so they switched to French, with Maria Fyodorovna translating. "As a democrat Gorky speaks of art with dissatisfaction, narrow and hasty in his judgments; judgments in which the mistakes are so deeply dissolved that you are quite unable to fish them out." Gorky the man made a more favorable impression: "He possesses a great and touching kindliness (that kindliness which always makes it impossible for the great Russians to remain artists), and it is very moving to find on his completely unsophisticated face the traces of great thoughts and a smile that breaks through with an effort."

No record survives of Gorky's immediate impressions, but Desnitsky, who must have been one of the morose Russians who paid no attention to Rilke, recalled "a comically puzzled expression" on Gorky's face during the conversation. Drawing on Desnitsky's recollections, Alexander Kaun, Gorky's American biographer, wrote in 1931 that Gorky "showered his visitor with questions as to his familiarity with a number of German and French writers. Rilke's answers were to the effect that he had met this man once or twice, that he was not acquainted with the other, that the third had sent him his book, that the fourth was a charming fellow, and that they were quite friends, and so on." Gorky was shocked by the gaps in his guest's reading. Many years later, Gorky recalled the meeting with Rilke with scorn: "When one meets men of letters, concerning literature one receives by the way of a reply not an evaluation of the author's work but comments such as these: 'He's a nice chap, a gay blade, a drunkard, a ladies' man.' This reminds me of Rainer Maria Rilke. When he was asked 'What do you think of Peter Altenberg?' he replied, 'I think I once had lunch with him on the Prater.'" Altenberg was a popular author of short stories set in Vienna; Gorky must have expected his guest to be brimming with opinions about him. Altenberg was not a giant, but how could Rilke have been in doubt as to whether he had lunched with him?

Rilke's letter to Karl von der Heydt radiates arrogance: one might say that the mistake in his ridiculous assertion that kindliness prevents great Russians from remaining artists is so deeply dissolved that it cannot be fished out. Yet he did perceive the essential, irreconcilable opposition between himself and the "democrat Gorky." He wrote to Heydt, "You know my persuasion that the revolutionary is the diametrical opposite of the Russian: that is, the Russian is supremely qualified to be one, much in the same way that a lace handkerchief is very nice for mopping up ink, taking for granted, of course, a complete misuse and ruthless misconception of its true properties!" Gorky is arrogant, too, in his dismissal of Rilke's critical powers because he said he thought he had had lunch with Peter Altenberg. The younger, less experienced guest was nervous; he wrote to Heydt about his difficulties speaking Russian "under the stress of the moment." Some writers prefer to reserve serious criticism for written expression and not to waste their powers on table talk. Yet Gorky must have felt Rilke's supercilious conceit, and if his guest made any reference to his mysterious certainty that he was Russian in his soul, one may easily imagine how Gorky would have received such a fanciful notion. More likely, Gorky realized at once that he was meeting the sort of man capable of likening the Russian people to a lace handkerchief, in other words a milksop who could never comprehend the great historical struggle that was taking place. No doubt he was happy when his tiresome guest left so he could go down to the inn with the lads and have a few laughs.

GORKY'S SOJOURN IN Capri presents a unique puzzle: although he stayed there for seven years, and evidently loved the place, the island had no discernible influence on his creative work. It was one of his most prolific periods, yet the novels and stories he wrote there are all set in wintry Russian darkness. He and the Russian writers and thinkers who visited him in Capri were too busy thrashing out their polemical disagreements to take much notice of their surroundings, and when they did, it was only to test and refine their evolving political philosophy. The Russian cadre was not standoffish so much as isolated, both by language and by their all-consuming political mission. As a result, apart from Rilke's arrogant account of his afternoon chez Gorky, the surviving testimony is sparse.

Again, the most vivid impressions come from Compton Mackenzie, in his memoirs. When he called on Gorky, he wrote, the house "was full of Russians talking incessantly and playing chess." He and Gorky often went together to the little cinema in the village. Conversation was difficult because Mackenzie's Italian was as limited as Gorky's French. Nevertheless, Mackenzie thought that Gorky enjoyed their nights at the movies, "a restful contrast to the incessant talking of the refugees from Tsardom in his own house." Mackenzie described him as "a tall lanky man, his head always out-thrust as he walked."

Norman Douglas recorded a dramatic incident he experienced with Gorky and Maria Fyodorovna. When they stopped by his house for a visit one day, no sooner had Douglas poured them a drink than "there was a loud bang at the door, and the woman who ran the small wine shop close by . . . rushed in to tell us that a foreigner had shot himself on the Punta Cannone," formerly the Malerplatte, the Painters' Plaza, very nearby. The foreigner was a young visitor named Heinrich Lieber, who had called on Douglas a few days before to seek his advice about an affair of the heart.

Lieber, in the terminal stage of an incurable disease, had conceived a great passion for a Capriote youth who did not reciprocate the feeling. Lieber told Douglas that he had no reason to live except to have that boy: "It was his last hope of joy on earth, and rather than suffer disappointment he would kill himself and be done with it." Now he had made the attempt.

Douglas and Gorky ran to the Punta Cannone and found Lieber "writhing on the ground with one of those absurd Browning pistols beside him." The bullet had gone straight through him. It had missed the heart, but he was bleeding badly. There was no time to be lost. Douglas wanted to get a shutter from his house and use it as a stretcher to carry Lieber down to the village, but Gorky did not rise to the occasion: "After a minute or two he sat down on the wall, rolled himself a cigarette, and began to smoke. I can still see him sitting there and letting his eyes wander over the landscape, which is certainly worth looking at from the Punta Cannone. There he sat with that careworn countenance of his, smoking. Gorky was bored. He was bored with this exhibition; he had gone through enough of that kind of thing." A neighbor showed up and took charge of the situation, and soon Lieber was on his way to the hospital in Naples, where he survived the wound.

Gorky's house was virtually a hostel for a ceaseless flow of Russian visitors, not all of them revolutionists. When Feodor Chaliapin, the great bass of the opera stage, came to Capri, in 1917, Gorky ghostwrote his autobiography for him, out of friendship. Gorky's most prominent guest was Lenin himself. After Lenin's death, in 1924, Gorky wrote a slim book of reminiscences, which provides rare glimpses of the revolutionary leader in repose. In Gorky's telling, Lenin never took a moment's holiday from his historical mission; every word he spoke was infused with ideology. In *Days with Lenin*, Gorky wrote that Lenin possessed a magnetic quality "which drew the hearts and sympathies of the working people to him."

Lenin endeared himself to the island's fishermen by mastering the art of fishing "with the finger," using the line without a rod. He spoke no Italian, but the local folk, "who had seen Chaliapin and many other outstanding Russians, by a kind of instinct put Lenin in a special place at once. His laugh was enchanting—the hearty laugh of a man who, through being so well acquainted with the clumsy stupidity of human beings and the acrobatic trickery of the quick-witted, could find pleasure in the childlike artlessness of the simple in heart." A fisherman named Giovanni Spadaro, an old man with a great white beard like Tolstoy's (who had been a favorite model of Christian Wilhelm Allers), declared, "Only an honest man could laugh like that."

In Capri, Lenin was always gathering economic and sociological data for his evolving ideology. "He asked in detail about the life of the Capri fishermen, about their earnings, the influence of the priests, their schools," Gorky wrote. "I could not but be surprised by the range of his interests." When Lenin found out that the local priest was the son of a poor peasant who had been sent to study at a seminary on the mainland and then returned to the village, he commended this policy to Gorky as a clever way of commanding the proletariat's loyalty to the church.

The Russians in Capri spent little time with other expatriates. Gorky wrote, "With equal enthusiasm [Lenin] would play chess, look through *A History of Dress*, dispute for hours with comrades, fish, go for walks along the stony paths of Capri, scorching under the southern sun." Frequently, after a long and bitter political wrangle, he would plunge into a game of chess, but "when he lost grew angry and even despondent, like a child." A chess match between Gorky and Lenin in Capri was recorded; Lenin lost.

Apart from being furiously productive at his writing, Gorky principally occupied himself in Capri with opening a school for the proletariat. "The primary work of the revolution I considered to be the creation of the conditions which would lead to the development of the cultural forces of the country." With that objective in view, he established the Free Association for the Development and Spread of Positive Science and invited prominent Russian scientists to come to Capri to teach there. The academy provoked a quarrel that was the beginning of his falling-out with Lenin. Here, Gorky understates the case: "I differed from the Bolsheviks on the question of the value of the role of the intelligentsia in the Russian Revolution." Lenin, in fact, loathed the intelligentsia. His view, of course, was that the primary work of the revolution was the total annihilation of every vestige of the ancien régime. No one, least of all Lenin, could doubt Gorky's loyalty. In the early days of the struggle, the royalties from his novels and stage plays, such as *The Lower Depths*, a sensational worldwide hit, were one of the Bolsheviks' major sources of funding. Yet Lenin did not care if the workers read books. He thought that teaching chemistry to Italian fishermen was a stupid waste of money and time.

Gorky was in a unique position to question the leader of the revolution about its nihilistic tactics. In *Days with Lenin*, he recounts a "repulsively memorable" anecdote about an event that occurred after his sojourn in Capri, when peasants occupied the Winter Palace of the Romanovs, near Petrograd, and "a great number of priceless Sèvres, Saxon, and oriental vases had been befouled by them for lavatory use." Yet Lenin was intolerant of any criticism of the tactics of his revolution, which committed outrages that went far beyond the use of imperial vases as chamber pots. "What do you want?" he demanded of Gorky. "Is it possible to act humanely in a struggle of such unprecedented ferocity? Where is there any place for soft-heartedness or generosity?" Gorky for his part took a dim view of Lenin's unconditional patriotism. In Capri, while Lenin was watching fishermen disentangle their nets, which were torn and snarled by sharks, he remarked, "Our men work more quickly." When Gorky cast doubt on this observation, Lenin retorted in vexation, "H'm, h'm. Don't you think you are forgetting Russia, living on this bump?"

Lenin missed the mark: Gorky never forgot Russia. He seems to have been indifferent to the classical heritage of Capri. A great walker, Gorky must have visited Villa Jovis once in his seven years' residence on the island, but if he did, he never wrote about it. He read everything he could get his hands on, but the stories and novels he wrote in Capri do not take in even a glimpse of the world beyond the frontiers of Mother Russia.

He wrote a novel in Capri he called *The Spy*, better known in English as *The Life of a Useless Man*, which reflects the powerful influence of Dostoyevsky. The first half of the book is a suspenseful narrative about an indecisive weakling, Klimkov, an orphan from a rural village who works at a bookshop that is under the control of the tsarist secret police. The shop's owner entraps progressive intellectuals by luring them into the back room of his shop, where he sells them radical books proscribed by the regime and then tips off the police, who supplied him with the books in the first place. Klimkov, in love with his employer's mistress, helps her murder him; the police uncover the plot and blackmail Klimkov into working for them as a spy.

Up to this point, the novel is firmly in the tradition of Dostoyevsky's great "pamphlet novel" satirizing radical nihilism, translated as *The Possessed*, *The Devils*, and *Demons*: Gorky's novel excites the reader's imaginative participation as much by the play of ideas as it does with its narrative of espionage and betrayal. *The Spy* also bears a strong resemblance in theme and narrative technique to Conrad's novel *The Secret Agent*, which was published in the same year, 1907. It appears that the two writers never met in Capri, although their stays there overlapped. The similarity may be attributed entirely to Dostoyevsky's influence on them.

The second half of *The Spy*, however, makes flat reading. Gorky fails to solve the problems entailed by narrating a long novel from the point of view of a contemptible character. Now working for the imperial secret police, Klimkov time and again meets workers drawn to the radical cause, minor characters brimming with joie de vivre, who are far more lovable than his tormented colleagues in the ranks of the spies; time and again he betrays the workers, which leads to a bitter disillusionment that ends with suicide. Klimkov's disillusionment does not build; it is simply restated. The attractive working-class characters are all very much alike, and the vicious, demoralized spies also lack vivacity. The novel was banned in Russia and only permitted to be published there in 1917, in an expurgated edition. The book was poorly received by the Bolsheviks, undoubtedly reflecting Lenin's personal view. One may surmise that simply humanizing an imperial spy was enough to make the book appear insufficiently revolutionary.

A second novel Gorky wrote in Capri was even more pernicious in Lenin's eyes. *The Confession* takes on the theme of religion, which was one of the toughest obstacles to enlisting peasants in the Russian Revolution. In the novel, Gorky advanced a theory he called "God-building," a hopeless attempt to find a middle ground that would unite Marxism and Christianity, by finding God in the nobility of the proletariat. The proposition was sketchy enough intellectually, and Lenin, an uncompromising atheist, hated it. In his view, the problem was deeper than the church itself; the very impulse to believe in God contributed to the enslavement of the masses. When Gorky returned to Russia after the victory of the Bolsheviks and the establishment of the Soviet Union, Lenin exiled his old friend and host, as the tsar had done, for doctrinal errors.

The widespread disenchantment (not to say disgust) with Stalin's regime in the postwar era made Gorky the equivalent of a nonperson in the West, and he has found few champions in the post-Soviet era. The music of the Soviet Union never suffered from an equivalent opprobrium; Prokofiev and Shostakovich continued to be performed in Western concert halls almost without interruption. We take note of the great debate about Shostakovich, ongoing and unsettled, about whether the composer was a martyr of Stalinism or a complicit participant in the regime, but his Symphony No. 5 in D

Minor, for example, is a thrilling expression of triumph that any listener can take pleasure from without considering who or what is having the triumph. Likewise, Soviet poster art makes its shocking graphic impact whether or not the viewer is sympathetic to the ideology it proclaims, though it is still capable of provoking controversy. *A Revolutionary Impulse: The Rise of the Russian Avant-Garde*, an exhibition at the Museum of Modern Art in 2016–17, was condemned by many visitors for failing to address the political objectives that the works served.

It is ironic that Gorky should now languish in comparative neglect, apart from *The Lower Depths*, an enduring staple in world theater, for he was not a Soviet writer. Born Alexei Maximovich Peshkov, in 1868, he was orphaned at the age of eleven and ran away from his grandmother's home. He spent his adolescent years as a hobo, associating with the vicious, hard-drinking tramps who would populate his early fiction and plays. In 1892, he adopted the pen name Gorky, which means "bitter," to express his anger at the wretched conditions endured by the Russian working class, which had not improved materially since the tsar abolished serfdom, in 1861. Gorky's junior by two years, Lenin at that time was an obscure legal clerk in Samara, at the beginning of his own intellectual progress toward socialism. Gorky's first book, a collection of short stories and essays published in 1898, had an immediate and spectacular success. Barely in his twenties, Gorky was embraced by Chekhov and Tolstoy, who proclaimed him the voice of the rising generation of Russian literature.

If the principal source for the life of Jacques d'Adelswärd-Fersen is a gossipy roman à clef by a writer who made his name as an apologist for pederasty, and that for many periods of Romaine Brooks's life the unedited manuscript of a flawed memoir, which may have passages of pure invention, in the case of Maxim Gorky the reader confronts a challenge closer to that of studying the life of Tiberius, which is hopelessly complicated because every document in the record is governed by a political agenda. Gorky's pre-Soviet writings presented no problems to the Bolshevik censors, nor did his memoirs of his youth, which conclude before he met Lenin, but interpreting *Days with Lenin* and other works published after the rise of Stalin poses a problem similar to that of disentangling reliable information about imperial lives from the vilifications of the neo-republican historians. Moreover, in Gorky's case the false scents thrown across the trail, what would come to be known as disinformation, were the author's own work.

In some passages of *Days with Lenin*, the party-line propaganda is so heavy-handed that one may surmise that the clumsiness is deliberate, to enable the knowledgeable reader to recognize its inauthenticity as an authorial expression. When Gorky describes his conflict with Lenin over the role of the intelligentsia, after he has summarized his own beliefs, which culminated in the creation of his science academy in Capri, he concludes, "So I thought in 1917—and was mistaken. This page of my reminiscences should be torn out. But 'what has been written by the pen cannot be cut down by the ax'; and 'we learn by our mistakes' as V. Ilyitch [Lenin] often repeated." It is also possible that Gorky reached this conclusion himself, for the rationale for the Free Association for the Development and Spread of Positive Science had a shaky intellectual basis. However, his confession of ideological error and quotations from the apotheosized leader of

the revolution are obviously intended to establish his conformity with Stalin's recently fabricated doctrine of Marxism-
Leninism.

Gorky's voice is heard more clearly in this address to the
reader, in the narrative of his dispute with Lenin about the
tactics of the revolution, which is just as relevant more than
a century after the First World War as it was when the book
was new:

> I challenge anyone to say frankly how far he approves
> of, and how far he is revolted by, the hypocrisy of
> the moralists who talk about the bloodthirstiness
> of the Russian Revolution, when they not only showed
> no pity for the people who were exterminated during
> the four years of the infamous Pan-European War,
> but by all possible means fanned the flame of this
> abominable war to "the victorious end." Today the
> "civilized" nations are ruined, exhausted, decaying,
> and vulgar petty bourgeois philistinism, which is
> common to all races, reigns triumphant.

Considering the lives and works of Maxim Gorky and his
comrades in the context of Capri forces us to confront a
problem that spans Augustus's frolics with the boys at the
Greek gymnasium and the theatrical fetes of Baron Fersen
and Marchesa Casati: the dreams of freedom and beauty of
most foreign visitors to Capri were paid for with inherited
wealth and protected by aristocratic position. There were exceptions: Norman Douglas, who was paid seventy pounds for
South Wind and never got a penny more in royalties, lived by
the fruit of his labors (with, it is true, many a free lunch laid

on by his rich friends), but most of the artists and writers who found what they were seeking in Capri never faced a day of want. Fersen could write fiction and poetry that found few readers and publish *Akademos* in a lavish production thanks to his fat steel shares. Romaine Brooks is a partial exception: her independent spirit was evident in her impoverished early life, but the perfectionism of her mature career as a painter was enabled by her grandfather's millions.

Gorky and Lenin came to Capri in the course of their pursuit of freedom of a more basic sort, and on a global scale, but in one important respect their lives there were not significantly different from those of Fersen and Brooks. Gorky was a self-made man, and while his tastes were not luxurious, he never let his sympathy for the workers' struggle get in the way of a comfortable style of living. In 1909, seeking more spacious quarters for the ceaseless influx of houseguests, he moved into Villa Behring, an imposing pink pile that towers above the village. It was previously the home of Emil von Behring, the German bacteriologist who won the first Nobel Prize in Medicine, in 1901, for his discovery of an antitoxin for diphtheria. It was there, on the villa's elegant terrace overlooking the Gulf of Naples, that Gorky and Lenin played their chess games. It was just the sort of paradox that inspired Orwell to write, in *Animal Farm*, "All animals are equal, but some animals are more equal than others."

NOT ALL OF Gorky's regular visitors in Capri were revolutionists. Ivan Bunin, one of Gorky's closest friends despite his opposition to the Russian Revolution, visited him in Capri for three consecutive winters (1912–14). The two writers eventually fell out over politics, but Gorky's warm feelings for Bunin personally and his admiration of his work never diminished (another proof, perhaps, that Gorky was ill-suited to the Soviets' doctrinaire strictures). Bunin, the first Russian to win the Nobel Prize in Literature, was a man of the world, as much at home writing about French schoolgirls and a suicide in Algeria as about Russians of any class. Born to wealth, he received a classical education and began his career as a poet, winning his first Pushkin Prize in 1903, when he was thirty-three. Yet he is better known as a writer of short fiction. In his stories, Bunin is a realist in the same sense that Flaubert is: his social observation has a startling, razor-sharp precision and never flinches, yet it is expressed in supple, delicate prose that aspires to the state of poetry. *The Gentleman from San Francisco, and Other Stories*, a slim volume of Bunin's stories published in 1922 by the Hogarth Press (which also published Gorky's *Reminiscences of Tolstoy*), might take the lead position on a critic's list of neglected masterpieces of twentieth-century literature.

The title story, in its translation by Samuel Solomonovich Koteliansky and D. H. Lawrence, may be perfect. It is superbly Flaubertian: every sentence tells, and every sentence is perfectly formed, or near enough; one must creep through the pages with a magnifying glass to find a word that might be cut or changed. Bunin wrote the story in 1915, inspired, he said, by seeing the cover of Mann's *Death in Venice* in a bookshop. His working title was "Death in Capri," and the story takes as its theme, literally, "See Capri and die." The nameless gentleman from San Francisco, a captain of industry (the industry, too, is nameless), sails to Europe

with his wife and daughter in search of culture and an il-
lustrious son-in-law. After a rough passage to Capri, he
checks into his hotel (the Quisisana, also not identified
by name), dresses for dinner, and has a fatal stroke while
waiting for his family in the reading room, which throws
the hotel into an uproar. The story ends with his bloated
corpse, in a makeshift coffin constructed from crates used
for soda-water bottles, stowed in the deepest hold of the same
ship that had just brought him to Europe, on its homeward
journey.

Bunin's observation of Americans in Europe has both
the deadly accuracy and the humanistic generosity of middle
Henry James; as a meditation on death and human vanity, it
resembles *Death in Venice* (which Bunin presumably read at
some point after he saw the book in a shop window); and its
verbal picture painting possesses the luminous precision of
northern Baroque genre painting. Tolstoy lays on a rich mass
of detail in his fictional worlds, but in Bunin's story the
reader never has a sense of reading a catalogue of physical
features. Rather, details accrete in spiraling complex sen-
tences that seem to grow organically around the subject. In
this description of a transatlantic cruise ship, Bunin creates a
diptych of the class struggle that dispels even the faintest
aroma of ideology by putting all human striving into a natu-
ralistic context:

> Outside, the ocean heaved in black mountains; the
> snow storm hissed furiously in the clogged cordage;
> the steamer trembled in every fiber as she surmounted
> these watery hills and struggled with the storm,
> plowing through the moving masses which every now

and then reared in front of her, foam-crested. The siren, choked by the fog, groaned in mortal anguish. The watchmen in the look-out towers froze with cold and went mad with their superhuman straining of attention. As the gloomy and sultry depths of the inferno, as the ninth circle, was the submerged womb of the steamer, where gigantic furnaces roared and dully giggled, devouring with their red-hot maws mountains of coal cast hoarsely in by men naked to the waist, bathed in their own corrosive dirty sweat, and lurid with the purple-red reflection of flame. But in the refreshment bar, men jauntily put their feet up on the tables, showing their patent-leather pumps, and sipped cognac or other liqueurs, and swam in waves of fragrant smoke as they chatted in well bred manner.

The story's action in Capri spans less than twenty-four hours, but Bunin hits many of the high points. When the gentleman and his family arrive in the Piazzetta, its likeness to an opera set is remarked, inevitable because it is so very apt. Tiberius has a brief star turn, bringing with him a hint of the author's feelings about events in Russia, and beyond: "On that island two thousand years ago lived a man entangled in his own infamous and strange acts, one whose rule for some reason extended over millions of people, and who, having lost his head through the absurdity of such power, committed deeds which have established him forever in the memory of mankind; mankind which in the mass now rules the world just as hideously and incomprehensibly as he ruled it then."

In his sketch of the island's foreign residents, Bunin takes an oblique, affectionate dig at his compatriots, "a few Russians who had settled in Capri, untidy and absent-minded owing to their bookish thoughts, spectacled, bearded, half-buried in the upturned collars of their thick woolen overcoats." Bunin's theme is philosophical, the tragic destiny of human life, viewed in comic terms. He was influenced by Hindu religious texts, and his story illustrates the doctrine of the illusoriness of phenomenal reality. On the transatlantic voyage, the passengers included "an exquisite loving couple, whom everybody watched curiously because of their unconcealed happiness: he danced only with her, and sang, with great skill, only to her accompaniment, and everything about them seemed so charming! and only the captain knew that this couple had been engaged by the steamship company to play at love for a good salary." In Capri, Giovanni Spadaro, the fisherman who befriended Lenin, makes a cameo appearance as "the tall old boatman Lorenzo, thorough debauchee and handsome figure, famous all over Italy, model for many a picture," who is paid by the village to stand around and strike picturesque poses, puffing on his clay pipe, his scarlet bonnet slipping over one ear.

By the time of his death, in 1953, Bunin's reputation had begun its decline into relative obscurity. Like Rilke, he isolated himself from history, a declaration of intellectual independence that might have been more acceptable in the Bohemian-Austrian poet than in a Russian writer who was nurtured by the tsarist regime. Bunin was a classicist, almost purely so, as much isolated from contemporary currents in literature as he was from worldly affairs. In an autobiographical note, he once explained his lack of a wide readership, despite an early, resounding success with the critics:

> I took no part in politics and, in my works, never touched upon questions connected with politics. I belonged to no particular literary school, called myself neither decadent nor symbolist nor romantic nor naturalist, donned no mask of any kind, and hung out no flamboyant flag. Yet during these last stormy decades in Russia, the fate of a writer frequently depended upon such questions as: Is he an opponent of the existing form of government? Has he come from "the people"? Has he been in prison, in exile? Or, does he take part in the literary hubbub, in the "literary revolution"?

Bunin was never jailed or exiled. He did not settle anywhere for long but was rather on a nearly constant tour of the Mediterranean world, from the Levant to North Africa. He was Russian, but Russianness did not define him. Being agnostic about the revolution was not really an option, either in his time or in our own. In the (approximately) post Communist era, we make an impossible demand on twentieth-century Russian writers: they cannot be tsarist, yet neither can they be Stalinists, which leaves a vaporous middle terrain that offers uncertain refuge.

One successful artistic effort to resolve these extraliterary considerations, though it has its own peculiar flaws, is *Coup de Grâce*, a short novel by Marguerite Yourcenar. In the summer of 1937, as Europe coasted toward another great war, she came to Capri with a new lover, an American graduate student named Grace Frick, who would become her lifelong companion and intellectual partner. The women rented La Casarella, a small house on the footpath that leads to Villa Jovis, where Yourcenar wrote most of the first draft of the novel. It was not Yourcenar's first visit to Capri. Nine years before, she had composed an elegant, richly phrased ode there about Tiberius's retirement. "Caprée" follows the Tacitean model of the emperor as an exhausted libertine, orchestrated in a sympathetic, somber key: "Debauchery and death mingle in the air he breathes." Yourcenar's Tiberius inhabits a unique solitude, for "having becoming a god himself, he no longer believes in the gods"—a spiritual dilemma that anticipates her magnificent imagining of a later emperor, in *Memoirs of Hadrian*.

Yourcenar and Frick's sojourn in Capri in 1937 was a sort of honeymoon. The women had met in Paris, where Yourcenar was recovering from a disastrous love affair with a gay man, which would provide the emotional background to *Coup de Grâce*. They found the island mostly abandoned by its foreign residents, who had repatriated with the rising threat of war. Yourcenar wrote that Capri was once again "a small Italian village, where you feel far from everything. After the departure of the excursion boats in the evening, it returns to a slightly indolent tranquility. The isolation and the light metallic chirping of crickets are favorable both for rest and for work." She composed her new novel by day, and in the evening the lovers strolled down the Via Tragara to view the Faraglioni by moonlight.

Coup de Grâce is a morality tale about a freelance Fascist of noble birth who fights with the White Russians against the Bolsheviks. Like *The Spy*, it is fiction with a repellent protagonist, but the author lays no ideological burden on the work. Yourcenar describes Erick von Lhomond as "one of those men who were too young in 1914 to have done more than brush with danger, but who were transformed into soldiers of fortune by Europe's postwar disorders, and by their personal anxieties as well, their incapacity for satisfaction or resignation, either one." The main story takes place at a railway café, in 1937, where von Lhomond, wounded in the Spanish Civil War while fighting with Franco's Nationalists, tells a group of travelers about his experiences nearly twenty years before in Courland, the westernmost province of Latvia and thus a remote frontier of the Russian Revolution.

Yourcenar's narrator makes no attempt to justify von Lhomond's political convictions; his "hostility to the Bolsheviks was a matter of caste." As he tells his story, von Lhomond alludes to historical events with the assured familiarity of a participant, but his real story is one of love, his love for a family, gentry in the backwoods of Courland, with whom he spent his summers as an adolescent. He idolized Conrad de Reval, a boy his own age. The sentimental evocation of swims in the lake at dawn, "noonday rests in the hay," overnights at Lettish farms, where the peasants gave their best featherbeds in the "great room" to their highborn guests, portrays an intensely romantic friendship. Throughout the novel, Conrad remains a dreamy cipher, a Baltic counterpart to the doomed youths of *A Shropshire Lad*. "One could readily imagine him at thirty," the adult Erick says, as "a humdrum country squire, pursuing farm girls, or boys; or even, in the postwar times, a poet cut to the order of T. S. Eliot or Jean Cocteau, and frequenting Berlin bars." The irony, the unreliability of the narrator, is crucial. Nothing in

Conrad's adult behavior supports the telegraphic hints that the physical aspect of the boys' friendship could ever progress beyond those noonday naps in the hayloft. Erick's lopsided crush is the main source of his own incapacity for satisfaction or resignation.

Conrad's sister, Sophie, is an invisible child in Erick's idyllic dream of his youth, but after the armistice, when he returns to Courland to serve in the campaign to suppress the Reds, she "was no longer a lump of a girl; she had real beauty." Always brooding, she spent the evenings "in savage poking at the drawing-room fire, sighing the while like a heroine in Ibsen utterly fed up with life." The cause of Sophie's frustration is that she is in love with Erick, her brother's former playmate and now his comrade in arms. "Why is it," Erick asks, "that women fall in love with the very men who are destined otherwise, and who accordingly must repulse them, or else deny their own nature?" In a desperate effort to get Erick's attention, Sophie takes to heavy drinking and degrades herself in casual sex with the loyalist soldiers who are billeted at the manor house. Erick cannot return Sophie's love, but he nonetheless has a great capacity for jealousy and torments her cruelly. When she kisses another officer at a Christmas dinner, Erick slaps her so hard that she falls and has a nosebleed.

Sophie's alienation becomes complete when she deserts her family and her hopeless love to join the Reds. She loves, or conceives a spiteful passion for, a radical bookstore clerk and absconds at dawn to join him in his cause. The Bolsheviks ultimately triumph, of course, but as Erick leads the loyalists in retreat, Conrad is wounded and dies a horrible death in his friend's arms. In his final action in the conflict in Latvia, Erick captures a group of Bolshevik soldiers hiding in the hayloft of a barn, which includes Sophie. He tries to spare her execution, but she scorns this sentimental gesture. In the final scene, when Sophie's turn comes, she stops the executioner, the former majordomo of her ancestral home, and tells him that she wants Erick to carry out the sentence. Erick shoots her in the face. He concludes the book by saying that at first he thought that she intended her request to be the final proof of her love, but later he understood that "she only wished to take revenge, leaving me prey to remorse. She was right in that: I do feel remorse at times. One is always trapped, somehow, in dealings with women."

Coup de Grâce, the book, is itself an act of revenge, that of the author against the man she loved. Like Sophie, Yourcenar was besotted with love for a man who could not love women, André Fraigneau, her editor at Éditions Grasset. She had already written one book about his brutal rejections, the long prose poem *Fires*, published in 1936. Yourcenar wrote in a preface to *Coup de Grâce* that the novel was based on a true story, claiming that the characters of Erick, Sophie, and Conrad "remain much as they were described to me by one of the best friends of the principal person concerned." We have no reason to doubt her veracity, but the book is plainly autobiographical, and the key is not difficult to decipher: Yourcenar herself is Sophie, and vain, cruel Erick von Lhomond is André Fraigneau. Conrad is a shadowy character because he is a generalized representation of Yourcenar's male rivals for Fraigneau's love.

After her stay in Capri with Grace Frick, Yourcenar completed and revised *Coup de Grâce* in Sorrento. It is a fascinating little novel, quite as grim to read as it sounds in synopsis. The author had suffered at the hands of a misogynist and took no interest in sparing the reader pain. The book presents a problem for some contemporary readers in its disregard of moral certainties about Fascism. Yourcenar copes with the hazards posed by a protagonist who holds despicable views simply by evading them. In *Coup de Grâce*, the harshness of her portrait of Erick von Lhomond is entirely confined to his private conduct. Like most loyalists of any ancien régime, von Lhomond makes no intellectual rationale for his partisanship; he was born with it. When he describes the extreme cruelty of "the highly specialized Letts who served the Reds as hangmen," who "perfected the art of torture in a manner worthy of the most celebrated Mongol traditions," he sounds admiring. In Marguerite Yourcenar's reading of history, inhumanity possesses no ideology.

~~~~~

THE ARTISTS AND WRITERS resident in Capri during the First World War were all exiles of one sort or another, the Russians in the strictest sense, and the others for reasons of their own, in some cases simply to avoid the inconvenient nastiness of the war, which left Capri unbruised. In "The Gentleman from San Francisco," written in the midst of war, Bunin's characterization of the Russians in Capri as "untidy and absent-minded owing to their bookish thoughts" was a wicked insider's joke for readers who had some knowledge about the background of Gorky's exile and the identity of his visitors. If they were absent-minded about their appearance, it was only because their thoughts were concentrated on great events and causes, and their bookishness, far from being an escape from the world, was their arsenal in these intellectual battles. Yet in the years preceding the next world war, Capri ceased to be a backwater and got swept up in the mainstream of ideological conflicts that would once more bathe Europe in blood.

Specifically, Fascism arrived. As early as 1922, before Mussolini's March on Rome and accession to power, there were Fascist demonstrations in the Piazzetta. Il Duce made a triumphant visit to the island in 1925, which persuaded him to make the island a showplace of Fascist values. In 1926, he installed as mayor a Neapolitan nobleman, Marchese Marino Dusmet de Smours, who was married to an heiress from California, a zealous Christian Scientist. Mussolini gave Dusmet all the money he asked for to upgrade the island's infrastructure. The Fascist mayor paved the main roads for the first time, took measures to prevent dangerous rockfalls on Via Krupp, and extended the pier at the Marina Grande so that ships could dock there in stormy weather. These improvements made Dusmet a popular leader, but when he used the bells of Santo Stefano to summon party members to meetings at city hall, the *parocco* locked the campanile and reserved the use of the carillon for church services. Another of the Fascists' goals in Capri was to clean up the morals of the foreign residents, in particular to round up and expel pederasts, a campaign enthusiastically supported by the American marchesa. (As usual, the lesbian community was never a target of the moralists.)

In the 1930s, Capri became a favorite holiday destination for the Fascist elite. Nazis, too: Field Marshal Hermann Göring conceived a strong fancy for the island, and as a souvenir brought his favorite tenor, Giuseppe Savarese, home with him to sing for Hitler in Berlin. In 1937, an exhibition in Rome that set out to prove one of Mussolini's favorite themes, the parallels between Fascism and imperial Rome, highlighted Capri's role in this connection. The exhibit gave rise to a series of patriotic, pseudo-scholarly events on the island, such as a jamboree to celebrate the two thousandth anniversary of the birth of Augustus. The most prominent Fascist to take up permanent residence in Capri was the gadfly journalist and author Curzio Malaparte, though labeling him a Fascist is problematic, for his career was an exemplary proof of the rapid, effortless mutability of Fascist ideology; later, he renounced it and espoused Maoist Communism.

Born Kurt Erich Suckert, in 1898, he was the son of a German dyer in Prato and his Milanese wife. He received a classical education at the Liceo Cicognini, D'Annunzio's alma mater, which was broadened by an immersion in Futurism at cafés in Florence, including the Giubbe Rosse, the movement's informal headquarters. Young Suckert dabbled in every extreme of the political spectrum. Still in his teens, he served in the First World War as a commander in the Battle of the Marne, supporting the Allies against the final German offensive on the western front. He served with distinction and was awarded the Croix de Guerre. After the war, Suckert worked as a journalist, stalking famous artists and intellectuals in pursuit of interviews and useful connections. He launched his own movement, a retread of Nietzsche he called Oceanism. Oceanism proclaimed as its motto, "Usefulness is not necessary in life." It did not attract a following—what was the use of joining?—and earned him a reputation as an opportunistic intellectual snob. That did not present a problem for the Fascists, who recognized his talent and recruited him as a rhetorician for the movement, which was always searching for a respectable rationale. In 1925, Suckert signed the *Manifesto of the Fascist Intellectuals*, adding his name to those of D'Annunzio and Luigi Pirandello.

Pirandello later remarked, "Fascism is like an empty tube, you can put whatever you want in it," a truism proved by Kurt Suckert's career. He tacked to every ideological breeze that blew through the movement and quickly rose to a position of power as a writer and editor of nationalist publications. When Mussolini ordained in 1926 that "a Fascist writer must have an Italian name," Suckert dutifully adopted the nom de guerre Curzio Malaparte, a diabolical inversion of Bonaparte, taking the "evil side" in opposition to Napoleon's "good side." At the age of thirty, Malaparte was appointed to the position of top editor at the Naples daily *Il Mattino*; three months later, he ascended even higher, taking charge of *La Stampa*, the newspaper of Fiat, in Turin. At the same time, he was a prolific author of books, notably *Technique du coup d'état*, a sympathetic study of the Machiavellian tactics of revolutionists including Napoleon, Trotsky, and Mussolini. Malaparte was sedulous in his flattery of Il Duce, but he made more enemies than friends in his rise through the ranks of the party. After the police intercepted letters he had written that ridiculed Mussolini's heir apparent, the air marshal Italo Balbo, Malaparte was arrested on charges of anti-Fascist activities and defamation, and sentenced to five years' exile in Lipari, a tiny rock off the coast of Sicily.

He passed the time there reading Homer in Greek, but the obscurity was intolerable to his vanity. "Too much sea, too much sky for such a small island and so restless a spirit," he said. He pleaded a medical excuse, and through the influence of his friend Galeazzo Ciano, Mussolini's minister of foreign affairs, Malaparte got his exile relocated, first to Ischia, Capri's neighboring island to the north, and then to Forte dei Marmi, a seaside resort in Tuscany. He prospered in his disgrace: in Forte dei Marmi, he occupied (and later bought) Villa Hildebrand, a modern palace with frescoes by Arnold Böcklin, which had previously been D'Annunzio's residence. In 1937, Malaparte launched *Prospettive*, a journal in the luxurious style of Henry Luce's *Fortune* magazine, which was subsidized by the Culture Ministry. It was a successful venture by any measure. Its contributors included André Breton, Federico García Lorca, and James Joyce, who gave Malaparte his Italian translation, in collaboration with Ettore Settanni, of the Anna Livia Plurabelle episode of *Finnegans Wake*. *Prospettive* outlived Fascism and continued publication until 1952.

After a visit to Capri in 1937, Malaparte decided to build a house there. He commissioned Adalberto Libera, an Italian architect who had designed public buildings for the Fascists, to create the initial designs for a monumental, radically modernist house. Malaparte took charge and improvised many major alterations during the construction. By the time it was completed, in 1943, it was very much what Malaparte called it, "una casa come me," a house like me, an allusion to a collection of autobiographical fantasies he had published with titles such as "Woman Like Me," "Dog Like Me," and "Saint Like Me." Casa Malaparte, as it is usually known, is one of the most famous private houses of the twentieth century, as familiar an icon of Capri as the Faraglioni, the majestic stone stacks off the island's southeast coast, which it overlooks from a steep, isolated crag on the island's south-eastern coast.

Malaparte's reputation as a writer rests upon two remarkable books he wrote during and soon after the Second World War: *Kaputt*, published in 1944, which is based upon his experiences on the eastern front, in Poland, Rumania, the Balkans, Finland, and the Baltic states, when he was a correspondent for *Corriere della Sera*, Milan's prestigious daily newspaper; and *The Skin* (*La Pelle*, 1949), which narrates episodes in his service as a liaison officer attached to the American high command in Naples immediately after liberation. The books are not widely read outside Italy. Because Malaparte was both a Fascist and later a Communist sympathizer, everyone in the postwar era has had grounds to despise him, and the books' savage irony and misanthropic black humor, with many passages of dyspeptic misogyny, make them a hard sell for the leisure reader as much as for university curriculums.

The history of the manuscript of *Kaputt* is a tale of adventure straight from a spy novel by Graham Greene or Eric Ambler, which Orson Welles might have filmed, casting himself as the slippery, amoral protagonist. In a preface, Malaparte writes that he began the book in the Ukraine in 1941, at a farm adjoining the former House of the Soviets, which was by then occupied by the SS. His host was a Communist pig farmer, whose daughters sat under an apple tree in the garden reading Herodotus in Greek. Before the Gestapo came to arrest him because of his dispatches in *Corriere della Sera*, Malaparte had sewn the manuscript of *Kaputt* inside the lining of his uniform. He resumed work on the book in Poland until he was reassigned to Finland, again transporting the manuscript in his coat. He finished it, except for the last chapter, while he was there.

Before his return to Italy, in 1942, Malaparte divided the manuscript into three parts and gave them to Spanish and Rumanian diplomats posted in Helsinki. When the pages arrived safely in Italy, he hid them in the perimeter wall of the newly completed Casa Malaparte. In 1943, he went back to Finland to resume his reports for the newspaper, until the day he heard the news of Mussolini's fall, when he returned to Rome. On this journey, he concealed his manuscript in shoes with hollow soles. Two days after his arrival, he was arrested yet again, still wearing the shoes that had the pages of his book, and confined in the notorious Regina Coeli prison. After his release, he wrote, "I wanted to go home, I wanted to go to Capri, to my lonely house high above the sea." In his refuge at Casa Malaparte, he wrote the final pages of *Kaputt* while he waited for the arrival of the Allies.

I have said that his books are based upon his observations as a war correspondent and a military officer, a deliberately vague description, for determining the precise relationship between text and history is one of the principal challenges these books pose. In *Kaputt*, the atrocities of the Nazi occupation are described in vivid, horrible detail, at times almost rhapsodical in tone, which creates a perceptual dissonance that cannot easily be resolved, because the historical realities also defy belief. The book begins on an elegiac note, in a long, melancholy Swedish twilight at the palace of Prince Eugen, Duke of Närke (whom Jacques d'Adelswärd-Fersen would have met on his visit to Stockholm in 1902). Malaparte torments the prince, a noted painter, with grisly war stories expounded in exquisitely shaded prose haunted by Proust. In an aside, Malaparte writes,

> There is something strange in Swedish nature, the
> same sort of madness that is in the nature of horses.
> There is also the same gentleness, the same morbid
> sensitiveness, the same free and abstract fancy. The
> equine character, the equine madness of the Swedish
> landscape, is revealed not only in the great, solemn,
> incomparably green trees of the forests but also in the
> silky gloss of the vistas of water, woods, islands, and
> clouds, in the light and deep airy vistas in which a
> transparent white lead, warm vermilion, cold blue,
> damp green, and shiny turquoise compose a clear and
> elusive harmony, as if the colors never rested long on
> the woods, meadows, and waters but flitted instantly
> away like butterflies.

The reader is lured into the belief that *Kaputt* is a factual memoir mixing the exquisite and the macabre with sophisticated artistry, until the third chapter, when Malaparte describes a bizarre natural phenomenon, again involving horses, in a deadpan narrative that purports to be scientific. A herd of horses of the Soviet artillery, trapped by a forest fire in the dead of Finnish winter, stampeded into a lake. "Suddenly, with the peculiar vibrating noise of breaking glass, the water froze. The heat balance was broken, and the sea, the lakes, the rivers froze. In such instances, even sea waves are gripped in mid-air and become rounded ice waves suspended in the void." This freakish phenomenon captured the horses and transformed them into a living crystal sculpture. "The lake looked like a vast sheet of marble on which rested hundreds upon hundreds of horses' heads." A dazzling image, an unforgettable symbol of the paralysis wrought by war, yet impossible, surely; it cannot be possible; yet like many passages in *Kaputt*, it hovers on the knife-edge of plausibility, giving the reader pause.

In Malaparte's tour of Axis atrocities across the eastern front, the overlay of irony is hammered to a delicate lamina that approaches the fineness of gold leaf, gruesome substance and nightmarish invention becoming almost indistinguishable. In one infamous passage, Malaparte interviews Ante Pavelić, the Fascist dictator of the State of Croatia, a Nazi puppet regime. Taking the title Poglavnik, a Croatian word approximating Führer or Duce, Pavelić began as the heroic leader of the Ustaše, or Ustashi, the Croatian nationalist movement. However, after the Nazis installed him in Zagreb, he instituted a program of genocide against Serbs, Jews, and Romanies that rivaled those of his patrons in monstrous bloodlust. Malaparte begins audaciously, by painting a sympathetic portrait of the Poglavnik. When he had met him on a previous occasion, Pavelić appeared to him to be a good-natured man. "His stupid air seemed to me shyness, goodness, simplicity, and a peasant-like way of facing facts, people, and things as if they were physical elements—material, not moral elements—belonging to his physical, not his moral world."

When he met Pavelić at his office in Zagreb, Malaparte was mindful of the crimes he had committed in the course of his rise to power but entertained the possibility that "while unhesitatingly countenancing extreme methods for the defense of his people's freedom, he was horrified by bloodshed."

Pavelić gravely tells his visitor, "I shall rule my people through goodness and justice." The political situation in Croatia has grown worse, with widespread resistance to the imposition of this good and just regime. "The pale, almost ashen face of the Poglavnik was marked with a sorrow that was deep and sincere. How grievously this excellent man must suffer, I thought." The Italian minister, Raffaele Casertano, arrives, and the two Fascists discuss the latest dispatches from the front. Partisan rebellion is raging throughout Croatia, but Pavelić promises the Italian that his valiant *ustashis* will soon subdue the guerrillas.

Then Malaparte lobs a bomb into the web of ironic sympathy he has spun around his subject:

> I gazed at a wicker basket on the Poglavnik's desk. The lid was raised and the basket seemed to be filled with mussels, or shelled oysters—as they are occasionally displayed in the windows of Fortnum and Mason in Piccadilly in London. Casertano looked at me and winked, "Would you like a nice oyster stew?"
>
> "Are they Dalmatian oysters?" I asked the Poglavnik.
>
> Ante Pavelić removed the lid from the basket and revealed the mussels, that slimy and jelly-like mass, and he said smiling, with that tired good-natured smile of his, "It is a present from my loyal *ustashis*. Forty pounds of human eyes."

Is it a gruesome fantasy or a real war crime? Like the implausible climatic phenomenon of a "broken heat balance" that caused a lake to freeze so quickly that horses are imprisoned in ice, the moral impossibility of collecting human eyeballs as tribute creates an insufferable trial to the imagination. Reading *Kaputt* requires the willing suspension of disgust as well as disbelief, forcing the reader to contemplate the ability of humankind to abandon the basic instincts of decency. The horror of horrors in *Kaputt* is not among the acts of cruelty it narrates but rather the capacity of those who perpetrate crimes of pure evil to believe that they are just, that they are doing good. After a wrenching visit to the ghetto in Warsaw, where the Jews were confined in conditions of almost unimaginable degradation, 1.5 million people starving in a district previously inhabited by 300,000, the sense of dread plunges deeper with Malaparte's account of a dinner the same evening, which Ludwig Fischer, the Nazi governor of Warsaw, gives in honor of Hans Frank, governor-general of occupied Poland. The scene evokes the grotesque gaiety of Prince Prospero's ball in Poe's story "The Masque of the Red Death."

As she carves a roasted deer with a Nazi flag stuck in its back, Frau Frank says with a dainty shudder that she hates going to the ghetto because it is so *schmutzig*, so dirty. "As for the filth," her husband comments, "it cannot be denied that they live under deplorable conditions. A German would never tolerate living like that." Another guest, the Nazi governor of Cracow, adds, "As far as hygiene, the living Jews are more contagious than the dead." Governor Fischer pours golden gravy over a great slab of venison and says that his main concern is for the children: "Unfortunately, there is little that can be done to reduce the children's death rate in the ghettos," which exceeded 50 percent. On his visit to the ghetto earlier in the day, Malaparte watched as two little girls fought each other savagely, bloodying each other's faces over a scrap of raw potato.

Previously, when Malaparte called on the Franks at Wawel, the royal palace of Cracow, a roasted boar was brought to the dinner table, posed ferociously amid a tangle of forest brambles. After dinner, Frau Frank took Malaparte on a tour of the palace, pointing out the magnificent antique furniture and carpets, the royal collection of paintings and sculpture. Finally, she admitted him to the governor's private study, a whitewashed room with nothing in it but a Pleyel grand piano. She told Malaparte that before Frank made a crucial decision, or when he was weary or oppressed by duty, he shut himself up there to play Schumann, Beethoven, and Brahms. Smiling with affectionate pride, Frau Frank said, "He is an artist, a great artist, with a pure and delicate soul. Only such an artist as he can rule over Poland." Malaparte rarely draws conclusions; they are almost always, as in this case, so obvious that it is an insult to the reader to state them openly. Indeed, the scarcity of explicit outrage in *Kaputt* is one of the book's most outrageous elements.

What prevents the book from becoming a depressing excursion through a familiar hell is the almost ecstatic beauty of the writing—not only in the sense of beautiful prose, and there's plenty of that, but also in the mastery of tone, the complex symmetry of the book's construction, and above all its freshness. In the years after the war, many books would document the horrors in a fullness of detail, but Malaparte wrote from personal observation in 1943, two years before the liberation of Auschwitz, Dachau, and the other Nazi death camps, when the outcome of the war was still in doubt.

Readers who may feel that they have "done" the Holocaust, the all-too-vague term embracing a wide spectrum of moral depravity and terrible suffering, will confront it as if for the first time in the pages of *Kaputt.*

The Skin, Malaparte's phantasmagoric memoir of his service in Naples after it was liberated by American and British troops, in October 1943, describes privation on a par with that of the Warsaw ghetto, intertwined with a pitiless analysis of the havoc unintentionally wrought by American good intentions. In this book, the element of fantasy is more pronounced than in *Kaputt*, punctuated by scenes of blackest humor, such as a pilgrimage to view the last remaining virgin of Naples. After queuing for an hour with Allied soldiers, Malaparte and his American friend pay a dollar each to enter a grimy hovel, lit by oil lamps, where a young girl with the eyes of an old woman sits on display, like a statue of Athena in an ancient Greek shrine. Posed amid wax figurines of the Holy Family and lithographs of scenes from *Cavalleria rusticana* and *Tosca*, the girl sits smoking a cigarette, until the impresario gives her a cue, and she lifts her red silk dress and spreads her legs, giving the customers a glimpse of her maidenhead.

The book's principal themes unite in the symbol of the Siren of the Naples Aquarium. After they liberated the city, the Allies prohibited fishing in the gulf, so there was not a sardine to be had. When General Cork, Malaparte's apparently fictional commander of the American forces, "a true American gentleman," entertains official guests, he orders fish to be caught in the only available source, the Naples Aquarium, the most important singular collection of marine life in Europe after that of Munich. Eisenhower was served the giant octopus presented to the aquarium by the emperor Wilhelm II of Germany, and rare dragonfishes, a gift from the emperor Hirohito, were served to a party of American senators. By the night that Malaparte dined with General Cork and a group of American dignitaries (including a general in the Women's Army Corps named Mrs. Flat), the aquarium's collection was almost depleted. They were served its last prize, the famous Siren, "a very rare example of that species of 'sirenoids,' which, because of their almost human form, gave rise to the ancient legend about the Sirens." The dinner reaches its outrageous climax when the anthropomorphic fish is served: "The majordomo, assisted by the footmen, deposited the tray in the middle of the table, in front of General Cork and Mrs. Flat, and withdrew a few steps. We all looked at the fish, and we turned pale. A feeble cry of horror escaped from the lips of Mrs. Flat, and General Cork blanched. In the middle of the tray was a little girl, or something that resembled a little girl." The boiled Siren lay on a bed of greens, encircled by a wreath of pink coral stems.

With a perfectly pitched Swiftian mock naïveté, Malaparte bathes the rot of war in cheap sweet perfume. In the wreckage of Naples, the most heavily bombed city in Italy during the war, he writes, he often saw a body prepared for burial amid wreaths of flowers, and it was often the corpse of a child. But before General Cork's dinner, he had never seen the body of a little girl encircled by coral:

> How many poor Neapolitan mothers would have
> coveted such a wonderful wreath of coral for their
> own dead babies! Coral stems are like the branches of
> a flowering peach tree. They are a joy to behold; they

lend a gay, spring-like air to the dead bodies of little children. I looked at that poor boiled child, and I trembled inwardly with pity and pride. A wonderful country, Italy! I thought. What other people in the world can permit itself the luxury of offering Siren mayonnaise with a border of coral to a foreign army that has destroyed and invaded its country?

Several scenes in *The Skin* are set in Capri. After Malaparte invited General Cork for a visit at his new house there, the general considered it "his own personal rest camp." He would have regarded Capri as a perfect paradise, except that it "lay prostrate beneath the heel of female tyrants—an elect band of 'extraordinary women,' as Compton Mackenzie calls them. All of them Countesses, Marchionesses, Duchesses, Princesses, and the like, and mostly no longer young, though still ugly, they constituted the feminine aristocracy of Capri. And as everyone knows, the moral, intellectual, and social tyranny of old and ugly women is the worst tyranny of all." If the reader can get past the rank misogyny, which may be ironic but not ironic enough, *The Skin* offers some moments of high-camp hilarity. Malaparte imagines the soirees of these female tyrants, dressed in tweed jackets and purple velvet capes, their wrinkled brows swathed "in lofty turbans of white or red silk, richly decked with gold clasps, precious stones, and pearls," who remained faithful to D'Annunzio and Debussy, for them the Schiaparellis of poetry and music.

At a fete to welcome the American liberators, General Cork is called upon to open the ball with the first lady of the island, but no one had told him who it was. "While the Quisisana orchestra played 'Stardust,' General Cork gazed one by one at the mature Venuses," until he saw a dark, saucy-looking girl, mingling with the maids at the door of the buttery. She was Antonietta, who ran the hotel's coat check. The general swept past the titled ogresses and opened the ball in the arms of Antonietta. Malaparte concludes, "It was a colossal scandal, and the Faraglioni are still quivering from its impact."

The master of Casa Malaparte became accustomed to uninvited visitors, who turned up on his doorstep in the hope of having a look at the house. In *The Skin*, he tells the guests at the Siren mayonnaise dinner about the time Field Marshal Erwin Rommel came to visit him, in the spring of 1942, shortly before the Battle of El Alamein. The story is certainly pure invention. Malaparte gives Rommel the full tour, and "when we returned to the vast hall with its great windows, which look out on to the most beautiful scenery in the world, I offered him a glass of Vesuvian wine from the vineyards of Pompeii." Rommel toasts his host and asks him if he designed the house himself. Malaparte lies and says that he bought the place just as it was. "And with a sweeping gesture, indicating the sheer cliff of Matermania, the three gigantic rocks of the Faraglioni, the peninsula of Sorrento, the islands of the Sirens, the faraway blue coastline of Amalfi, and the golden sands of Paestum, shimmering in the distance, I said to him: 'I designed the scenery.'"

The final twist in Malaparte's restless ideological metastasis was an embrace of Maoism, in the years preceding his death in 1957, of lung cancer. He attributed his illness to his exposure to mustard gas in the First World War, though in almost every photograph of him that survives he has a cigarette planted in his mouth. In a quixotic gesture intended to strengthen relations between East and West, he left Casa Malaparte to the Chinese people in his will. His family, unimpressed by this beau geste, challenged the will and eventually won control of the house, in the early 1970s. They have been good caretakers and have restored the house to its pristine condition. They might even have enhanced its power as a legend by their decision to make visits there virtually impossible.

—

THE MANAGER OF Casa Malaparte, a member of the Suckert family, advises that the house "cannot be understood without seeing it in person," a stale truism all the more pointless because the only way to follow her advice, it seems, is to pay a fortune to rent it by the day to film a perfume commercial there. The house is one of the most popular tourist sights in Capri, in the same sense that the Turin Shroud attracts millions of visitors: even Nicolino Morgano, the owner of the Quisisana Hotel, was unable to secure me an invitation to visit Casa Malaparte at a week's notice when I was in Capri. The only options available to tourists intent on getting a look at Casa Malaparte are an overland trek, which gets you a peek through the trees at a distance of about a hundred yards, or an expensive boat trip, which brings you closer in terms of a GPS reading, but the house's site atop a hundred-foot cliff permits only a view of the top edge of the seaside facade and gives no sense of the layout.

The site Malaparte chose was Punta di Massullo, a narrow, rocky promontory that sticks like a finger into the sea, pointing to the Sorrento peninsula and flanking the Faraglioni. He bought the land from a fisherman for ten thousand lire, saying he wanted to breed rabbits there. It was yet a greater coup that he got permission to build a house in a district of the island where private residences were prohibited, which he contrived through the influence of his old friend Galeazzo Ciano, who had previously arranged his release from his gilded cage of exile in Forte dei Marmi. Adalberto Libera executed the preliminary design for the house, followed by a revision submitted for approval to the island's planning commission, but after construction began, Libera disappeared from the scene. Recently published correspondence supports the thesis that the final design was Malaparte's own, in collaboration with the builder.

Libera had designed a modernist building in harmony with traditional Capriote architecture, but Malaparte conceived the house as a unique work that defied categorization among the jungle of isms that proliferated in European architecture in the mid-twentieth century. Casa Malaparte has lived up to its creator's ambition, steadily gaining prestige since his death: it is an enigmatic icon, if the two qualities can coexist in a single work. Bruce Chatwin described the impact of Malaparte's masterpiece with a series of metaphorical questions: "A Homeric ship gone aground? A modern altar to Poseidon? A house of the future—or the prehistoric past? A surrealist house? A Fascist house? Or a Tiberian refuge from a world gone mad?" Casa Malaparte is a brute monolith, a masonry box painted Pompeii red, sparingly fenestrated, which occupies its geological plinth with a ponderous majesty that justifies Chatwin's comparison to an ancient warship. The building's most striking feature is the trapezoidal stairway that slopes gently from the ground to the roof platform, which is a long, unrailed rectangle inflected only by a freestanding whitewashed wall, a windbreak in the shape of a comma or ear.

The interior is made for deep conversations and heavy psychodrama, a destiny achieved when Jean-Luc Godard shot *Le mépris* (*Contempt*), his film based upon Alberto Moravia's novel *Il disprezzo*, at Casa Malaparte. The house's spare, elegant furnishings were designed by Alberto Savinio, the painter and writer who co-founded the Metaphysical school of art with his brother, Giorgio de Chirico, and Carlo Carrà. The majolica pavements resemble the stones of an ancient Roman road, graced with the motif of a lira coin, a theme borrowed from Goethe's *Italian Journey*. Among several ingenious innovations in the house, a glass-bottom fireplace provides a view of the sea when it is not in use, and when it is, it functions as a signal to visitors approaching by boat that the house is occupied. The living room has four large windows, among the earliest picture windows in Europe, which frame spectacular, perfectly composed views of the Faraglioni and the Sorrento coast, justifying Malaparte's grandiose boast that he had designed the scenery.

After the war, he hosted the intellectual and artistic elite of Europe at Casa Malaparte. Camus and Picasso stayed there, among many others. One of his most frequent visitors was Alberto Moravia, whom he had hired as a foreign correspondent based in London, when he was the editor of *La Stampa* and Moravia was wanted by the Italian police for "anti-Fascist activities." The maverick Fascist and the ardent Communist were close friends, to the continuing surprise of no one more than themselves. Moravia often came to Capri for long stays. He wrote one of his best books there, a short novel called *Agostino*, about a sheltered middle-class boy's loss of innocence when he becomes involved with a gang of feral youth on the beaches of the Sorrento coast.

Contempt is one of Moravia's most widely read battle-front dispatches from the war between the sexes, based upon his tormented marriage to Elsa Morante. It tells the story of Molteni, a writer who dreams of writing literary stage plays but undertakes hackwork for the cinema to pay for a com-fortable modern apartment for his bored, sexy, utterly con-ventional wife, Emilia. Battista, a crass film producer, hires Molteni to write a screenplay based upon *The Odyssey*, to be directed by a German director, "certainly not in the same class as the Pabsts and the Langs" but an artist deserving of respect. Battista wants a sword-and-sandal blockbuster, but Rheingold, the director, wants to make a film based upon his interpretation of Homer's poem. Rheingold's premise is that Penelope was unfaithful to Odysseus, which prompted him to leave her and join the siege against Troy. In the second half of the novel, work on the film script begins in Capri, where Battista seduces Emilia, mirroring Rheingold's con-ception of *The Odyssey*. In the denouement, Emilia leaves Molteni and dies in a traffic accident after her return to the mainland.

In Godard's film, the protagonist is Paul Javal, a French writer living in Rome, played by Michel Piccoli, yet as in most of the director's films the protagonist is actually Go-dard himself. His wife, Camille, played by Brigitte Bardot, likewise becomes Bardot, with nude scenes that mark the peak of her filmic incarnation of Aphrodite; Rheingold is

Fritz Lang, playing himself; and Battista is transformed into Jerry Prokosch, a heavy-handed caricature of the American barbarian, played by Jack Palance, whose leering pursuit of Camille verges on the ludicrous. Thus none of the principal characters in a story about the making of an Italian film in Italy is Italian.

Godard's *Contempt* has been analyzed and puzzled over by film critics and scholars as much as their counterparts in architectural history have spun theories about Casa Malaparte. The film makes a stunning impact with its fusion of big ideas, expressed in dialogue that alternates between sharp, staccato blasts and elaborate monologues, filmed in a gorgeous, romantic flood of saturated Technicolor. The ravishing flood of symphonic music, by Georges Delerue, almost Mahlerian in its intensely moving blend of the ecstatic and the tragic, is the binding agent in this cinematic fresco. The real star of the film is Casa Malaparte, with its bespoke scenery. Raoul Coutard's photography created the definitive image of the house, which may outlast the building itself. When the film was shot, in 1963, the house was in a state of mild disrepair, the red stucco peeling and the iron grates rusting, which only adds to the illusion of permanence, by creating the sensation that the building is as old as the cliff it is built on.

The two works are not in competition, but there is no doubt that Moravia's novel presents a more nuanced psychological narrative in its subtle palette of ironies than the film does. The reader is aware, even if Molteni is not, that he is pimping Emilia to advance his career. Battista is a complex character, eager to be taken as a serious participant in the creative process; Jack Palance's Jerry Prokosch is a contemptible human gorilla. The dramaturgical catastrophe of Godard's film, the car crash that kills Prokosch and Emilia, is shocking cinema, whereas the final pages of Moravia's novel are a rich synthesis that weaves together the themes of disappointed love, the classical conception of destiny, and the indestructible power of Capri as a primordial land of dreams, floating beyond the limits of ordinary human experience. In a vivid daydream that begins at the Marina Piccola, Emilia returns to Molteni, who has not yet learned of her death. She declares her love for him and explicitly offers every reassurance that he has sought from her in vain until then. Overjoyed, he takes the phantom Emilia by boat to a grotto to consummate the rebirth of their love, but he gets lost in the cavern's gloom. He awakens from the enchantment to find himself alone, wrapped in sea mist and tormented by the echo of his own voice.

THE MOST DISTINGUISHED writer who sought refuge in Capri after the Second World War was Pablo Neruda, who came to the island as a political exile, as Gorky had done. Neruda became an international literary celebrity at the age of twenty with the publication of *Twenty Love Poems and a Song of Despair*, in 1924, one of the most widely read books of poetry in the twentieth century. A zealous Communist, in his twenties Neruda served Chile as a diplomat in Burma, Java, Argentina, and Spain. After his return to Chile, in 1943, he was elected to the Senate. Five years later, when the right-wing government of González Videla outlawed the Chilean Communist Party, he was forced into hiding, in a series of urban basements and forest encampments. After more than a year of life underground, he escaped to Argentina on horseback, riding over a high pass in the Andes.

In his exciting *Memoirs*, originally published with the title *Confieso que he vivido* (I confess that I have lived), Neruda wrote, "In the course of these wanderings from place to place as an exile, I came to a country I had never visited, and I learned to love it deeply: Italy." In Milan, Florence, Genoa, and Venice, he recited his poems at crowded public events, followed by ceremonies where he was feted and made an honorary citizen. After champagne toasts, "between embraces and hand-kissing, I would finally make it down the front steps of the city hall," where the police, "who never gave me a moment's rest, would be waiting for me in the street." Neruda was warmly embraced by socialist municipal authorities, but the constabulary did not approve of the dangerous allusions to peace and the people's struggle in his poetry. After he was lionized by civil officials, the police would send him on to the next jurisdiction like a tramp.

It was a genteel persecution. "The police," he wrote, "never mistreated me but hounded me without respite." It all came to a head in Naples, where the police took him into custody at his hotel and informed him that he had to leave Italy immediately. Apologizing profusely and carrying his bags, they put him on a train out of the country. When Neruda stopped in Rome to change trains, there was an enormous throng of well-wishers waiting on the platform. "I saw great commotion and confusion. Armfuls of flowers advanced toward the train, raised over a river of heads. 'Pablo! Pablo!'"

With the arrival of their hero, the crowd became unruly. Neruda glimpsed prominent writers and painters among them, including Alberto Moravia and Elsa Morante, who struck a policeman on the head with her silk parasol. Carlo Levi, author of *Christ Stopped at Eboli*, presented him with a bouquet of roses. The police begged Neruda to quell the fury of the mob, which chanted, "Let the poet stay! Let the Chilean stay!," but he was powerless. Finally, a superior arrived, granting Neruda permission to stay in Italy. "I left the station, sad to be walking on the flowers the battle had scattered everywhere." The next morning, he received a cable from a stranger, Edwin Cerio, Capri's native historian, naturalist, and architect, inviting him to come to Capri as his guest.

Neruda, who defended Stalin and Stalinism to the end of his life, was a more faithful Communist than lover. In exile he was traveling with his mistress, Matilde Urrutia. He had sent his wife, Delia del Carril, home to Chile, ostensibly to prepare for his triumphant return from exile. Delia herself had hired Matilde to nurse Neruda when he was stricken with phlebitis in Mexico City, where he was serving as Chile's consul general. The two lovers arrived in Capri on a winter's night. "The coast loomed through the shadows," Neruda wrote, "whitish and tall. What would happen? What would happen to us?" When they arrived at the house Cerio had prepared for them, he was waiting, "standing in the glow of a burning candelabra," a tall, white-haired man wearing a white suit. He welcomed the lovers to their house, Casetta Arturo, overlooking the Marina Piccola, and left them with the promise that they would not be disturbed.

"Matilde and I took refuge in our love," wrote Neruda. "The small island, divided into a thousand tiny orchards, has a natural splendor too much commented on but strictly true." They became a part of "the hidden Capri," discovering "where to find the good wine and where to find the olives that the natives of Capri eat." Pablo and Matilde's sojourn on the island was an idyll of illicit love borrowed from an over-wrought melodrama by D'Annunzio. In *My Life with Pablo Neruda*, Matilde Urrutia wrote, "I have always said that I have experienced a taste of the perfect life and that, yes, a paradise does exist: we had the good fortune to experience it when we lived in Capri."

Soon after they arrived, Matilde discovered that she was pregnant with Pablo's child. Overjoyed, he told her, "Today I'm going to get a ring made that you will wear for the rest of your life." The ring was engraved, "Capri, 3 May 1952, your Captain." The night he gave her the ring, the couple performed a symbolic wedding by moonlight, with no guests, at their villa, bedecked with paper flowers the poet had made. "Pablo, in a very serious tone," Matilde wrote, "asked the moon to marry us. He explained to the moon that we were not able to marry on Earth, but that with her, the muse of all poets in love, we could be married." Humming the wedding march from *Lohengrin*, they went into the house to consummate their union.

Neruda called himself Matilde's captain in reference to a book of poems he completed in Capri, in which he imag-ines the island as a ship, with himself at the helm. Two months after the lunar wedding, he published *The Captain's*

Verses in Naples, anonymously, in the hope of protecting Delia del Carril, "sweetest of consorts, thread of steel and
honey," from learning about his infidelity. It was issued in a
luxurious limited edition of forty-four copies, printed on
handmade ivory paper. The production costs were paid by
the Italian Communist Party, in homage to an "exiled comrade and poet." The book's authorship "remained a secret for
a long time," Neruda wrote in his memoir, "as if the book
itself did not know who its father was. There are natural
children, offspring of natural love, and in that sense, *Los ver-
sos del capitán* was a natural book." One of the love poems he
wrote for Matilde in Capri, "Night on the Island" (La noche
en la isla), conceives of the island as a little bark, bearing the
dreaming lovers through a dark sea:

> All night I have slept with you,
> the two of us together at sea, on the island.
> Savage and sweet you were between the pleasure and
>   the dream,
> between fire and water.

As he often does in his mystical love poetry, Neruda mixes
intensely vivid concrete images with enigmatic abstractions.
The lovers are lost in time, united only in their dreams,
which connect above them like branches moved by the same
wind, and in the earth below, "like red roots that touch." In
sleep, Matilde's dream drifts apart from the poet's

> and searched for me
> across the dark sea
> like before,

when you did not yet exist,
when even before I caught a glimpse of you
I sailed at your side.

When they awake, they are entwined physically, in real time, yet the dream lingers. The poem concludes on a sensual, ecstatic note:

Your mouth,
quitting your dream,
gave me a taste of earth,
of seawater and seaweed,
from the depth of your life,
and I received your kiss
moistened by the dawn
as if it came to me
from the sea that surrounds us.

The association of Pablo Neruda with Capri was strengthened, albeit erroneously, by the popular film *Il postino* (1994), an Italian production directed by Michael Radford and Massimo Troisi. It is an old-fashioned romance in the tradition of *Cyrano de Bergerac*, in which a fictional Neruda, in exile in Capri, schools a timid, awkward young postman in the arts of love, helping him to overcome his shyness in the pursuit of the girl he likes. It is a classic example of the movies taking bold liberties with literature. *Il postino* is based on a short novel by the Chilean writer Antonio Skármeta, who set his story in Chile, at Isla Negra, Neruda's home for most of his life. Isla Negra is in fact not an island but a village on the coast, south of Valparaiso. The film's script, credited to five writers, relocated Skármeta's story to Capri for obvious reasons. The actors and crew were Italian; filming in Capri must have been cheaper than in rural Chile; and, mainly, anywhere you point a camera in Capri, it frames a stunning view.

NERUDA'S VISION OF a night of lovemaking in Capri
as a night at sea, the poet sailing on the island at the
side of his beloved, marks the end of an era, or two. Neruda
was the last major artist who came to Capri seeking a place
conducive to creativity and made it a theme of the work.
Norman Douglas died a few months before the publication
of *The Captain's Verses*, in 1952. Compton Mackenzie was
knighted that year, beginning his slow decline into a tartaned
caricature of a professional curmudgeon. Curzio Malaparte's
best work was behind him, too: in his final years, he produced a satirical revue called *Sexophone*, stood unsuccess-
fully for Parliament as a right-wing Republican, and toured
the Soviet Union and China as a Communist. Writers and
painters of distinction continued to visit Capri on holidays,
of course. Notable among them would be Graham Greene,
whose decades-long association with the island is told in
Greene on Capri, a memoir by Shirley Hazzard, who, with

her husband, Francis Steegmuller, befriended him on their visits there.

The only book Greene had a hand in that took Capri as its setting was the memoir of Elisabeth Moor, a Viennese doctor who practiced medicine on the island for fifty years. Dottoressa Moor, as she was known, who attended Norman Douglas in his final illness, was a flamboyant personality with a sexual appetite prodigious even by the lusty standards of Capri. In her old age, she lapsed into a deep depression after she witnessed the accidental death of her young grandson by electrocution, in a shoe shop in Zurich. Greene suggested that she write her memoirs as a therapeutic measure. He arranged a series of taped interviews, which were conducted in German by an anonymous Hungarian who had never met her and then translated into bad English. The task of editing this mess fell to the filmmaker and novelist Kenneth Macpherson, who had cared for Douglas in his old age. Macpherson died before he completed the job, and Greene took it over. He finished the book, revising it with a heavy hand—to the point of writing several passages himself narrating events that "did not appear on the tapes because the right questions were not asked." *An Impossible Woman: The Memories of Dottoressa Moor of Capri*, with an epilogue by Greene, was published shortly before Moor's death, at ninety. It is generally reckoned among Greene's weakest literary projects and has small value as a historical record, for Moor was a notorious prevaricator.

In the 1950s, Capri began a new life as a playground for film stars and fashion icons, giving up its air of mystery for tabloid glamour. Audrey Hepburn kittenish in Capri pants,

Elizabeth Taylor and Richard Burton lounging by the pool, champagne parties aboard Aristotle Onassis's yacht, Jacqueline Onassis pattering barefoot through the village: images such as these contributed to the boom in mass tourism that transformed the island. Inevitably, Capri succumbed to the global currents it had resisted for so long. James Money, an amateur archaeologist and devoted reader of Compton Mackenzie, wrote a compendious chronicle of the island's scandals, *Capri: Island of Pleasure*, which concludes with this lament: "The elegance of Capri life which was notable in the 'sixties and still evident in the 'seventies had vanished by the early 'eighties, when vulgarization, overcrowding, pressure on the island's facilities, and assault on the environment began to turn Capri into a Mediterranean version of Coney Island."

Money published his book in 1986. The number of short-term visitors has multiplied many times since then, and so have the complaints. Capri, once known as a remote destination, Goethe's "dangerous, rocky island," had become all too easy to get to by the end of the twentieth century. In 2016, the mayor of Capri proposed that the number of ferries from and to Naples be reduced, to relieve "problems of congestion which are doing irreparable damage to our reputation." Jostling in the Piazzetta may be a mild amusement, but when the place is so densely packed that one cannot enter, it's another thing. If the subject of Capri comes up among the French, they will smirk and sing the chorus of "Capri c'est fini" (Capri is finished), a catchy pop song recorded by Hervé Vilard in 1965, in which a young lover swears he will never return to the island. His disenchantment with Capri is caused not by overcrowding or a decline of elegance but rather by a broken heart, the end of his first love affair, which began there, but now the title has a broader implication.

To liken Capri to Coney Island is a stretch (unless one considers the funicular from the Marina Grande to the Piazzetta as a sort of carnival ride), and one man's vulgarity is another man's good fun. A more just complaint, often heard, is that Capri has become a shopping mall. That must be the impression carried away by day-trippers who browse the smart shops in the village and have an early dinner before catching the last ferry to Naples. Yet on my sojourn in Capri in the spring of 2016, I found the island to be in remarkably good form for a limestone rock four square miles in extent, with a year-round population of some thirteen thousand people who play host to millions of visitors annually. If I were looking for a complaint, it would be that the place is too perfectly pre-served, a trifle overscrubbed, every wall freshly painted and every flower box in full bloom—rather like a Las Vegas rep-lica of a quaint Italian village. But that would be peevish: since antiquity, the genius of the island has been hospitality, and a good host wants to keep the place looking its best.

A more profitable way of viewing Capri in the twenty-first century might be as a museum, not an awesome mauso-leum like Venice, but a modest provincial museum, which has let the gift shop and food-and-beverage outlets take over. As I walked around the island, I found it easy to escape the mob (admittedly, not as thick in April as it would be a few months later), simply by venturing beyond the shopping dis-trict in the central village. Villa Behring, where Gorky and Lenin played chess, is now a middle-class apartment build-ing, fifty paces from the Piazzetta down a crooked stone lane, where I met no one but housewives doing their errands and children kicking a soccer ball. When I strolled up to the Belvedere Cannone, the former Malerplatte, where German watercolorists once painted the views and Norman Douglas found Heinrich Lieber writhing on the ground after shooting himself with an absurd Browning pistol, it was deserted except for some local teenagers furtively smoking marijuana. Visitors attuned to the eccentric cultural legacy of Capri will find mementos of it at every turn in the island's winding footpaths.

If Capri is a museum, its curators are the publishers of Edizioni La Conchiglia, a small press that operates out of a narrow shop in the village, which opened its doors in 1981. Conchiglia has published more than 350 exquisitely designed books, most of them in a small format, with covers in Wedgwood blue and gray or shocking purple and pink. The Conchiglia catalogue comprises the best literature produced in Capri, including many works that had gone out of print long ago, as well as Italian translations of books by Jacques d'Adelswärd-Fersen, Norman Douglas, Compton Mackenzie, and the rest. One recent title, by Francesco Durante, a native of Anacapri, is a comprehensive literary history of the island, starting with the Greek poet Blaesus, born in Capri in the sixth century B.C., of whose work but a single verse survives ("Pour out for us seven cups of your sweetest [wine]"), down to the present day. The index of the book has 494 names.

Conchiglia is a family business run by Riccardo Esposito, his wife, Ausilia Veneruso, and their son, Vincenzo Sorrentino. I met Riccardo Esposito one day when he saw me wandering down Via le Botteghe, trying to find the shop. He presented an extravagantly romantic appearance, wearing a cashmere scarf wrapped around his neck and a pince-nez like Yeats's, dangling on a black velvet ribbon. Esposito is a native of the island, descended from a family of hoteliers and restaurateurs, and a distinguished writer himself, who has taken as his theme the transformation of the island from a legendary international cultural enclave to a byword of chic.

He led me to his shop and sat me down in the one little chair, and there we talked as best we could in his bad English and my worse Italian. He reminisced about Moravia in Capri, "serious, very serious, solitary. You saw him go around the island with a great burden on his shoulders." Esposito made a stirring defense of Malaparte, which elicited a cheer from his wife, sitting in the office behind us. He proudly told me about meeting Ezra Pound in Venice, in 1969.

"Capri was an international laboratory for the avantgarde," he said, "a place where ideas were born, a new artistic vision, and given to the world." With an air of resignation, sad but not bitter, Esposito concluded, "In the past, intellectuals and artists came here to live. Now people come just to use our name. Now Capri is a brand."

Where do they go now? I asked. Where is the laboratory for a new artistic vision today?

He lifted his shoulders and eyebrows in eloquent synchrony. "Yes, where is it?"

NOTES AND
BIBLIOGRAPHY

In addition to citing the sources of quotations, these notes incorporate the bibliography of my research, with occasional brief comments about the works I consulted and grateful acknowledgment of assistance from colleagues and friends. I did much of the research for this book in libraries and archives in Capri, Paris, and London, but I often had recourse to electronic books. I live in Indonesia, a country that lacks research libraries and well-stocked bookstores, and many of the texts I write about are easily obtainable online. Therefore, in these notes I provide page numbers only for books that actually have pages; for electronic books, I cite chapters or other markers where possible. Of course, one advantage of electronic books is that a passage may easily be located by a global search.

In quotations, apart from silently changing British to American usage in modern texts, I follow the spellings of the original, in the belief that archaic forms and competing scholarly notions of correct usage hold some interest, but I have freely edited punctuation in the belief that it does not (and often does not reflect the writer's intentions at all but is rather imposed by the publisher). In other words, all the quotations here are verbatim and faithful to their sources, with omissions noted by ellipses, but I groom them as it suits me.

Unless otherwise noted, translations are my own.

~~~~

PAGAN LIGHT, my title, comes from Norman Douglas's *South Wind*. The phrase makes several appearances in the novel as Douglas's attempt to encapsulate the source of Capri's transformative effect on visitors, yet none of them quotes very well. In the first occurrence, Mr. Keith, a wealthy, worldly hedonist long resident in Nepenthe, Douglas's fictional Capri, encounters Bishop Heard, Douglas's protagonist, while he is swimming in the sea. Mr. Keith invites him aboard his luxurious boat and delivers a witty discourse expounding the author's views on life and opinions about life on Capri. He mentions Denis Phipps, a melancholy undergraduate who has confided in the two older men. Mr. Keith (his full name in the novel) remarks, "Have you seen Denis lately? We must be friendly to that young man, Heard. I don't think he is altogether happy in this clear pagan light." Later in the book, the bishop, full of doubts about his vocation after his experiences in Nepenthe, seeks Keith's advice. "You seem to have a quarrel with Moses and his commandments," the bishop says. "I want to listen to the opinions of a man so different from myself as you are. It may do me good." He concludes by quoting Keith back to himself: "I think I could stand almost anything in this landscape—in this clear pagan light, as you call it."

3 *Goethe attempted to visit there*: Johann Wolfgang von Goethe, *Italienische Reise*, chap. 53.

7 *"the sage surrenders"*: Norman Douglas, *South Wind* (London: Martin Secker, 1917), chap. 39.

7 *"Come hither, renowned Odysseus"*: Homer, *Odyssey* 12.184–91.

9 *Apragopolis*: The location of Suetonius's Apragopolis is an insoluble problem. In his *Vita divi Augusti* 98.4, Suetonius writes, "Vicinam Capreis insulam Apragopolim appellabat," which would ordinarily be translated "an island in the vicinity of Capri called Apragopolis." However, there is no inhabited (or habitable) island in the vicinity of Capri, much less one large enough to accommodate a polis, a city or small state. Classical scholars have offered several theories to explain this passage, none of them satisfactory. One scholar proposed an emendation in the text that enabled it to be translated "the neighboring part of the island of Capri," that is, the part facing Campania, where the Marina Grande is located and where Augustus built his villa. I have followed this reading: it is sketchy Latin, but at least it makes sense. For a full discussion of this issue, see Walter Brooks McDaniel, "Apragopolis, Island-Home of Ancient Lotos Eaters," *Transactions and Proceedings of the American Philological Association* 45 (1914): 29–34.

9 *"were adorned not so much"*: Gaius Suetonius Tranquillus, *Vita divi Augusti* 72.

10 *"the first paleontological museum"*: Norman Douglas, *Siren Land* (London: Martin Secker, 1929), chap. 4.

15 tristissimus hominum: Gaius Plinius Secundus, *Naturalis historia* 28.5.23.

15 *"For the first time"*: Douglas, *Siren Land*, chap. 4.

16 *"for the most part"*: Publius Cornelius Tacitus, *Annales* 4.57.

16 *"The solitude of the place"*: Ibid., 4.67.

19 *"In the years that he went into exile"*: Ibid., 1.4.

19 *One modern military historian*: David L. Woods, *A History of Tactical Communication Techniques* (Orlando, Fla.: Martin-Marietta, 1965). Also see John Kingman, "The Isle of Capri: An Imperial Residence and Probable Wireless Station of Ancient Rome," *National Geographic*, Sept. 1919, 224.

20 *"The more intent"*: Tacitus, *Annales* 4.67.

20 *"In Capri, they point out"*: Suetonius, *Vita divi Tiberii* 62.2.

21 *"Like a royal despot"*: Tacitus, *Annales* 6.1.

22 *"On retiring to Capri"*: Suetonius, *Tiberius* 43. On the life of Gilles de Rais, I consulted Jean Benedetti, *Gilles de Rais* (New York: Stein and Day, 1972).

24 *"He hath his boys"*: Ben Jonson, *Sejanus, His Fall*, act 4, scene 5, lines 392–95, 398–401.

24 *"This Emperor hath no son"* and Charles Dunster's note: John Milton, *Paradise Regained*, ed. Charles Dunster (London: T. Cadell, 1795), 196–97.

25 *"the only writer"*: Francine du Plessix Gray, *At Home with the Marquis de Sade* (New York: Penguin, 1999), 11.

26 *"The palace is perched"*: Marquis de Sade, *Juliette*, trans. Austryn Wainhouse (New York: Grove Press, 1968), 992–95.

27 *"a fanatic sparkling with wit"*: Unsigned review, *Analytical Review* (London: J. Johnson, 1790), 568. See also Edwin Bowen, "Did Tacitus in the Annals Traduce the Character of Tiberius?," *Classical Weekly* 6, no. 21 (1913): 162–66.

28 *"that the first Pope"*: John Rendle, *The History of That Inimitable Monarch Tiberius* (Exeter: Trewman and Son, 1813), 432.

28 *"foreigners had been coming"*: Compton Mackenzie, *Vestal Fire* (London: Hogarth Press, 1985), 93.

29 *"possessed of much fondness"*: Thomas Spencer Jerome, *The Orgy of Tiberius on Capri: Source of the Story: A Paper Read at the International Congress of Historical Studies, London, April 1913* (Rome, 1913). A copy of this privately printed pamphlet is held by the library of the Centro Caprense Ignazio Cerio. .

32 *Thomas Jerome's life began*: For information about Jerome's life, I consulted John G. Winter's preface to Thomas Spencer Jerome, *Aspects of the Study of Roman History* (London: Mills & Boon, 1914), iii–ix, and Carlo Knight, *L'avvocato di Tiberio* (Capri: La Conchiglia, 2004).

34 *"His pictures—picturesque corners"*: E. F. Benson, *Final Edition* (London: Hogarth Press, 1988), 113.

35 *"The rooms were lofty"*: Allan McLane Hamilton, *Recollections of an Alienist* (New York: George H. Doran, 1916), 173.

35 *"After I left"*: Ibid., 174.

36 *"One evening he was sitting"*: W. Somerset Maugham, *Collected Short Stories* (New York: Penguin, 1978), 4: 173–75.

37 *"When [Scudamore, the character based on Jerome] came to Sirene"*: Mackenzie, *Vestal Fire*, 94.

38 *"said to Jerome"*: Quoted in John G. Pedley, *The Life and Work of Francis Willey Kelsey* (Ann Arbor: University of Michigan Press, 2012), 291.

39 *"He set to work"*: Mackenzie, *Vestal Fire*, 93–94.

40 *"difficult to express"*: Thomas Spencer Jerome, *Roman Memories in the Landscape Seen from Capri* (Rome: Mills & Boon, 1914), xxiii.

41 *"has a distinguished ancestry"*: Michael Schmidt, *The Novel: A Biography* (Cambridge, Mass.: Harvard University Press, 2014), 656.

41 *"My generation was brought up"*: Ibid.

42 *"comely outlines were barely"*: Douglas, *South Wind*, chap. 1.

42 *"very beautiful but also"*: Virginia Woolf, *The Voyage Out* (London: Duckworth, 1915), chap. 21.

44 *"with such precision"*: Douglas, *South Wind*, chap. 21.

45 *"We of the South"*: Ibid., chap. 39.

46 *Born in Thüringen*: The best source for the life of Norman Douglas is Mark Holloway, *Norman Douglas: A Biography* (London: Martin Secker & Warburg, 1976).

47 *"could endure the society"*: Paul Fussell, *Abroad* (Oxford: Oxford University Press, 1980), 130.

47 *"Niotcsoohoan brand of naughtiness"*: Ibid., 120.

51 *"I want to lay a few simple flowers"*: Wilde to Turner, Oct. 15, 1897, quoted in James Money, *Capri: Island of Pleasure* (London: Hamish Hamilton, 1986), 55.

51 *"a great connoisseur"*: Wilde to Robert Ross, Oct. 19, 1897, quoted in ibid.

51 *"a man, accompanied by a younger man"*: Roger Peyrefitte, *The Exile of Capri*, trans. Edward Hyams (London: Panther, 1969), 15–16.

53 *"those beings who, incapable"*: Ibid., 7.

58 *"Thirteen, blond, with precocious eyes"*: Poem quoted in full in Will Ogrinc, *Frère Jacques: A Shrine to Love and Sorrow* (2006), semgai.free.fr/doc_et_pdf/Fersen-engels.pdf, accessed June 24, 2018. Ogrinc's little book is the best, authoritative source for information about Fersen's early life and the Black Masses scandal.

59 *"Cycladian girls, pretty Greeks"*: Jacques d'Adelswärd-Fersen, *Ébauches et débauches* (Paris: Léon Vanier, 1901), 18. Most of Fersen's books are available for download in good scans from the website of the Bibliothèque nationale de France.

61 *"throbbed the naked"*: Quoted in Robert Aldrich, *The Seduction of the Mediterranean* (London: Routledge, 1993), 123–24. Aldrich's book is a fascinating, wide-ranging study of homosexual fantasy in the literature of the Mediterranean world.

62 *"It was a marvel"*: Achille Essebac, *Luc* (Paris: Ambert, 1907), 76–77.

64 *Morand later confided to a friend*: Jacques Chardonne, Morand's close literary colleague and a fellow Nazi collaborator. Paul Morand and Jacques Chardonne, *Correspondance I* (Paris: Gallimard, 2013), 746–47.

66 *"arrested the Baron d'A."*: "Un scandale parisien," *Le Figaro*, July 10, 1903, 4.

66 *"Baronne Axel d'Adelswärd"*: "Regina," "La vie de Paris, L'Île de Puteaux," in ibid., 1.

67 *"Contemporary anxiety over"*: Nancy Erber, "Queer Follies: Effeminacy and Aestheticism in *Fin-de-Siècle* France in the Case of Baron d'Adelswärd Fersen and Count de Warren," in *Disorder in the Court*, ed. George Robb and Nancy Erber (Houndmills, U.K.: Macmillan, 1999), 188.

70 *a pornographic novel*: A.-S. Lagail, *Les mémoires du baron Jacques: Lubricités infernales de la noblesse décadente* ("Priapeville": Librairie Galante, 1904).

71 *"I don't shake hands with pederasts"*: Paul Morand, *Venices*, trans. Euan Cameron (London: Pushkin Press, 2012), 42.

71 *"Graeco-Preraphaelitico-Modernistic bric-à-brac"*: Peyrefitte, *Exile of Capri*, 8.

71 *"rich poetaster"*: Shirley Hazzard, *Greene on Capri* (New York: Farrar, Straus and Giroux, 2000), 93.

73 *"a virtually unique manifestation"*: Ogrinc, *Frère Jacques*, 19.

73 *"He found himself beautiful"*: Jacques d'Adelswärd Fersen, *Black Masses: Lord Lyllian* (Norwich, Vt.: Asphodel, 2005), 23. This excellent translation (unattributed, apparently a group effort led by the publisher), beautifully printed and designed, is the only major full-length work by Fersen published in English.

74 *"I teach these youngsters"*: Ibid., 139.

75 *"You elevated my heart"*: Ibid., 170–76.

79 *"overran the island"*: Hamilton, *Recollections of an Alienist*, 176–77.

79 *"If you have come to Capri"*: I am grateful to Cornelia Biegler-König for this translation of Platen's poem.

81 *"The Persian* ghazal": Thomas Mann, *Essays of Three Decades,* trans. H. T. Lowe-Porter (New York: Knopf, 1947), 264–65.

83 *"Brønnum's akten":* Personal communication from Adam Lüders, with the author's thanks.

83 *"One's body glows":* August Bournonville, *My Theatre Life,* trans. Patricia N. McAndrew (Middletown, Conn.: Wesleyan University Press, 1979), 94.

83 *"The entrance to the cave":* Mark Twain, *The Innocents Abroad,* chap. 30.

85 *"in so cosmopolitan a city":* John Clay MacKowen, *Capri: The Island Revisited,* ed. Anna Maria Palombi Cataldi (Beaconsfield, U.K.: Beaconsfield, 2012), 124. The principal interest of this new edition of MacKowen's guidebook to Capri is Dr. Cataldi's biographical sketch of the author, the best source of information about his life.

88 *"negresses and cannibals":* Fersen, unpublished letter dated Aug. 4, 1904, "aboard the English steamship Doric," recipient unverified. I am grateful to Raimondo Biffi, in Rome, for supplying me with copies of Fersen's unpublished correspondence.

88 *"a house in the sun":* Viveka Adelswärd, *Alltför adlig, alltför rik, alltför lättjefull* (Copenhagen: Carlsson, 2014). Here, I quote an English synopsis kindly given to me by the author.

89 *"a favorite spot of mine":* Norman Douglas, *Looking Back* (London: Chatto & Windus, 1933), 359–60.

91 *"With his childlike freshness".* Ibid., 361.

94 *"Their villa above the Grande Marina":* Quoted in Compton Mackenzie, *My Life and Times: Octave Four, 1907–1915* (London: Chatto & Windus, 1965), 183.

94 *"Carlyle once said":* Mackenzie, *Vestal Fire,* 47.

95 *"My only memory":* Compton Mackenzie, *My Life and Times: Octave Five, 1915–1923* (London: Chatto & Windus, 1966), 138.

95 *"in the dusty rear":* Henry James, *Notes on Novelists* (New York: Charles Scribner's Sons, 1915), 318. James's appraisal of Compton Mackenzie's work is warm but measured, and expressed in convolutions so complex that it resists sensible quotation except in full.

96 *One popular book about Capri:* Money, *Capri.* James Money's book is an encyclopedic catalogue of the island's scandals, entertaining but fatally flawed as a source of information. He frequently quotes Mackenzie's novels as though they were historical chronicles, and even attributes dialogue from the novels as quoted speech by the real people he supposes to be the models of Mackenzie's characters; yet he never concedes that he is doing so. Money follows the same dubious practice with Roger Peyrefitte's

Exile of Capri. The reader must refer to Money's footnotes to find out if a quoted passage comes from a nonfiction book or a novel.

97 *"make extravagant gestures"*: Jacques d'Adelswärd Fersen, *Et le feu s'éteignit sur la mer* . . . (Paris: A. Messein, 1909), chap. 13.
97 *"The people in Capri annoyed"*: Ibid., chap. 16.
97 *"the little painter"*: Ibid., chap. 21.
99 *"The two maidservants"*: Peyrefitte, *Exile of Capri*, 200.

101 *"Intelligence beamed from his eyes"*: Mackenzie, *Octave Four*, 244.
105 *"No doubt one of his family"*: Ibid., 245.

106 *"If it is true"*: Quoted in Ogrinc, *Frère Jacques*, 36.
109 *"was torn between feelings"*: Ibid., 39.
109 *"He dined, and as he was lighting"*: Douglas, *Looking Back*, 365.

112 *"Yet perhaps one evening"*: Jacques d'Adelswärd Fersen, *Ainsi chantait Marsyas* (Paris: Vanier, 1907), 16.
112 *"a smoking room"*: Jacques d'Adelswärd Fersen, "L'extase," *Akademos* 1, no. 9 (1909): 321–26.
113 *"Tonight I sing of opium"*: Jacques d'Adelswärd Fersen, *Hei Hsiang: Le parfum noir* (Paris: Albert Messein, 1921), 5.
114 *"I would wish to live"*: Ibid., 22.
115 *"To be granted dreams"*: Peyrefitte, *Exile of Capri*, 7.
116 *"Miles asked for a mirror"*: Jacques d'Adelswärd Fersen, *Le baiser de Narcisse* (Reims: L. Michaud, 1912), 18.
116 *"slowly at first"*: Ibid., 20.
117 *"with a charming, childlike gesture"*: Ibid., 21.
117 *"It is in a bungalow"*: Jacques d'Adelswärd Fersen, "Lontaine-ment," in *Paradinya* (Paris: Pan, 1911), 9.
119 *"opium-tainted cigarette"*: Oscar Wilde, *The Picture of Dorian Gray*, chap. 1.
120 *"Crime belongs exclusively"*: Ibid., chap. 19.

123 *"We want no part of it"*: Filippo Tommaso Marinetti, "Le Futur-isme," *Le Figaro*, Feb. 20, 1909, 1.
124 *"the refuge for indispensable disorders"*: Quoted in Money, *Capri*, 167.
124 *"little gentleman, hunchbacked"*: Fortunato Depero, *Fortunato Depero nelle opera e nella vita* (Trent: TEMI, 1940), 203.
126 *"Our too intense participation"*: Filippo Tommaso Marinetti and Bruno Corra, *L'isola dei baci* (Capri: La Conchiglia, 2003). Many quotations from the short novel, in my translation, follow in se-quence, except as noted.

130 *"The warm, soft lilac twilight"*: Ibid., 45.

131 *"a youthful way"*: Bruno Giancarlo, "Tacito e il Futurism," *Rivista di Cultura Classica e Medioevale* 50, no. 2 (2008): 394.

132 *"epiphany of the irrepressible germination"*: Ugo Piscopo, *Capri Futurista* (Naples: Alfredo Guida, 2001), 10–13.

My principal source for information on the life of Romaine Brooks is the unpublished typescript of her memoirs, circa 1950, archived by the Beinecke Rare Book and Manuscript Library at Yale University. The Beinecke typescript is untitled; other versions of the memoir are titled "No Pleasant Memories." The best biography of the artist is Cassandra Langer's *Romaine Brooks: A Life*, published in 2015, which is concise yet thoughtful and thought-provoking, well researched, and elegantly written. Meryle Secrest's biography of Brooks, *Between Me and Life*, published in 1974, is dated in its approach but remains an invaluable resource.

136 *"At the end of the last century"*: Romaine Brooks, unpublished memoir (Beinecke Library, Yale University, ca. 1950), 150. Throughout this section, many quotations from the typescript follow in sequence, with exceptions noted.

136 *"arrogance, unusual culture"*: Ibid., 3.

137 *"rhythmic calls and responses"*: Ibid., 159–61.

139 *"Mr. Burr's face"*: Ibid., 162–63.

140 *"always planning diversions"*: Ibid., 166–67.

142 *"frigid and labored"*: Benson, *Final Edition*, 115.

142 *"devoid of any rendered magic"*: Ibid., 177.

142 *"Came for lunch"*: Benjamin Taylor, *Naples Declared* (New York: Penguin, 2012), 151.

142 *"coming along one day"*: Mackenzie, *Octave Four*, 233.

143 *"inexcusably indolent"*: Benson, *Final Edition*, 243.

144 *"He became very angry"*: Brooks, Beinecke typescript, 162.

146 *"I gazed at her spellbound"*: Ibid., 177.

148 *"When for the last time"*: Ibid., 198.

149 *"Festival of San Costanzo—an Island Carnival"*: Quoted in Harold E. Trower, *The Book of Capri* (Naples: Emil Prass, 1906), 303.

151 *"From where he lay"*: W. Somerset Maugham, *The Mixture as Before* (New York: Doubleday Doran, 1940), 110.

151 *"I decided to forgo"*: Brooks, Beinecke typescript, 200.

153 *"Mrs. Brooks has returned"*: Knight, *L'avvocato di Tiberio*, 96.

153 *"Enough for meat"*: Money, *Capri*, 130.

153 *"Of all the painters"*: Brooks, Beinecke typescript, 205.

155 *John Singer Sargent*: For information about the artist's life and sojourn in Capri, I consulted Stanley Olson, *Sargent: His Portrait* (New York: St. Martin's Press, 1986).

156 *"the slightly 'uncanny' spectacle"*: Henry James, "John S. Sargent," *Harper's Magazine*, Oct. 1887, 683–91.

156 *"One generally feels used up"*: Olson, *Sargent*, 68.

156 *"an Anacapri girl"*: Evan Edward Charteris, *John Sargent* (New York: Charles Scribner's Sons, 1927), 48.

158 *disgrace of Friedrich Alfred Krupp*: My principal source for the *Fall Krupp* is Dieter Richter, "Friedrich Alfred Krupp auf Capri: Ein Skandal und seine Geschichte," in *Friedrich Alfred Krupp: Ein Unternehmer im Kaiserreich*, ed. Michael Epkenhans and Ralf Stremmel (Munich: Beck, 2010). I also consulted the sensational and censorious account in William Manchester, *The Arms of Krupp* (New York: Little, Brown, 1968), 221–32.

161 *"It was one thing"*: Brooks, Beinecke typescript, 207.

162 *"gens du monde ever seeking"*: Ibid., 212.

162 *"Blond and boyish"*: Ibid., 205.

163 *"fairy tale of life"*: Ibid., 214.

165 *"These pensive portraits"*: Meryle Secrest, *Between Me and Life* (London: Macdonald and Jane's, 1974), 197.

166 *"What I called grown-up games"*: Brooks, Beinecke typescript, 224.

167 *"to give a portrait"*: Ibid., 212.

168 *"the masculine soul"*: Richard von Krafft-Ebing, *Psychopathia Sexualis*, trans. Franklin S. Klaf (New York: Arcade, 1965), 264.

169 *"Venetia Ford! So that was"*: Radclyffe Hall, *The Forge* (Bristol, U.K.: Arrowsmith, 1929), chap. 6.

170 *Gabriele D'Annunzio*: My principal sources for information about the writer's life were Lucy Hughes-Hallett, *Gabriele d'Annunzio: Poet, Seducer, and Preacher of War* (New York: Knopf, 2013), and Jonathan Galassi, "The Writer, Seducer, Aviator, Proto-Fascist, Megalomaniac Prince Who Shaped Modern Italy," *New Republic*, Feb. 9, 2014.

170 *"a frightful gnome"*: Cassandra Langer, *Romaine Brooks: A Life* (Madison: University of Wisconsin Press, 2015), 55.

170 *"the great* lapidé *of our times"*: Brooks, Beinecke typescript, 242–55.

174 *"I have seen many things"*: Whitney Chadwick, *Amazons in the Drawing Room: The Art of Romaine Brooks* (Chesterfield, Mass.: Chameleon Books, 2000), 23.

174 *"ivory face with gemlike eyes"*: Langer, *Romaine Brooks*, 71.

175 *"the figure of Sebastian"*: Thomas Mann, *Death in Venice*, trans. H. T. Lowe-Porter (London: Martin Secker & Warburg, 1955).

176 *"The violent transformation"*: Chadwick, *Amazons in the Drawing Room*, 23.

176 *"I come, I ascend"*: Ibid.

177 *Rubinstein visited D'Annunzio in Arcachon*: Michael de Cossart, *Ida Rubinstein (1885–1960): A Theatrical Life* (Liverpool: Liverpool University Press, 1987), 60–61.

177 *"seemed to me more beautiful"*: Brooks, Beinecke typescript, 258.

178 *"The Venus lay"*: Hall, *Forge*, chap. 8.

179 *"For the first time"*: Chadwick, *Amazons in the Drawing Room*, 26.

179 *"The Weeping Venus"*: Brooks, Beinecke typescript, 281.

180 *"believed that sensuality flourished"*: Langer, *Romaine Brooks*, 47.

180 *"Friendship came to me"*: Brooks, Beinecke typescript, 277.

182 *"There comes before me"*: Ibid., 238.

184 *"I am a cynic"*: Langer, *Romaine Brooks*, 94.

185 *"one is indispensable to the other"*: Francesco Rapazzini, *Élisabeth de Gramont: Avant-gardiste* (Paris: Fayard, 2004), 339.

185 *"Lily, Natalie, and Romaine"*: Langer, *Romaine Brooks*, 99.

187 *"The offender was usually of a masculine type"*: Allan McLane Hamilton, "The Civil Responsibility of Sexual Perverts," *American Journal of Insanity* 52 (1896): 505.

189 *"A plumbago ramped"*: Benson, *Final Edition*, 115.

189 *"Long mornings of swimming"*: E. F. Benson, *As We Were* (London: Longmans, Green, 1930), 291.

193 *"I shut myself up"*: Secrest, *Between Me and Life*, 284.

193 *"A heat wave"*: Ibid., 285.

194 *"every one of the characters"*: Mackenzie, *Octave Five*, 138.

195 *"a Swedish mathematician"*: Compton Mackenzie, *Extraordinary Women* (London: Hogarth Press, 1986), 231.

196 *"These dinner-parties of Rosalba's"*: Ibid., 263.

197 *"When the dusty road"*: Ibid., 275.

197 *"a young Neapolitan"*: Ibid., 101.

198 *"I know that you have not bathed"*: Langer, *Romaine Brooks*, 97.

199 *"The masculine side"*: Mackenzie, *Octave Five*, 152.

200 *"I want to cry"*: Ibid.

201 *"the destroyer of mediocrity"*: Daniela Ferretti, "A Coré, distruttice della mediocrità," in *La divina marchesa: Arte e vita di Luisa Casati*, catalogue of an exhibition at the Palazzo Fortuny, Oct. 4, 2014–March 8, 2015 (Milan: 24 Ore Cultura, 2014), 17. The beautifully produced catalogue of this extraordinary exhibition is the best source on the life and work of Luisa Casati.

204 *"She wore an astrologer's hat"*: Mackenzie, *Octave Five*, 175–76.

206 *"a prey to his black whims"*: Curzio Malaparte, *Kaputt*, trans. Cesare Foligno (Pickle Partners, 2015), chap. 1.

206 *"You are quite right, Mrs. Mackenzie"*: Mackenzie, *Octave Five*, 128.

209 *"an abandoned farmyard"*: Secrest, *Between Me and Life*, 353.

209 *"I shall always serve"*: Langer, *Romaine Brooks*, 106.

211 *"What's the use?"*: Secrest, *Between Me and Life*, 382.

213 *"a Scot (born in Austria)"*: Frederick R. Karl, *Conrad: The Three Lives* (New York: Farrar, Straus and Giroux, 1979), 578. Among the many cradle-to-grave biographies of Conrad, I prefer Karl's.

214 *"I've done nothing"*: Ibid., 577.

215 *"a good European"*: Joseph Conrad, "Il Conde: A Pathetic Tale," in *A Set of Six* (London: Methuen, 1908).

216 *Modern critics have been attracted*: See Jeremy Hamilton, *Sexuality and the Erotic in the Fiction of Joseph Conrad* (London: Bloomsbury, 2007), and Sylvère Monod, "Rereading 'Il Conde,'" *Conradian* 30, no. 1 (Spring 2005): 118–26.

217 *Conrad's Polish biographer*: Zdzislaw Najder. Zygmunt Szembek's grandson is Zygmunt Mycielski, letter to Najder dated March 12, 1981. See Hamilton, *Sexuality and the Erotic*.

219 *"the best single piece of writing"*: Quoted in David Ellis, *D. H. Lawrence: Dying Game, 1922–1930* (Cambridge, U.K.: Cambridge University Press, 1998), 6.

219 *"Douglas tall and portly"*: D. H. Lawrence, *Memoir of Maurice Magnus* (Santa Rosa, Calif.: Black Sparrow Press, 1987), 30.

220 *"a gossipy, villa-stricken"*: Mark Kinkead-Weekes, *D. H. Lawrence: Triumph to Exile, 1912–1922* (Cambridge, U.K.: Cambridge University Press, 1996), 556.

220 *"in the black dark"*: Lawrence, *Maurice Magnus*, 40.

222 *"A Plea for Better Manners"*: Ibid., 105–32.

223 *"Certainly Magnus was generous"*: Ibid., 136.

224 *"would sometimes say a good word"*: Mackenzie, *Octave Five*, 166.

224 *"Warmed by Capri wine"*: D. H. Lawrence, *The Woman Who Rode Away, and Other Stories*, ed. Dieter Mehl and Christa Iansohn (Cambridge, U.K.: Cambridge University Press, 1995), xxxvi.

224 *"There was a woman"*: Ibid., 5.

225 *"There was a man who loved islands"*: Ibid., 151.

225 *"a granite island in the Channel"*: Ibid., xxxix.

225 *"What idiotic self-importance!"*: Ibid., xxxviii.

227 *"Always I grow really melancholy"*: Rainer Maria Rilke, *Selected Letters*, trans. R. F. C. Hull (London: Macmillan, 1947), 106–7.

228 *"Where the few stony paths"*: Ibid., 118.

228 *"This is Greece"*: Ibid., 122.

228 *"rises and subsides"*: Louise Bogan, "Rilke in His Age," *Poetry* 50, no. 1 (April 1937): 39.

230 *"The fact that Russia is my homeland"*: Rainer Maria Rilke to Lou Andreas-Salomé, *Rilke and Andreas-Salomé: A Love Story in Letters*, trans. Edward Snow and Michael Winkler (New York: Norton, 2008), 85.

231 *"Alexei Maximovich laughed to tears"*: Emanuel Salgaller, "Strange Encounter: Rilke and Gorky on Capri," *Monatshefte* 54, no. 1 (Jan. 1962): 20.

231 *"I have seen Gorky"*: Rilke, *Selected Letters*, 129–30.

232 *"a comically puzzled expression"*: Salgaller, "Strange Encounter," 17–18.

234 *"was full of Russians"*: Mackenzie, *Octave Four*, 185.

234 *"there was a loud bang"*: Douglas, *Looking Back*, 488–89.

236 *"which drew the hearts"*: Maxim Gorky, *Days with Lenin* (Honolulu: University Press of the Pacific, 2004), 27–28.

236 *"With equal enthusiasm"*: Ibid., 38.

237 *"when he lost grew angry"*: Ibid., 26.

237 *"The primary work of the revolution"*: Ibid., 32.

238 *"repulsively memorable"*: Ibid., 35.

238 *"Our men work more quickly"*: Ibid., 51.

238 The Spy: Maxim Gorky, *The Life of a Useless Man*, trans. Moura Budberg (New York: Carroll & Graf, 2000).

239 *It appears that the two writers never met*: Karl, *Conrad*, 612.

242 *"So I thought in 1917"*: Gorky, *Days with Lenin*, 33–34.

243 *"I challenge anyone to say"*: Ibid.

246 *"Outside, the ocean heaved"*: I. A. Bunin, *The Gentleman from San Francisco, and Other Stories*, trans. D. H. Lawrence, S. S.

Koteliansky, and Leonard Woolf (New York: Thomas Seltzer, 1923), 11–12.

249 *"I took no part in politics"*: I. A. Bunin, *The Village*, trans. Isabel Hapgood (London: Martin Secker, 1923), 8–9.

249 *she came to Capri with a new lover*: For Marguerite Yourcenar's visit to Capri with Grace Frick in 1937, see Ciro Sandomenico, *Il "viaggio di nozze" di Marguerite Yourcenar a Capri* (Naples: Liguori, 2001), excerpted in *L'Isola*, Aug. 2004.

250 *"Debauchery and death mingle"*: Marg [Marguerite] Yourcenar, "Caprée," *La Revue Bleue*, Dec. 21, 1929, 371.

251 *"one of those men"*: Marguerite Yourcenar, *Coup de Grâce*, trans. Grace Frick (London: Black Swan, 1983).

253 "Coup de Grâce, *the book, is itself an act of revenge"*: As this book went to press, a biography of Grace Frick was published (Joan E. Howard, *We Met in Paris: Grace Frick and Her Life with Marguerite Yourcenar* [Columbia: University of Missouri Press, 2018]), which speculates that Yourcenar's love affair with André Fraigneau may have been a fabrication. My analysis of *Coup de Grâce* as an autobiographical work is based upon the established narrative of Yourcenar's life. This issue, among many other enigmas in the author's life, cannot be resolved until Yourcenar's private papers are unsealed, in 2037—if ever.

255 *Specifically, Fascism arrived*: For the Fascist era in Capri, see Ciro Sandomenico, "Capri al tempo di Mussolini," *L'Isola*, Dec. 5, 2005.

257 *"Fascism is like an empty tube"*: Davide Spina, "The Good, the Bad, and the Malaparte," *AA Files*, no. 72 (2016): 5.

257 *"Too much sea"*: Ibid., 7.

259 *The history of the manuscript of* Kaputt: Malaparte, "The History of a Manuscript," in *Kaputt*.

261 *"There is something strange"*: Malaparte, *Kaputt*, chap. 1.

261 *"Suddenly, with the peculiar vibrating"*: Ibid., chap. 3.

262 *"His stupid air"*: Ibid., chap. 12.

264 *"As for the filth"*: Ibid., chap. 5.

267 *"a very rare example"*: Curzio Malaparte, *The Skin*, trans. David Moore (Pickle Partners, 2015), chap. 6.

268 *"lay prostrate beneath the heel"*: Ibid.

269 *"when we returned to the vast hall"*: Ibid.

270 *"cannot be understood"*: Spina, "The Good, the Bad," 17.

271 *"A Homeric ship"*: Bruce Chatwin, *Anatomy of Restlessness: Selected Writings, 1969–1989* (New York: Viking, 1996), 162.

273 *"certainly not in the same class"*: Alberto Moravia, *Contempt*, trans. Angus Davidson (New York: New York Review of Books, 1999), 79–80.

276 *"In the course of these wanderings"*: Pablo Neruda, *Memoirs*, trans. Hardie St. Martin (New York: Farrar, Straus and Giroux, 1977), 211–15.

278 *"I have always said"*: Matilde Urrutia, *My Life with Pablo Neruda*, trans. Alexandria Giardino (Stanford, Calif.: Stanford University Press, 2004).

278 *"Today I'm going to get a ring"*: Adam Feinstein, *Pablo Neruda: A Passion for Life* (London: Bloomsbury, 2004), 276.

279 *"sweetest of consorts"*: Neruda, *Memoirs*, 216.

279 *"remained a secret"*: Ibid., 215.

284 *"did not appear on the tapes"*: Mike Hill and Jon Wise, *The Works of Graham Greene* (London: Bloomsbury, 2015), 2:235.

285 *"The elegance of Capri life"*: Money, *Capri*, 242.

285 *"problems of congestion"*: The mayor of Capri quoted is Gianni De Martini, in a post by Kathy McCabe, on italytravel.com, a website of Perillo Tours, Aug. 8, 2016.

287 *One recent title*: Francesco Durante, *Il richiamo azzurro* (Capri: La Conchiglia, 2000).

ACKNOWLEDGMENTS

Foremost among the colleagues and friends who assisted my research for this book are Cassandra Langer, the author of a fine biography of Romaine Brooks, who gave me good advice and made some essential corrections to my manuscript while I was working on it; and the late Will Ogrinc, who carefully reviewed my biographical sketch of Jacques d'Adelswärd-Fersen. Ogrinc's untimely death in 2018 deprived the community of Fersen scholars of their brightest and most learned authority, and me of the opportunity to thank him personally for his invaluable corrections.

I am grateful to Matthew Gurewitsch, who interrupted his tour of Java to translate Rilke's "Lied vom Meer" when I needed it, in short order, yet with a timeless elegance. For help with my translations, I offer warm thanks to Nigel Barley and Cornelia Biegler-König. For their assistance in picture research and verifying elusive points of information, my thanks go to Tiziana Alvisi, Raimondo Biffi, Geoff Drutchas, Jérôme Merceron, Giulia Napoleone, and Antonia Soriente.

I am grateful to many new friends in Capri for their generous hospitality and advice, particularly Don Vincenzo Simeoli, Anita de Pascale, Tonino Gargiulo, and my friends at Edizioni la Conchiglia, Riccardo Esposito, Ausilia Veneruso, and Vincenzo Sorrentino. Thanks to Dott.ssa Anna Maria Palombi Cataldi, director of the library of the Centro Caprense Ignazio Cerio, for granting me full access to the archive there. Nicolino and Carmen Morgano were very kind to receive me at Villa Cercola, an experience that enriched my understanding of life on Capri in its glamorous heyday.

For their hospitality and good company when I was carrying out my research, I offer thanks to Agnès Montenay, in Paris; to Richard Fairman, in London; to Fabrizio Ottaviani, in Rome; and to Nina Schwalbe and Sally Girvin, in New York. I am grateful to these old friends who offered valuable corrections and comments: John Finlay, Mark Livingston, and Adam Lüders.

As ever, I am grateful to my agent, Katinka Matson, for her loyal and astute guidance.

At Farrar, Straus and Giroux, I am indebted to Ileene Smith for her sensitive and perceptive edit of my manuscript, and to Jonathan Galassi for his enthusiastic support of this project from the beginning. Jackson Howard was a steady and reliable guide in the journey from manuscript to book. I give thanks to Ingrid Sterner, once again, for vital corrections and improvements to the text, and to Katie Hurley, the production editor, for gathering all the errant editorial strands into a coherent text. I offer grateful admiration to Na Kim for the brilliant cover.

Finally, I wish to express my warmest deep affection to my dedicatee, my best friend and partner, Rendy, and his family, who have taken me to their hearts as one of their own, despite my outlandish ways. Without their love and support, I could not do what I do.

INDEX

ILLUSTRATION CREDITS

Illustrations follow page 180.

1: (*Top*) Courtesy of the British Museum; (*bottom*) courtesy of the Bibliothèque nationale de France, photograph by the author

2: (*Top*) Courtesy of the Bibliothèque nationale de France, photograph by the author; (*bottom*) photograph by the author

3: (*Top*) Photograph by the author; (*bottom*) courtesy of Ignazio Cerio Museum

4: Bentley Historical Library, University of Michigan

5: (*Top*) Courtesy of Will Ogrinc; (*bottom*) photograph by the author

6: Photographs by the author

7: Courtesy of Comune di Capri

8: (*Top left*) Courtesy of Anita de Pascale; (*right and lower left*) courtesy of Comune di Capri

9: Photographs by the author

10: Photographs by the author, with permission of Palazzo Fortuny, Venice

11: (*Top*) Courtesy of George Wickes Collection, University of Oregon Libraries; (*bottom*) Courtesy of Morgano Hotels Capri

12: (*Top*) Copyright Centre Pompidou, MNAM-CCI, Dist. RMN-Grand Palais / image Centre Pompidou, MNAM-CCI; (*bottom*) Smithsonian American Art Museum, Washington, DC / Art Resource, NY

13: (*Top*) Public domain; (*bottom*) courtesy of the Denver Art Museum
14: Morgano Hotels Capri
15: Photograph by the author, with permission of Museo Casa Rossa, Anacapri
16: (*Top*) Morgano Hotels Capri; (*bottom*) photograph by the author

A NOTE ABOUT THE AUTHOR

Jamie James is the author of several books of nonfiction, including *The Glamour of Strangeness*, *Rimbaud in Java*, and *The Snake Charmer*. He has contributed to *The New York Times*, *The New Yorker*, *The Wall Street Journal*, *Vanity Fair*, and *The Atlantic*, among other publications, and he previously served as the American arts correspondent for *The Times* (London). The recipient of a Guggenheim Foundation grant, he has lived in Indonesia since 1999.